IRIDESCENCE OF LITERARY PARADIGMS

JINU GEORGE & SARAN S.

Copyright © Jinu George & Saran S.
All Rights Reserved.

ISBN 979-888521936-5

This book has been published with all efforts taken to make the material error-free after the consent of the author. However, the author and the publisher do not assume and hereby disclaim any liability to any party for any loss, damage, or disruption caused by errors or omissions, whether such errors or omissions result from negligence, accident, or any other cause.

While every effort has been made to avoid any mistake or omission, this publication is being sold on the condition and understanding that neither the author nor the publishers or printers would be liable in any manner to any person by reason of any mistake or omission in this publication or for any action taken or omitted to be taken or advice rendered or accepted on the basis of this work. For any defect in printing or binding the publishers will be liable only to replace the defective copy by another copy of this work then available.

Contents

Contents

Contents

Foreword

Prof. Dr. B. Keralavarma
Member of the MG University Syndicate
Dean of Languages and Literature
Kerala Kalamandalam Deemed to be University for Art and
Culture, Associate Professor (Retd) Dept. of English
Govt. College Kottayam, Kerala.

This book testifies to the academic competence, zeal and maturity of the editors Jinu George and Saran S. It is a unique venture, publishing a book of research papers every month- a daring undertaking. As wholesome as daring, it encourages both production and dissemination of knowledge. And that is what an institution of higher education stands for. Above all, it occasions a continual engagement with contemporary intellectual pursuits.

I am impressed by the richness and variety that the book proudly offers to the academic community, by the amazing spectrum of topics that one comes across in the book. It is heartening to note that a good deal of research is going on in all the domains of social and literary theories. Being concerned with the puzzling questions faced by the society we live in augurs well for the future. A few of the papers are concerned with the bitter experiences of the vulnerable sections of society. A couple of them engage directly with the two-fold oppression that Dalit women are subjected to. While this is a singeing issue, the experiences of women, in general, are so alarming as to deserve equal academic attention and public support. One of the contributors takes up for examination the peculiar transgender issue. No issue of academic merit is left out. Environment, particularly man's brutal encroachment into the sacred realm of nature, climate change which occurs in the aftermath of such heedless violation, find adequate treatment here. It is dealt with in the context of science fiction.

A few words about criticism before I conclude. Students generally find criticism abstruse and formidable. One of the reasons for this phobia is that they are never properly initiated into the processes of criticism. The general impression among students is that criticism is a sort of appreciation of works. Their business usually does not go beyond writing an appreciation for examination. Literature is no longer a thing for elite appreciation although at the bottom the question of aesthetics is still relevant. Criticism has become a vehicle of critiquing social structures and practices. Students of social sciences will find in literature as fertile and intriguing a ground for creative investigation as in approved textbooks for study. Thus the periodic publication of papers in book form will, in the long run, cause students to choose from the sparkling array of essays topics of their interest for regular discussions and debates. I wish all the very best for this laudable venture undertaken by the editors.

• • •

FOREWORD

Editor

Dr. Jinu George
Associate Professor
Dept. English, St. Peter's College, Kolenchery
Member, PG Board of Studies & Research Guide
MG University, Kottayam, Kerala

Dr. Jinu George, Associate Professor, Department of English, St.Peter's College, Kolenchery has been a promising contributor to research-oriented articles on English language and literature, especially in the field of edifices one that is trodden by the less. He is an active participant in research-oriented seminars/webinars conducted under the aegis of various universities and has proved his erudition in editing many literary publications. He has submitted a project to UGC on Web-Quest which is an analytical and intellectual presentation of contemporary digital trends in the teaching and learning scenario. He had served as Associate Professor at the University of Garyonius, Libya. He is at present a member of the P.G. Board of Studies and research guide at Mahatma Gandhi University, Kottayam. His area of interest is ELT and Eco-Linguistics. He is the author of a number of articles published in various national and international journals and has recently published a book titled *English Language Teaching: A Modern Taxonomy* (2021).

Editor

Saran S.
Assistant Professor in English
University Extension centre Pathiyoor
University of Kerala, Thiruvananthapuram

Saran S. (MA, Ph. D.) is a writer, Poet, Nature Activist, Teacher, and Research Scholar. He has completed his Doctoral Research from the Department of English, M. S. University in 2020. Currently, he is working as an Assistant Professor in the Department of English, University Institute of Technology Pathiyoor, University of Kerala. His areas are Comparative Literature, Cultural Studies, Film Studies, Psychoanalytical Studies and Eco Studies. He is the author of several articles published in various national and international journals as well as six academic books on topics of current interest like English Language, Film Studies, Partition Studies and Cultural Studies. He also authored a collection of poems and short stories. He also edited twenty international books. He is the chief editor of Edit Academic, an advisory board member in *The Creative Launcher*, international, open access, peer-reviewed refereed, e-journal in English and also Editorial Board Member in *ShodhKosh: Journal of Visual and Performing Arts* (UGC-CARE Listed Journal).

Contributors

1. "A Neuro-Psycho Analytical Study of Characters in Harold Pinter's *The Birthday Party* with Special Reference to Stanley and Meg" - **Dr Mini V. S.**, Assistant Professor, Dept of English, St.Xavier's College for Women, Aluva.

2. "Disrupting Gender Stereotypes through Media: A Critical Study of the Malayalam film *Sara's*" - **Dr. Anjali Abraham.**, Assistant Professor, Department of English, M A College, Kothamangalam, Kerala.

3. "I Shall Not Hear The Nightingale: A Socio-Psychological Study of Human Insights" - **Dr. Reji George.**, Associate Professor of English, Department of English, Shri Trikamjibhai Chatvani Arts and J. V. Gokal Trust Commerce College.

4. "A Cultural Study on Indian Ethnic Inclusiveness" - **Dayaram R Meshram**, R. D. Collage Allapalli Dist.Gadchiroli.

5. "Narrative Technique in the Novels of Hemingway"- **Jesfert Aagy**, Lecturer, Gariyonis University, Benghazi, Libya.

6. "Freedom at Midnight: Disruptive Spatiality of Normative Disjuncture and Deceptive Will of Resistance" - **Jesto Thankachan.**, Assistant Professor, Department of English, St. Peter's College, Kolenchery.

7. "Dismantling Utopia to Dystopia: The Anthropocentric Greed and Environmental Catastrophe in J. G. Ballard's *The Drought*" - **Lismin P. Samuel**[1] & **Roopa Jose**[2], Al-Azhar College, Thodupuzha, St. Joseph's College, Moolamattom.

8. "Narratology, Its Features: A Study Based on Indian Narratology" - **Ramdas V. H.**, Assistant Professor & Research Scholar, Department of English, Ilahia College of Arts and Science, Research Scholar in Sree Sankara University of Sanskrit.

9. "Registering Resistance: Representation of the Othered Dalit Women in Baby Kamble's *The Prisons We Broke*" - **Radhika Raj**

P., Assistant Professor, Department of English, Baselios Poulose II Catholicose College, Piravom, Ernakulam, Kerala.

10. "Job Stress of College Teachers Especially After Covid-19 Pandemic" - **Sanil Thomas.**, Commerce Department, Yeldo Mar Baselios College, Puthuppady, Kothamangalam, Ernakulam,Kerala.

11. "Nature and Culture; A Journey into the Wild in Sean Penn's Film *into The Wild*"- **Ms. Sarah** Santhosh., Assistant Professor, Department of English, The Cochin College, Kochi, Kerala.

12. "Ontological Existence of Transwomen: A Study on a Revathy's *Truth about Me:* A Hijra Life Story" - **Shahina N.**, Assistant professor, Safa College of Arts and Science.

13. "Tracing the Things' Fallen Apart: A Case of Igbo Cultural Identity Reflected in the Comedy Series Mark Angel Comedy" - **Sindhu Thomas**, Assistant Professor, Department of English, Baselios Poulose II Catholicos College, Piravom, Ernakulam, Kerala.

14. "From Desires to the Becoming: Analysing Sexual Prejudice and Hypocrisy in Jeanette Winterson's *Oranges are Not the Only Fruit*" - **Sneha K.**, Assistant Professor, PG Department of English, Yuvakshetra Institute of Management Studies, Mundur, Palakkad, Kerala.

15. "Mapping Popular Science Narratives: A Reading of V. S. Ramachandran's *The Tell-Tale Brain*" -**Urmila K.**, Assistant Professor of English, University College, Thiruvananthapuram.

16. "Infringement of Rudimentary Rights: An Analysis of Khaled Hosseini's *A Thousand Splendid Suns*"- **Anakha Saji.**, Department of English and Centre for Research, Sacred Heart College (Autonomous), Cochin.

17. "Nation and Cinema: Tracing Paths of Intersections Between Indian Cinema and Postcolonial India" - **Treesa Petreena**, Ph. D. Research Scholar, St. Xavier's College for Women.

18. "An Anonymous Signature: Understanding Guess Who Graffiti" - **Lakshmipriya A. S.**, CMS College, Kottayam.

19. "Pastoral Power and Reform of the Indian Woman: A Reading of

Introduction

Iridescence of Literary Paradigms

Gone are the days in which research and teaching were seen as two separate entities-- the former for the elite and the erudite, and the latter for lay teachers. Things have changed. This unique collection of articles which I am privileged to introduce to the lovers of English language and literature proves that an era has come that research and publication are currently perceived as a self–undertaken effort in improving their pedagogical outputs. 'Publish or Perish' has become the order of the day and anyone with spontaneous skills is left with no other options.

The book *Iridescence of Literary Paradigms* is compiled not on the fringes of any rigid area of categorization. In one sense this is the 'Muse with Cause' since contributors have responded to diverse themes namely ELT, Eco-Linguistics, Performance Studies, Media Studies, Cultural Studies, Discourse Analysis, Feminism, Eco-Critical Studies etc... which emerged as specialized branches in our discipline. The total range of this collection is very wide and the modes of expression varied.

Contributors have given free play to their research temperament to enrich it by adding their own robust and valuable contributions. The collection reflects the pull of the past and the pressure of the present, the force of both of which are inescapably ought to be reconciled in a neat manner-- when a truly creative mind is tested. A scholar who is sharp and clear in his vision will naturally see the future in the making and reconcile with the two to meet the emerging challenges in the research realm of language and literature.

The birthmark of 'Free Thinking' is evident in almost all compositions of this collection. The collection proves that the contributors are rendering great service to the development of the research field and the contemporary literary scenario. I earnestly hope that this pioneering venture will yield enduring benefits to the cause of nurturing and sustaining the realms of English language and literary studies.

A NEURO-PSYCHO ANALYTICAL STUDY OF CHARACTERS IN HAROLD PINTER'S THE BIRTHDAY PARTY WITH SPECIAL REFERENCE TO STANLEY AND MEG

Dr Mini V. S.
Assistant Professor, Dept of English
St.Xavier's College for Women, Aluva

ABSTRACT

Harold Pinter has been described as an existentialist dramatist and a playwright of the ambiguous. The Birthday Party is one of the most outstanding plays written by him. Although the play puzzled critics and audiences alike at its production, many noticed signs of greatness in it. The play has elements of mystery that never gets solved. The atmosphere of terror which pervades the play despite its rich comedy is perhaps its most striking aspect. Stanley Webber and Meg are two important characters in the play. The paper attempts to explore Meg who suffers from a psychological disorder and Stanley who shows symptoms of neurotic problems.

• • •

A Neuro-Psycho Analytical Study of Characters in Harold Pinter's *The Birthday Party* with Special Reference to Stanley and Meg

Harold Pinter, the English playwright who achieved international fame known for his "comedies of menace" is one of the most complex and challenging post-World War II dramatists. Besides being a playwright, he was also a screenwriter, actor, director, political activist and poet. In awarding the Nobel Prize for Literature in 2005, the Swedish Academy noted that Pinter occupies a position as a modern classic is illustrated by his name entering the language as an eponymous adjective. The supra-realistic dialogues in his plays and the menace in them, more than any other aspect of the work, have made the term "Pinteresque" extremely significant in the world of modern dramatic literature. Much of his work emphasizes the fear lurking around the corner. He conveys to us a sense that peace is only an illusion that is subject to sudden destruction by the appearance of an intruder: maybe a neighbour, a stranger or a figure from the past. The meaninglessness of the human condition has been presented very truthfully in Harold Pinter's early plays. Pinter himself admitted in a dialogue about the play The Birthday Party that the play is a comedy because the whole state of affairs is absurd and ineffective.

Symbolically, the play The Birthday Party represents the youth who have given up the outside unfriendly world. So, the characters presented in the play are idle, sleepy, and dirty most of the time. Stanley, the protagonist is given refuge by the elderly couple in the boarding house. He usually wakes up late in the day and reflects upon the post-war young London generation. Such individuals are filthy, chaotic and blemish on family and society. These individuals have dragged families towards terror and anxiety. The personal and family dignity of such individuals is devalued and lost. Harold Pinter's plays still puzzle the audience and critics after several years of acquaintance with his work. Pinter in his play The Birthday Party expresses his vision of looking at the milieu of the modern age. He employs psychological devices to present discontented and vicissitudes of life. Among these six, Goldberg and McCann are the antagonists who exploit other characters. They treat Stanley badly, who gets lost in thoughts, makes vigorous efforts to think, imagine and speak but is powerless to do so.

The Birthday Party is a mysterious play because we are ignorant of Stanley's purpose of anguish and nervousness; and Goldberg—McCann's mission. The audience, as well as McCann, remain unaware of their intention to visit the boarding house. The pair brings an aura of suspense and menace to the audience. Goldberg and McCann ironically represent Jews and Irish respectively, two of the most oppressed, persecuted communities that become tormentors The play is labelled as 'Comedy of Menace' due to its hilarious and tormenting terror going through its scenes and episodes. In most events, the audience is amused at the ambiguous menace of Stanley.

Kirby, one of the renowned critics states: "The Birthday Party enacts with precision a textbook case of a mental breakdown" (164). The play depicts the mental and nervous breakdown of post-war individuals and the ontological predicaments that human society profusely experienced. Pinter, as we know, has made an in-depth study of human psychology to understand the most internal state of the human mind. So, he should be called the dramatic psychologist because at all stages he investigated the human mind. "The psycho-analytical approach helps in understanding the play and its impact and effect on the audience" (Esslin 8)

His characters suffer from psychological imbalance and are seen performing unexpected activities. The ideological stance or philosophical model of thinking i.e. existentialism with which his works are associated contain the clarity and soundness of his ideas, grandeur of thoughts and glittering eloquence with proper diction. The dramatic techniques connect his plays with the modern theatrical movement i.e. The Theatre of the Absurd. His plays reflect psychological thought that depends on, "what the characters say, wish to say, ought to say or don't say, trusting the author's power to breathe life into his dramatis personae and create characters who are consonant with his own ideas" (Almansi and Henderson 14). Esslin regarding the play argues:

Stanley appears to have lost his sense since Goldberg and McCann entered the house, but after analysing the play it is noticed that they had tried to put Stanley out of the absurd, terror, and anxiety from which he was suffering. They want to put a live soul in his body to let him live a free and responsible life which he has given up. At last, Stanley has become a wretched figure, alive corpse, unable to utter a single word and is ultimately dragged out of boarding house by Goldberg and McCann. So Stanley is kidnapped, tortured and taken away in a car by them. (17)

The childless and old couple, Meg and Petey live at a dilapidated boarding house in a seaside town, where Stanley Webber has found refuge. Meg gives excessive attention and care to Stanley. Petey is a deck chair attendant who usually spends his time outside neglecting his ambitious and desirous wife at home. Stanley's birthday party is celebrated at the request of the two outsiders, Goldberg and McCann about which Stanley himself does not know. Of the two men who have come to take Stanley away, Goldberg rapes Lulu. Despite Petey's efforts, Stanley is taken away by the intruders and the play ends with Meg's return from the market who is ignorant of Stanley's departure.

At the beginning of the play, Meg is very happy to hear from the newspaper the news of childbirth. Her curiosity suggests a childless woman's over-excitement at the news of a delivery. Meg is not just content to know about the birth but is eager to know the sex of the child. She is disappointed to know that it is a girl, not a boy.

Petey: Someone's just had a baby

Meg: Oh, they haven't! Who?

Petey: Some girl

Meg: Who, Petey, who?

Petey: I don't think you'd know her

Meg: What's her name?

Petey: Lady Mary Splatt

Meg: I don't know her

Petey: No

Meg: Oh, what a shame. I'd be sorry. I'd much rather have a little boy. (11)

From the above dialogue, it can be inferred that Meg always wanted to be the mother of a son. Stanley partially fulfils this psychological desire. But she behaves both as a mother and a tart to him. And this is evident from her keenness to know whether Stanley takes the cornflakes and the tea just as she had done with her husband. In another scene that is revealing, Meg's amorous and erotic intentions can be seen. In reply to Meg's query whether the fried bread she has served is "nice", Stanley describes it as "succulent". Meg appears to be offended by the word which should not be said to "a married woman".

Meg: The fried bread

Stanley: Succulent

Meg: You shouldn't say that word.

Stanley: What word?

Meg: That word you said

Stanley: What, succulent?

Meg: Don't say it! (17)

Meg goes into the kitchen and she "ruffles his hair" which itself constitutes her erotic feelings. Her pouring tea "coyly" and her desire to be reassured, "Am I succulent?", and her allotment of Stanley's room where she had "some lovely afternoons"- all these go to prove that her attitude to Stanley is less holy than a mother's. She is "sensual" as "she strokes his arm." Her erotic nature is noticed by Stanley himself when she enters his "bedroom and wakes him up." And when she strokes his arm Stanley "recoils from her hand in disgust, stands and exits quickly" (19) When Stanley is standing smoking at the window, "she crosses behind him and tickles the back of his neck". She longs to accompany her.

Stanley (punishing her). Get away from me.

Meg: Are you going out?

Stanley: Not with you

Meg: But I'm going shopping in a minute.

Stanley: Go

Meg: You'll be lonely, all by yourself

Stanley: Will I?

Meg: Without your old Meg.... (19)

Psychoanalysts describe those who obtain sexual excitement by contact with another person as a frotteur:

The infantile reaction to cuddle and rub against...seems to become a perversion in some cases, and when it does so the sexual satisfaction is obtained by rubbing against objects in crowds and so on. It is not uncommon to find young men who feel intense sexual excitement when caressing a girl and ejaculate in so doing. Should they attempt to have intercourse they invariably have premature ejaculation or else are impotent. From the behavioristic point of view, this is a case of over-excitation, and indeed it may be found to occur temporarily in those who have been deprived of intercourse overlong. (Clifford 73-74) Sigmund Freud himself has written upon frotteurism as a "fore-pleasure", or one of the pleasures which increase sexual tension and the urge of the partners on to the final culmination of the sexual act. That contact could be a partly acquired reaction through nursing and cuddling in infancy.

As Clifford points out, Hence we long to clasp in our arms those whom we tenderly love. We probably owe this desire to inherited habit, in association with the nursing and tending of our children, and with the mutual caresses of lovers. With the lower animals, we see the same principle of pleasure derived from contact in association with love. (74)

In this sense, Meg can be recognized as a frotteurist who gets sexual pleasure by ruffling Stanley's hair, stroking his hand, tickling the back of his neck etc. Her acts may be an indication of the absence of sex in her life. Meg flirts with Stanley, trying to fill a second void in her life. Her marriage to Petey has settled into a mechanical routine, as their listless and absurd dialogue that opens the play reveals. Meg tries to win Stanley's approval of her as a woman, shamelessly fishing for compliments. Stanley, in his mildly perverse manner, responds by teasing her, knowing that she is both vulnerable and susceptible.

Stanley behaves in a rude way to Meg and we often doubt how a lodger gains such superiority over a hostess. His attitude to Lulu is not better. His clumsy appearance is noticed by her and refuses to wash when asked to. When he refuses to open the door for her she does it. She cannot understand why he stays at home all the time.

Lulu: Why don't you open the door? It's all stuffy in here
She opens the back door
Stanley(rising): Stuffy? I disinfected the place this morning
Lulu (at the door); Oh that's better.

Stanley: I think it's going to rain today. What do you think?

Lulu: I hope so. You could do with it. (25)

Pinter himself once said:

It was sparked off from a very distinct situation in digs when I was on the tour. The other day a friend of mine gave me a letter. I wrote him in nineteen-fifty something. Christ knows when it was. This is what it says, "I have filthy insane digs, a great bulging scrag of a woman with breasts rolling at her belly, an obscene household, cats, dogs, filth, tea-strainers, mess, oh bullocks, talk, chat rubbish shit scratch during poison, infantility, deficient order in the upper fretwork, fucking roll-on...Now the thing about this is that was The Birthday Party. I was in those digs and this woman was Meg in the play, and a fellow was staying there in Osbourne, on the coast. (qt.in Trussler 43-44)

But there is no instance regarding her sexual misconduct although she exceeds in her world as a hostess. Originated by a Scottish doctor, Cullen, the term connotes to the "sickness of motion and sense" (Russon 85). Stanley can be seen as a projection of such an individual whose personality has been crippled for his artistic vision by the cruel gods of society. His only crime was that he was indifferent to society and that he wished to retain his individuality. But the society did not allow him to live freely and it is this fear of society that made Stanley neurotic. Freud believed that the result of every neurotic impulse forces the patient out of real-life and alienates him from actuality" (55). The difficulty to communicate and establish a relationship with others can also be considered a symptom of neurosis. Stanley is an escapist who wants to run away from the norms of society and prefers to take refuge in the boarding house. Right from the beginning, he is detached from the world of reality. His conversation with Meg in Act 1, where he dreams to be a successful pianist exposes his dreamy nature and alienation from the world of reality. This points to the disordered condition of his mind.

Stanley: They are coming today

Meg: Who?

Stanley: They're coming in a van

Meg: Who?

Stanley: And do you know what they've got in that van?

Meg: What?

Stanley: They've got a wheelbarrow in that van. (14)

According to Stanley, the world outside had crushed him and is responsible for his failure in practical life. He says, "They carved me up. Carved me up. It was all worked out.... They want to crack me down on bended knees"(13). Burkman considers Stanley as a "caged animal waiting for the slaughter at the hands of the representatives of the establishment" (31). The repressions put by society cause neurotic disorders in individuals and that gets illustrated through Stanley's character in the play.

Works Cited

Pinter, Harold. The Birthday Party. London: Methuen, 1984.

Allen, Clifford. The Sexual Perversion and Abnormalities. London: Oxford UP, 1940.

Almansi Guido and Simon Henderson. Harold Pinter. London: Methuen Co. Ltd.1983.

Burkman, H C. The Dramatic World of Harold Pinter: Its Basis in Ritual. Ohio: Ohio

State University Press, 1971.

Esslin, Martin. The Theatre of the Absurd. London: Methuen Drama; 2001.

Freud, Sigmund. The Future of an Illusion. Trans Strachey J. New York W Norto &

Co.1989.

Kirby ET. Paranoid Pseudo community in Pinter's The Birthday Party. Educational

Theatre Journal 30.2 (1978): 157-164. JSTOR. 2 August 2018.

Russon, J. Human Experience, Philosophy, Neurosis and the Elements of Everyday Life.

New York: University of New York Press.2003

Trussler, Simon. The Plays of Harold Pinter: An Assessment. London: Victor

Gollancz,1974.

• • •

CHAPTER II

DISRUPTING GENDER STEREOTYPES THROUGH MEDIA: A CRITICAL STUDY OF THE MALAYALAM FILM SARA'S

Dr. Anjali Abraham

Assistant Professor, Department of English

M A College, Kothamangalam, Kerala.

ABSTRACT

Released on Amazon Prime, Sara's is the story of most Indian families but one that's rarely discussed, especially in mainstream cinema. It also brings to emphasis a textbook style kind of gender norms and stereotypes, sexual and reproductive rights, and has been critiqued for these too. This study is a critical analysis of the film using gender and sexual and reproductive rights lens. Sara's is a film about Sara (played by Anna Ben), a 25-year-old Associate Director from a relatively privileged background who dreams of directing a film. It focuses on her choices, be it those regarding boyfriends, profession, partner, and pregnancy, and in doing so, puts the limelight on challenging gender norms, exercising sexual and reproductive agency, and rights of women, in particular. It also subtly and systematically subverts gender stereotypes regarding the choice of profession and domestic roles.

Keywords: Sexual reproductive rights, gender stereotypes, gender equality, choice of profession and motherhood.

• • •

Disrupting Gender Stereotypes through Media: A Critical Study of the Malayalam film Sara's

Jude Anthany Joseph's Sara's is a Malayalam movie scripted by Dr Akshay Haresh, directed by Jude Anthony Joseph, produced by PK Murali Dharan and Santha Murali, and starring Anna Ben and Sunny Wayne. It is centred on Sara, played by Anna Ben, and how she's almost persuaded to sacrifice her career and dreams when she gets pregnant. An unconventional romantic comedy, the movie is a light-hearted take on how society and family pressurize young couples in matters concerning relationships, marriage and pregnancy. Without ever getting preachy, the film manages to make its point while addressing a few common social stigmas. From a very young age, Sara was clear that she didn't want to give birth. She's an aspiring filmmaker and when she meets Jeevan (Sunny Wayne), who also has a very similar opinion about not wanting to have kids; they hit it off. They fall in love and get married. As fate would have it, Sara accidentally gets pregnant and her decision to keep the child comes at the cost of her dream of finally becoming a filmmaker.

Gender equality, also known as sexual equality or equality of the sexes, is the state of equal ease of access to resources and opportunities regardless of gender, including economic participation and decision-making; and the state of valuing different behaviours, aspirations and needs equally, regardless of gender. Whoever we are, wherever we live, all the decisions we make about our bodies should be ours. Yet all over the world, many of us are mistreated for making our own choices and many more are prevented from making any choices at all. Sexual and reproductive rights mean we should be able to make our own decisions about our body, access sexual and reproductive health services including contraception, choose if, when and who to marry and decide if we want to have children and how many. They also mean our lives should be free from all forms of sexual violence, including rape, female genital mutilation, forced pregnancy, forced abortion and forced sterilization. Rights to reproductive and sexual health include the right to life, liberty and the security of the person; the right to health care and information; and the right to non-discrimination in the allocation of resources to health services and their availability and accessibility.

Of central importance are the rights to autonomy and privacy in making sexual and reproductive decisions, as well as the rights to knowledgeable consent and confidentiality about health services. This paper, through a critical study of the movie Sara's, illustrates issues that reflect a complete defilement of the above rights in varied forms, including maternal mortality, lack of procedures for legal abortion, inadequate allocation of resources for family planning, forcible population programs, spousal consent to sterilization, and occupational discrimination of pregnant women.

The right to autonomy in making health decisions in general, and sexual and reproductive decisions in particular, derives from the essential human right to liberty. One of the most expressive elucidations of the meaning of "autonomy" is that of Isaiah Berlin in his essay, Two Concepts of Liberty. For Berlin "liberty" in the ordinary sense is a "negative" right to freedom, in that one is entitled to be free in certain areas from the interference of others. "I am normally said to be free to the degree to which no man or body of men interferes with my activity." But "liberty" also has a "positive" sense. It is not merely freedom "from" but freedom "to" (Shalev). This positive right to freedom is "autonomy", in the sense that one is entitled to recognition of one's capacity, as a human being, to exercise choice in the shaping of one's life.

Even though the movie talks about a sensitive matter about a woman's right to embrace motherhood, it takes a light-hearted approach to make its point. The film doesn't try to showcase motherhood as a burden but it allows one to introspect on the sacrifices women have to make to raise kids. It also talks about how patriarchy has made raising kids solely a woman's job as the men are the breadwinner.

Sara's also gleaming the limelight on the discrimination of women in the film industry. From being turned down to direct her script because of her gender to being told that her duty, like that of most women, is to eventually have kids and raise them, the film doesn't hesitate to address uncomfortable questions. In the movie, there is a male gynaecologist with a better sense of understanding motherhood than most men. Anna Ben continues to impress with her choice of stories. She's slowly emerging as the flag bearer of films with unconventional storylines. With an appropriately energetic yet passive performance, she makes us empathize with her character but at the same time root for her. The supporting cast also does a very nice job in playing their respective characters.

Sara wants to achieve other things in life that are important to her. She is the opposite of the unaspiring and self-sacrificing women that mainstream Indian films and serials depict. The film features Sara's finding out about her accidental pregnancy right when she gets an opportunity to direct her first film. Both demand nine months of her time, but that is not the core of the film. Sara consistently has been shown to not want to have children, and neither does her partner. It seems that this is one of the things that brought them together.

Sara's character seems like a 'real' person and not an ideal woman within a heteropatriarchal framework. Sara's husband understands what she is going through both to the profession she is in as well as about the unwanted pregnancy. He is shown to struggle with his choices even as Sara makes hers. He had opted to not have children, based on his experiences babysitting for his older sister. But following his marriage and promotion, he is not too sure of the choice he made earlier. He is not the 'villain' in Sara's life, but a man struggling with the pressures of patriarchal expectations of masculinity, which have been depicted very well by the director.

The film is simplistic in its depiction of Sara at different stages of her possible future if she were to accept the prescribed gender roles using different women characters in the film. There is Jeevan's sister Sandhya, a single mother working in forensic medicine, trying to alter work and her two children. We also meet Jeevan's mother, a woman who lived her life only for her children. Yet her daughter does not want her in her life except as a child-minder. Sara directly challenges Jeevan's mother, who is pressurising her to continue the pregnancy, with "What have you achieved?" In another scene,

Sara goes to meet a retired woman actor she wants to cast in her film. This actor's husband laughs at his wife and says, "Give her a role, otherwise people will think that I am not giving her the permission to act". Sara stays quiet in front of the husband but mutters to herself, "Who says she needs your permission?" The film very subtly demonstrates how the actor herself is complicit in the patriarchal 'choreography' of life. This film's primary focus is on women being expected to become mothers and how that marginalises women or couples who choose to not have children. For such people, the men are questioned about their masculinity – equated with the ability to 'impregnate' and women are challenged about their femininity – equated with fertility.

Cultural and religious attitudes may value women according to their ability to produce children. Their health may consequently be endangered by repeated pregnancies spaced too closely together, often as the result of efforts to produce male children. Women who have not borne children may be cast out of marriages on the assumption that they, rather than their male partners, are infertile. Women may be deprived of access to health care that is unrelated to their reproductive functions, and their health needs may be considered secondary to those of their children or, in the case of pregnant women - to the health of their fetuses.

The right to reproductive choice means that women have a right to choose whether or not to reproduce, including the right to decide whether to carry or discharge an unwanted pregnancy and the right to choose their preferred method of family planning and contraception. The right to family planning education, information and services is key to reproductive choice, and central to women's sexual and reproductive health, especially given the risk of maternal mortality and the illegality of abortion in many countries.

The absence of an understanding of privacy in our cultural context is how family and friends come to know of Sara's pregnancy. Seeing Jeevan and Sara coming out of a gynaecologist's cabin, friends convey the information to Jeevan and Sara's family members with no regard for their privacy. The film talks about abortion from a sexual and reproductive rights- and choice-based perspective. Talking about abortion access for women within the framework of the Medical Termination of Pregnancy (MTP) Act and explaining the legal status of abortion in the country is a notable contribution of this film. There are hardly any mainstream films that portray abortion in a non-judgemental way. In the film, a male gynaecologist is willing to perform an abortion for Sara after counselling (as is required by the law). He mentions that it needs to be 'Sara's choice' more than it is Jeevan's as she would be the one to carry the pregnancy for nine months. He refers to contraceptive failure and the consequence as an 'accident'. He emphasises parenthood as a commitment and tells Sara the decision is more hers than anyone else's.

The fate of Sara's character in the story is a rare one. The film didn't expect her to misrepresent her career against what the family wants from her – motherhood. She is a person with dreams, who thankfully, can choose what she wants. In the film, she goes on to having an abortion and making her film, surrounded by her family, who have come to terms with her choices. The film breaks many stereotypes shown in mainstream Malayalam movies, one such example being that Sara wants to direct a thriller movie. The well-meaning producer of the film casually suggests that a heavy genre like a thriller would need an experienced male 'Director' and Sara asks him how much more experience one would need, listing her work.

In the film, Sara is a privileged woman from an upper-class family and has a supportive father and husband. So, when she stands firm in her decisions that do not conform to the heteropatriarchal ideal, she does not face much disagreement. The film contrasts Sara's situation with the lack of equal access to reproductive rights with that of a woman in the gynaecologist's waiting room who is pregnant with her fourth child. The film quietly supports feminism and stands for sexual and reproductive health and rights firmly. By matter-of-factly empathising with Sara, and not positioning arguments for and against, the film draws us into the complicated debate on reproductive rights. Sara's is a bold film that has the potential to make some people rethink their opinions. That mainstream cinema is handling issues relating to sexual and reproductive rights and choices indeed gives hope.

In the film, the director is telling the story from the woman's perspective. Given that Sara's revolves around a woman's right to abortion, there is no other way of telling this tale. It is Sara's decision and so we get to experience this film through her eyes. If you wonder why there is an apostrophe and s after her name, it is the director's way of giving her agency and emphasising that it is the woman's decision.

In all, Sara's directed by Jude Anthony Joseph is a film made from the female's perspective and the way she decides to deal with her ambitions, confusions, and dilemmas of life taking complete responsibility. The film is intelligent enough not to judge its key character for her early affairs or sex but has also been made with an obvious intention of not getting rated as a disturbing film. it disturbs and forces the youngsters to think about parenting in particular as it is one of the least discussed subjects in our social structure.

Benny's character is just one of the male characters in the film who think they give enough freedom to women in their lives. Like the producer, who announces he is 'not sexist' but doesn't want Sara to handle such a big film project. "You're a girl, you will find it very difficult," he says. Sara's is populated by several such 'progressive, non-sexist men. Popular film actor Anjali has quit cinema to attend to her duties as a wife and a mother. She seems to find happiness in her everyday household tasks at home and chooses little moments with her family over an offer that can fetch her a National Award. Or at least that's what she tells herself.

She is unwilling to accept a profound role in Sara's film, which would be perfect for her comeback. "I had already permitted her to do some television ads or become a judge in reality TV shows," (Sara's) says Anjali's husband, full of entitlement. He conveniently seems to forget that Anjali has her own free will. Screenwriter

Akshay Hareesh seamlessly directs Sara's story through the culvert of deliberate misogyny and this sort of casual sexism. When men support women to pursue their dreams, it always comes with a set of terms and conditions. In case there is a deadlock, it is up to the men to decide what's best for women. The ironies in this film need no explanation.

As much as this film is Sara's story, it is also the story of her husband Jeevan (Sunny Wayne). When Sara accidentally gets pregnant, she treats Jeevan with contempt. Jeevan, who never wanted to be a father, has now matured and wants to keep the baby. It is not an easy decision for Jeevan and it is supposed to be an emotional roller-coaster ride for him. But, the film hardly makes an effort to let us in on Jeevan's thoughts and emotions.

Fights over women's rights to sexual and reproductive health have been vital in advancing women's human rights in general. When reproductive health is understood to involve more than just the biological workings of a woman's womb, we arrive at "women-centred" approaches to sexual and reproductive health. A woman's right to reproductive autonomy is often reduced because of her status in society. Enjoyment of this right depends on her right to act as an independent adult of full legal capacity to participate in civil society and to be free from discrimination in its various forms. Conversely, without the right of reproductive choice, all other human rights - civil and political, economic and social - have only limited power to advance the well-being of women. Thus the film Sara's plays a role in the struggle for women's rights by trampling on the existing gender stereotypes.

Works Cited

Praveen S.R. "Sara's movie review. A Commendable attempt at shaking a societal norm." The Hindu, 6 July 2021. https"//www.thehhindu.com/entertainment/reviews/saras-movie-review-a   -commendable-attempt-at-shaking-a-societal-norm/article35144221.ece.

Sara's. Directed by Jude Anthany Joseph, July 2021. Amazon Prime Video.

Shalev, Carmel. "Rights to Sexual and Reproductive Health-the ICPD and the convention in the Elimination of All Forms of Discrimination Against Women." www.un.org/women watch/daw/csw/shalev.htm. March 18, 2018

Vettikad, Anna M.M. "Sara's Movie Review: A Brave Film on Women's Reproductive Rights with its own share of Unconscious Bias." First post, 14 July 2021.www.firstpost.com/entertainment/saras-movie-review-a-brave film-on-women's-reproductive-rights-with-its own-share of-unconscious-bias-9805611.html.

Bio-Note

Dr. Anjali Abraham joined the English department of M. A College (Autonomous) Kothamangalam as Assistant Professor on 11th October 2010. She took graduation and post-graduation from U.C College Alwaye. In 2005. She completed her M.Phil in English Language and Literature from S.S.U.S, Kalady. She was awarded a Doctorate in 2009 in English language and literature from Sree Sankaracharya University of Sanskrit, Kalady, and her thesis entitled Writing the Black Woman: A Study of Race and Gender in Alice Walker's Novels. She has published in various national and international journals. She has participated in and presented various research papers at seminars and conferences at the national and international levels. She worked as guest faculty in Govt. Law college, Ernakulam and S.S.U.S, Kalady. Her areas of interest include Phonetics, Indian literature and Black Literature. She has created her own YouTube channel and created e-content for online classes.

• • •

CHAPTER III

I SHALL NOT HEAR THE NIGHTINGALE: A SOCIO–PSYCHOLOGICAL STUDY OF HUMAN INSIGHTS

Dr. Reji George
Associate Professor of English, Department of English,
Shri Trikamjibhai Chatvani Arts and J. V. Gokal Trust Commerce College.

• • •

Kushwant Singh, the most well-read, columnist, author and journalist was born on 2nd Feb 1915, in Haldia (now in Pakistan). He initially began his career as a lawyer and but soon he switched over to writing. Despite being from a business family, he never showed his inclination towards business or construction. On the contrary, he developed the task of writing and published his first novel 'Mano – Manjra' which was later known as *The Train to Pakistan*. Initially, this work did not receive its due acceptance and praise but gradually it established Singh's genius as a novelist. *The Train to Pakistan* won Grove Press Award in 1954. This award motivated him to try another novel and gradually 'the Stone Started Rolling' and another three novels such as like *I Shall Not Hear the Nightingale* (1959), *Delhi* (1990) *and The Company of Women* (1999) won enough fame and name for Kushwant Singh. The speciality of Kushwant Singh is that he unhesitatingly writes on controversial issues and tries to present the real subdued human sentiments and emotions explicitly. He is equally popular for his acerbic pen, wit, humour and also for satires on social issues. In his novel, *I Shall Not Hear the Nightingale* the social custom, atmosphere and family values system of pre-independence years has been beautifully presented. He has also boldly revealed the various paradoxes of human relations, subdued sentiments and its exhibitions in this work. According to Santha Rama Rao: "Khushwant is direct to the point of brutality, unsentimentally observant, and in his bold characterisation, he is ready to explore the least appealing aspects of human nature and relationship" (1).

The story 'I Shall Not Hear the Nightingale' moves around the Punjabi Sikh family of Buta Singh, who is a faithful magistrate of the British Raj. Contradictory to his beliefs and ideologies, his son Sher Singh becomes the leader of an anti-British group. The ideological conflict between a father and son is strikingly presented by Kushwant Singh. This reveals the tendencies and temperament of the new generation and also the ideological generation gap, that is to say, the Pro-British and the AntiBritish. The novel also reflects upon the personal lives of the freedom fighters. This novel beautifully reveals the various human psyche reflected through various characters in different situations and phases of life. The story exhibits the religious, spiritual and traditional psyche of the characters. It also depicts the traditions, celebrations and rituals of the Sikh community during World War II. Kushwant Singh has successfully made a creative rendering of the real. In this novel, he has attempted to explore the deep insight into the human psyche that faced trials, tribulations and temptations at various layers and phases of life.

The author has tried to explore and expose the hidden human and natural psychological reflections, insights and responses very meticulously and quite naturally. He has boldly exposed the extramarital relations and subdued natural human instincts through various characters and situations in which they are placed. The situation in the first chapter of the novel is rooted deeply in the characters and illustrates their mentality of young schoolboys who pretends to be youth and mature warriors. Their inner psychological repression against the British is reflected in the performance of 'baptism in blood' following the conformity of the ancient Hindu custom of dipping swords in the blood of the goat and laying them before Goddess Durga to be blessed. Thus, in the beginning, Singh presents the custom–ridden psychology of the younger generation during the Pre – Independence era. The incident where Sher Singh is reluctant to shoot and kill the crane (sarus), as he believed that "if one of a pair is killed, the other dies of grief" (2).

It is the culture, inculcations and nourishment of the family values that force Sher Singh to think so. Being brought up in a traditional Sikh family under the strict guidance and religious attitude of his mother – Sabharai, prevents him from killing a harmless bird. However, the influence of his friends like Madanlal and other youngsters changed the harmless psychological approach of Sher Singh. Later, we observe that the same Sher Singh attains the courage to kill even a fellow human being. We witness the transformed brutal mentality of Sher Singh. The very idea of patriotism is reduced to a sordid murder which Sher Singh commits to saving himself. However, Sher Singh neither owned the strength nor the manhood to cope up with the 'conflicting emotions of guilt and pride'The nature and deeper insight of a true, elderly housewife is reflected in the portrayal of Sabhrai- the wife of Bhuta Singh and an affectionate mother of Sher Singh. She embodies the Indian culture of her time. She is presented as a replica of common Indian housewives, who are generally, devoted to the services of family members and religious activities. She regarded

'The Granth Sahab' as her source of knowledge and encouragement. She was a woman with great maturity, a deeper understanding of life and true towards her conscience. When she returns from Simla, she realizes that something has gone wrong back at home and invades her serene and religious world of moral values. On her return, she comes to know about her son's arrest and wants to meet him in jail. Before proceeding, she reads the Granth Sahabcontinuously and she prays the entire night at the Golden Temple, takes a dip in the cold mater in preparation for seeing her son. She conveys the message of her husband to her son. However, she reveals the true feeling which her conscience conveyed. She said, "... my son had done wrong. But if he named the people who were with him, he would be doing greater wrong. He was no longer to be regarded as a Sikh and I was not to see his face again" (3).

It is this voice of truth and courage that elevates her status to a greater and higher position. Here, once again, the in-depth psychology of a conscientious mother is exhibited very naturally. She becomes the voice of truth and love and thus gives the correct advice. She is the spirit of the entire family. She is a woman with an extraordinary, profound and instinctive understanding of life. Kushwant Singh has minutely portrayed her matured sense of viewing and dealing with the issues of life. Kushwant Singh has exposed the deeper and hidden unfulfilled carnal physical desires of a married woman and married man. It is revealed in the physical intimacy and advances developed by champak (the wife of Sher Singh) and Madanlal (the friend of Sher Singh). Champak is presented as a woman with unfulfilled lust which is reflected in her extramarital affairs with Madanlal. Here, the author wants to draw attention to the drawbacks of joint Indian families where married couples are forbidden to meet openly for satisfying their physical quest. "Many young couples live with unfulfilled physical impulses 'resulting in an obsession with sex and in many perversions which result from frustration, sadism, masochism and most common of all exhibitionism" (4).

Such a psychological state of mind may lure them towards extramarital relations. One more example of the subdued physical urge of human beings is exhibited through the character of Shun no – the middle-aged maidservant. An interesting and shocking event emerges as Shunno was seen seeking the help of Peer Sahib (A Muslim saint) to get a cure for a mysterious disease. As she had no faith in eastern or western medicines, she sought the help of Peer Sahib. This encounter with Peer Sahib 'violates the rules of celibacy' and we see Shunno engulfed in sensual pleasure with Peer Sahib, it is strikingly explicit in the following narration by Kushwant Singh: "Here was a man twenty years younger, strong and virile with an untamed lust savagely tearing off the padding of respectability with which she had covered herself. He stirred up the fires of the volcano which had all but become extinct. It was wrong but was deliciously irresistible" (5).

The illicit physical relations with Peer Sahib and Shunno run counter with the illicit affairs of Madan and Champak. However, there is a difference in social stratification. Madan and Champak belong to the upper-class stratum of Indian hierarchical society and Shunno and Peer Sahib belong from the lower section of the society. The author attempts to depict and expose the "tearing off the padding of respectability". It is the ironic presentation of this stark reality and truth in all 'its horror and elemental passion'. The author opines that any socio-psychological suppression especially related to sensual dissatisfaction can cause very serious consequences. Kushwant Singh has tried to treat the theme of carnal desire at a psychological level which results in physical intimacy. Physical intimacy results out of love or attraction. Though it comes at a later phase, it remains one of the priorities for a balanced socio-psychological society. The author has boldly unveiled the stark and bitter truth of a society that exists in the real world and has poignantly satirized these kinds of people. In this novel, the author has courageously presented the personal life of freedom fighters. The novel also beautifully reveals the vivid traditional and cultural description of the Sikh rituals and traditions. In the present novel, Kushwant Singh has minutely explored the various socio-cultural spiritual, religious and psychological facets of the pre-independent Punjabi society with all its realistic representation. The 'nightingale' in the novel is a multi-dimensional symbol. The symbol of 'nightingale' in I Shall Not Hear the Nightingale is, thus, a symbol of realism.

Works Cited

Santha Rama Rao: The New York Times Book Review, December 13, 1959, P.36

Singh, Kushwant, I Shall not Hear the Nightingale, Delhi: Ravi Dayal Publisher, 1997,

Ibid, P. 208

Ibid, pp. 47-48.

bid, p. 159

Anand, T. S, "Sabhrai, The Maternal Women in I Shall not Hear the Nightingale.",

Mothers and Mother Figures in Indo English Literature, Ed. Usha Bande, Jalandhar: ABS

Publications, 1994.

CHAPTER IV

A CULTURAL STUDY ON INDIAN ETHNIC INCLUSIVENESS

Dayaram R Meshram

R.D Collage Allapalli Dist.Gadchiroli

ABSTRACT

The main objective of this paper is to investigate the role of ethnic inclusiveness in Indian English literature. Man and culture are both different sides of the same coin and they both embody each other. Etheric Inclusiveness in Indian literature is different from another post-colonial language. Cultural ethnic discrepancies may be accommodated in social, Political and Economic arrangements. It means enables people to live their originality consciously and without authorization the other cultures. This paper to study in the form of a survey will show the need for the district to include literature. Almost all the Indian English novelists huge clay to give the shape of world-class novels more over globalization has given birth of the hybrid culture. Like English novelist R.K. Narayan, Mulk Raj Anand, Raja-Raw, Vikram Seth, Arun Joshi, Amitao Ghosh, Khushwant Singh and all other males have successfully dealt with various topics in their fictions.

• • •

INTRODUCTION

Indian "Cultural Studies" designates a cross-disciplinary enterprise for analyzing the condition that affects the production, reception and cultural Significance of all types of institution Practice and product. A chief concern is to specify the functioning of the social, economic and political forces and power. The role of English in Indian literature is a curio Cultural Phenomenon. Ethnic culture consists of distinguishable individuals, within a majority and social system by sharing characteristics such as race, religion, language cultural modes. Ethnic culture with its distinctive subject matter. Ethnic cultural context and mclian literature are different. According to Ashcroff Bill and others, Diasporic fiction in English in the (1) Post-colonial period has not only been exciting but abundant but has undergone some fundamental transformation of theme and technique. And recent years, the Idea of ethnic-inclusiveness has become a powerful and controversial influence in a variety of social and cultural territories. This paper proposes to analyse and compare the multicultural elements.

Multiculturalism is so imminently bound up in many parts of the world with that practice and discourses which manage diversity Ethnic inclusiveness means different things in different contexts in Canada, the united states of America and the united kingdom the term is intertwined with questions of racialized difference that have so for not been given sufficient recognition India. Ethnicity differs from race, nationality religion and migrant status. Sometimes in subtle ways, but include facets of these other concepts. It follows that investigators who wish to study ethnicity on such underlying factors, especially language, religion country of birth and family origins. Assamese literature has a long and glorious history starting with the charyapadas which were Buddhist devotional songs writer between the 8th and 12th century A.D in the late 13th century. The most well-known pre vaishnavite period of Assam was Mahadev Kandali who rendered Valmiki's Ramayana India is cultured by more ethnic and religious groups than most other countries of the world. The Assam problem is primarily ethnic, the Punjab problem is primarily ethnic.

Ethnic Inclusiveness in Indian Cultural Literature English is considered to be a subsidiary official language that is often reserved for government and commercial purposes. Although India does not officially recognize racial or ethnic categories in the national census, it continues to be one of the most ethnically diverse populations in the world. Bradly ethnicities of India can be broken down into main groups based on their linguistic background, the two largest being in to Aryan and Dravidian for example many people belonging to Indo-Aryan ethnicities live in the northern half of the country, Dravidianlanguage commonly spoken include Tamil, Kannada, Telugu and Malayalam and 2

Indo-Aryan languages commonly spoken include Hindi, Bengali, Marathi, Urdu, Odia and Punjabi these labels of Indo-Aryan and Dravidian usually serve as a helpful way to categories the origins of Indian ethnic diversity, although they don't necessarily reflect people's identity. The word Ethnic was derived in the 14th century as a noun and in the 15th century as adjective meaning heathen from the Greek word ETHOS which means nation According to CHAMBERS 21ST century Dictionary ethic is relating to or having the common race of cultural tradition it is associated with an exotic especially non-European, racial or tribal group. Ajay Sahebrao Deshmukh in his book "ethnic angst" says that whenever any culture or ethnic group or civilization has an advantage over all others whether culturally or politically there programs of glorification has usually directed to the destruction of not just that ethnic group or civilization but also that of the other who have been drawn to cultural identity has become the major issue in the multicultural nations that clash arises in the multiethnic nation because the dominant culture is reluctant to absorb the immigrant cultures Both basic sidhwa and Mistryhave depicted the way hoe Parsi interacts with the rest of the world.

Sidhwas novel *The crow Eaters* talks about the Parsi community and their movement and migration to the UK and they try to be like the British on another side Mistry's novel family matters is about the middle-class family matters of a Parsi family living in Bombay it carries them of immigration. Alienation communal disharmony etc. Bapsi sidhwa likes to be called a Panjabi Pakistani Parsi woman. Her first two novels the bride and the crow eaters bought her recognition she is a prominent writer of the diaspora of Pakistan. Sidhwa deals with ethnic identity. She has taken up the issue of cultural differences and also discussed problems arising out of it in her novel The crow eaters in these words she has given information about the customs, ceremonies myth legends and various other aspects related to Parsi life, RobinsonMistry's family matters in India he shows the marginalized existence of Parsis. Which is threatened by the impact of modernity it presents longing for home and problem of homelessness and through the narration of domestic crisis in one middle-class family According to T.S Eliot is the spirit which motives ideas and customs The General ethos of the people they have to govern determines the behaviour of political (T.S Eliot P.25) to Pre-Independence era the British Rular expressed themselves in Englishman. And English employees covered the Indian milieu. Sir William Jones has composed 'Hymns to Hindu Deities Deen Mahomet also published his travelogue in English entitled The Travels of "deen mohamet" (3).

However, English language and literature introduced global affairs such as the American Revolution French Revolution as well as Voltaire and Rosseau the argument of Surendranath Banargee Sir Aurobindo, C. Y. Chintamani in the Newspaper Amrit Bazar Patrika. And the national congress leaders like Dadabhai Nauroji, M.G. Rande, G.K Gokhale, Motilal Neharu, Jawaharlal Neharu and M.K. Gandhi created introspective literature through their writings and speeches. Balabhai Desai M.A Jinnah, V.K. Krishna Menon and Dr, B.R. Ambedkar the well-known barristers elaborated Indian Perspective through their pleading in the court of law which was an essence of Indian ethos. Sir Aurobindo, Rabindranath Tagore, Puran high, Sarojini Naidu and Shri Anand Acharya the first generation of poets and writers in English from India played the role of a bridge between the western and Indian culture Besides the next generation Mulk Raj Anand, Raja Rao and R.K. Narayan. The novelist and the short story writers had closely explored Indianness' in the sentence Pattern, dialogues, feelings, reactions and themes by the early half of the 20th century. In the post-colonial period (1950-1980) Indian ethnic- Inclusiveness was associated with the social, political and economical Problems of India. Apart from Nissim Ezekiel, A.K. Ramanujan, R. Parthasarthy Pritish Nandy. A. K. Mehrotra, Arun Kolhatkar, Jayant Mahapatra, Dilip Chitre, Saleem Preeradina and Agha Sahid Ali also covered issues like everyday life it also shared the global aspects of Postmodernism that is parody intertextuality, literary cannibalism etc. Salman Rushdie, Vikram Seth, Allan Sealy, Shashi Tharoor, Bharati Mukharjee, Upamanyu Chatterjee, V.S Nainapal, Chetan Bhagat m Anita Desai, Arundhati Roy, and Amitav Ghosh are renowned literary figures in contemporary Indian English literature, they have covered a wide range of themes social, historical, romantic, conflict, freedom moment and the partition of the country. Their writings are instructive, expressing religious faith and urge for reformation.

Indian Ethnic Fiction

Jogesh Das's novel was titled Dawar Aru Nai (clouds Have Gone) this is the first Assamese novel set against the background of the tea-garden, Brinchi Kumar Baruahs Seuhi Patar Kalani (The Story of the Green Leaves) in1959 in this novel novelist reveals the deep plight and sufferings. In another novel by the same author titled Anami Nagini (1963) with this novel, the novelist tries to present the life and society of the Angami nagas. The third novel portrayed the life of the soldier against the background of the revolution Birendra Kumar Bhattacharjee is novel Iyaraingom was published in1960 the story is based on the Naya tribe residing in Manipur in1965, Pashupati Bharadwaj's novel 'Simsangar Dutipar ' (The two sides of the Simsang river) It describe the plight, pain and sufferings of the Garo community of the Mymensingh district of East Pakistan offer the partition India Amulya Barua wrote Ukhan Jangha (my treasure) based on the Khasi lifeworld in 1973 in 1996 Dhrubajyoti Bora's novel simantar sur (Tunes from the Border) was Published. The novel is set against the backdrop of the Arunachala Society in 1992 Uma Kanta Sharma wrote a novel Bharand Pakhir jak (A flock of Vulture-type Birds) whether he introduces relevant issues related to the question of ethnic identity.

Conclusion

In this present research in an attempt to study the various aspects of the fictional work and is confined to the study of the relationship of Indian people, how they live their life with different understanding and self-confinement to conclude this chapter provides an introduction in the current study, It defines the term ethos and that too Indian ethos this study's line of enquiry would also be further advanced by more ethnographic research which Focuses on space, place material and intangible culture, both within and without the context of organized events the process and criteria for selection of certain elements as "authentic" otherwise knowledge to passed down through generations. There is a saying "if "language is a plant literature is its flower" our country has a vast literature-rich culture and tradition.

Works Cited

Arthur Lewis, W (1954) The Principal of economic Planning (PP.10-11) London:

George Allen Unwin

Anand, Mulk Raj. Untouchable 2nd End. (London: Penguin Books (1940)

Ashcroft, Bill and Ahluwalia, D. pal's Edward said 2

nd (London: Routledge, 2001)

Bendrick, B. 1963 Indians in a Plural Society (Second ed. London) Her Majesty's

Stationary office

Bennet J.W.Ced 1975 The New Ethnicity: Perspective from Ethnologh. St. Paul.

New York: West Publishing co.

Benton, M. 1983 Racial & Ethnic commotion: Cambridge University Press.

Cambridge dictionary. Cambridge.org/English/ avatar

Das, Bijay Kumar, The Horizon of Nissim Ezekiel's Poetry Delhi: B.R Publishing

Corporation, 1995

Graddol, David, English next U. K British council. Digital Edition by the English

Company U.K ltd, 2006

Kannan C.T.1978 Cultural Adaptation of Asian immigrants: first and second

Generation, Bombay: India Printing works.

Krousi, E 1971 Ethnic minorities in Britain, London: Macgibbon and kee.

Macauley. T.B. "Munute by the Hon'ble T.B Macauley" 2 nd Feb 1835.

M.G Smith (eds.) 1965 Pluralism in Africa. Berkeley. Los Angles: university of California

Narayan, R.K. Aspects of Indian writing in English Naik M. K. Ed Delhi: the macmillian company of India ltd.1982

Narayan, R.K. The painter of signs (London: Penguin Books, 1982.)

CHAPTER V

NARRATIVE TECHNIQUE IN THE NOVELS OF HEMINGWAY

Jesfert Aagy

Lecturer, Gariyonis University, Benghazi, Libya

• • •

Hemingway received the Nobel Prize for literature in 1954 for his powerful style and mastery of art in modern narration. It is as a stylist that Hemingway commands the greatest respect among contemporary writers. The famous Hemingway style which he forged in the early twenties, has been imitated by many, though it seldom attained perfection as in the hands of Hemingway. Hemingway's style is unusual, special and different. He developed a style of his own, a tone that is no one else's. Though he has hundreds of disciples, one can easily distinguish them. Where did Hemingway get his style? Whom does it belong to? Critics have sensed to Hemingway some of the directness, harshness and candour of Mark Twain. We consider Mark Twain pre-eminently as a humorist. But there is often violence in his humour "Howells applauded, and was full of praise and endorsement which was in him and judicious. If he had manifested a different spirit, I could have them thrown out of the window. I like criticism, but it must be my way" (1).

Mark Twain was capable of looking at a subject with devastating accuracy of the death of his brother. He was able to say mingling compassion with force. The realism of Mark Twain reflects in the harshness of life on the American frontier, which developed a strong sense of realism among those who lived it. Hemingway, a generation later prefers a frontier kind of life. Born in a well-to-do suburban family outside the great city of Chicago. As an adolescent, he preferred the backwards of Northern Michigan. As a young man, and throughout his life, he lived and wrote about the frontier places of the world and the frontier experience of the human race; war, bullfighting, hunting and fishing in Cuba, Spain and Africa. Hemingway's style began as a deliberate reworking of his idiom of two other styles, one literary and the other non-literary. The non-literary style was that of a good newspaper and a feature writer, keenly observant and descriptive.

The literary style was that of Gertrude Stein - with a stress on the monosyllabic, small simple words and declarative sentences to achieve a pure statement with very little emotion, except for dry understated humour. Much of Hemingway's writings, especially the earlier ones, consists of simple declarative sentences like Gertrude Stein's. The first collection of his short stories, "In Our Time" is a classic example of short beautiful sentences; sometimes strung together with coordinating conjunctions. The first chapter of "A Farewell to Arms" is another well-known example. " In the last summer of that year, we lived in a house in a village that looked across the river and the plain to the mountains. In the bed of the river, there were pebbles and boulders, dry and white in the sun and the water was clear and swiftly moving and blue in the channels. Troops went by the house and down the road and the dust they raised powdered the leaves of the trees" (2). He adopted this style from Gertrude Stein who wanted him to cut out unnecessary details and focus the attention on the most important event in the narration. Hemingway's contribution to the art of narration is his dialogue. Words like "Charmingly" "Smilingly", "Hesitatingly" etc. are completely missing. And they are replaced by one simple word "said". A typical Hemingway dialogue runs like this: "What are you looking at? "Max looked at George "Nothing".

"The hell you were. You are looking at me. "

Maybe the boy meant it for a joke, Max ! " (3)

It is possible that there are very few adjectives and adverbs used. The greatest burden is put forward by the nouns and simple verbs. What the author was trying to achieve was not to give the reader what the author felt, but he was looking for the sequence of notion and acts which produces the emotion.

This style was not a revolt against 19th-century romanticism. The famous Hemingway style evolved as a reply to the crash of values after the 1st World War on the English Literary Scenario. The famous passage in " A Farewell to Arms" in which he states that words like patriotism and Glory appear Obscene to him because of the manifesto of the new writing that Hemingway was trying to out. He wanted the writer to use a maximum number of simplest words accurately. He believed that if the experience felt are deep and genuine, it can be expressed in a simple language without creating ambiguity and complication.

Even when the hero is suffering deeply, he would express his emotion in simple words like "damn it ", " hell with you " etc. This style, though it looks extremely simple, is not simple. It requires hard discipline and a deep understanding of language. Hemingway received the language of Huckleberry Finn, the colloquial American language. He also brought to literature the language of bar and brothel and the street. There are no declarative words to distract the attention of the readers. In one place Edmund Wilson remarks that Hemingway was influenced by Gertrude Stein's " conventional as well as her literary style" (4)

Among other personalities Hemingway liked includes Harold Leob, James Joyce, Ezra pound etc. In their thirties, his style changed. The old biblical austerity was replaced with a certain flexibility and ease that goes with confidence. The influence of the authorized version of the Bible is visible in Hemingway. But he had used that style for delineating contemporary society. Now the sentences have become longer, dramatic and situations become more and more complex and in fact, it was a movement towards the style of Faulkner. In "Green Hills of Africa" Hemingway goes more poetic. "If you save society, democracy, and the other things quite young and declining any further enlistment make yourself, you exchange the pleasant comforting stench of comrades for something you can never feel in any other way than yourself" (5)

This makes a break with the past austere style that Hemingway used for writing the condition of the contemporary man in " In Our Time ". During this period the adverbs and adjectives which he used in the past occupied their rightful place. The style is certainly relaxed. Not that he had discontinued the earlier style. It acquired flesh and muscle in addition to the skeletal bones that were predominant earlier. The vision that Hemingway had acquired in his old age is the maturation of the earlier tentative views that he had evolved and later rested in the arena of life. Similarly, his style reduces the English language to primitive elementary forms. As he had withdrawn from the complexities of life which baffled him in "For Whom the Bell Tolls" and "To Have and Have Not". Similarly, he also withdrew from the complexities of the language and started imitating the style that had evolved in the Twenties. It is a case of regression rather than development. When Faulkner was asked to comment on Hemingway's style, he remarked: "He has courage, he never crawled out on a limb. He has never used a word that might cause the reader to check with a dictionary to see if it is properly used." (6)

When Hemingway learned of Faulkner's adverse comment, he replied, "I use the oldest words in the English language when I write. People think I am an ignorant bastard that doesn't know the ten-dollar words. There are older better words, and if you use them in proper combination, you make it stick" (7). Whether Hemingway wrote in his early style, or his middle style he is unique among modern writers because he pressed his style into the service of his subject matter. His style had become the minimal representation of the moral attitudes of the author. In absence of any code, the style itself becomes the code. In Hemingway's writings, one can sense the bitter tussle going on in the mind between realism and symbolism. The symbolic effects in his novels are achieved through a suitable process of suggestions. Among the many which must be mentioned. We shall be concerned with only three, the weather, the emblematic people and the landscape. The best known of this is the first. Almost with poetic care, Hemingway builds up in the readers a mental association that came naturally enough to Hemingway himself. In his second experience of war and its aftereffects, he had personally watched the pitiful stream of refugees plodding through mud and sodden with rain during the memorable evacuation of civilian people from the city of Adrianople.

Anyone who reads "A Farewell to Arms " with a weather eye will eventually marvel as he watches the author playing with falling air as a symbol of imminent doom. Towards the close of the book, the weather warms and the rain arrives. For a whole miraculous winter, the lovers have gloried in their isolation, living happily in their high mountain fastness, surrounded by healthy cold air and snow, far from the mud and muck of war. Now at last the rain comes, some great change lurks, just beyond the lover's limited horizon. We just seem to sense that Catherine is in mortal jeopardy as in dew she is. Another manifestation of symbolic intent in the novel is the subtle way in which the author plays two levels of the landscape against each other. Without following it slavishly, he carefully establishes a pattern in which plains or lowlands are associated in the reader's mind with war, death pain, sadness or gloom. The high mountain regions an Abruzzin Switzerland, where the priest originated and Lausanne, where the lovers establish their temporary heart-land are carefully associated with pleasure and good life, joy and health or whatever stands opposed to the plains of Veneto where the war is being fought and the great retreat has been made. This poetic association of heights with pleasure and depths with pain is Hemingway's version.

In sum, we can suggest that " A Farewell to Arms' and "For Whom The Bell Tolls" are symbolic in undertone though there is a marked difference between symbols that operate in both the novels. The damp weather and rain in the previous novel are replaced by the warm sun which dominates the latter – the sun shining through the trees and warming the pine needled earth. The setting – except for the occasional huddling within the caves where the atmosphere was close, sullen as Pablo brooded drunkenly on his lost manhood, as tempers flared darkly, and death stalked ominously is out of doors. Their love was made and soldiers death received. Hemingway represents Maria as the child of the sun with her hair having the colour of ripened wheat, and she has the colour of burnt gold and her eyes gold with dark flakes in them. The sun is identified with their love:

" On the day Jordan and Maria made love the hot gold of the sun co-mingled with the heather smell of the earth and the cropped golden heir of Maria – blending into Van Goh – like a celebration of the sun so that the pulsing energy of the sun beat through the lovers into the earth and the earth moved. For Jordan Maria was the sun driving away the night and abolishing the loneliness: She was a life that held off death." (8)

Yet another association that Hemingway attributes to Maria is that of virgin Maria – her very name suggests the force of her love and will obliterate the violence that had been done to her and recaptured her virginity. Despite the Loyalist's official disapproval of the church is to the virgin that many of the partisans and even fascists turned in the presence of death. It was the young boy in El Sordo's Band, who as the planes swooped down uttered " Hail Mary": it was the enemy. Lt. Berrendo riding at the head of the column: prayed to the virgin for the soul of his friends. Again at the same moment, it was Anselmo, who caught the sight of the enemy column, and frozen by fear, prayed to the "Most kind, Most sweet, Most eminent Virgin." As we have noticed earlier, the sun, like the rain in "A Farewell to Arms " has been surprisingly been used as a dominant symbol of death. In the last chapter when all that has gone, the sun is curiously twisted with death. Jordan who has always the advent of the sun lay on the pine-needled earth and watched the first light of the sun dispelling the light mist, that obscured the outline of the bridge. As the bridge shone clear in the morning light, he heard the bomb drop, and he drew a long breath as if he expel the lonely feeling that came with the dealing of death and he prepared to shoot the sentry. The sentry stood in the road with the sun shining on him: " There was no mist on the road now and Robert- Jordan saw the man, clearly and sharply standing there on the road, looking at the sky. The sun shone brightly on the trees" (9).

" The Old Man and the Sea" is a classic example of Hemingway's style. The very title of the book suggests that the old man pictured against the vastness of the sea is a metaphor for the human condition. In the vastness of life like the sea, there are endless possibilities that lie hidden from the common eye. The old man suggests the total universe in which everybody has to go and take a chance " like any man, bird or fish".

Santiago's struggle against the marlin is suggestive of the endless struggle that man has to undergo in life. Survival in this context is not mere physical survival but it means survival with dignity and self-respect. It also means a life full of richness, meaning and beauty. Santiago kills the fish not merely for keeping him alive but for pride and self-respect. The fish is a symbol of what man can achieve and therefore without this achievement his life would have been meaningless. Only by participating in the duel action of killing the marlin and later defending the marlin against sharks, does he justify the title? In his defeat, there is no loss of true pride. He has dramatized the moral code that defeat is immaterial and what is important is that man should continue striving irrespective of the result. As Hemingway says: " But man is not made for defeat. A man can be destroyed but not defeated." (10)

Santiago also stands for a creative artist like Hemingway himself. It does not matter how many times he has proved himself in the past. Every day is a new day and every day he must prove himself. In Santiago's sufferings, Hemingway has created a beautiful metaphor for all times. To analyze the symbolic meaning of "The Old man and the Sea" is like dissecting a beautiful flower. So one can at the most suggest a few meaning which lies under the surface. Santiago has to kill his true brother and that is the tragedy of mankind. He is bound to carry the guilt of killing his brother in his subconscious mind. Similarly, sharks have many meanings. They symbolize the evil that exists in this world for its own sake. Other symbols are Marlin, the boy, Di Maggio and the lions. The boy is a powerful symbol of youth. Often he thinks about it and gets inspiration from it.

Di Maggio acts as a tonic on the waning spirit of the old man. Santiago draws constant inspiration from this base ballplayer. The lions in their grace and dignity help the old man to relax. These two embody the rhythm of life in which spurts of action must be followed by relaxation. Critics have pointed out that there is a close parallel between Santiago and Christ. Santiago's journey up the hill carrying the mast, lying on the bed with his arms spread, the fall of Santiago during his ascent, all have some close resemblance with Jesus Christ walking up the hill of Calvary carrying his cross on his shoulder. Hemingway used to rewrite his books and this enabled him to achieve perfection in his writings.

"I always rewrite each day up to the point where I stopped. When it is all finished, naturally you go over it. You get another chance to correct and rewrite when someone else types it, and you see it clean in type. The last chance is in this proof. You are grateful for this chance" (11). When Hemingway speaks of leaving things out, what he really means by it is rearranging them in a different way and giving them a different rhythm. The very letter of 27 July 1952, in which he expounded his iceberg theory to Longwell, is helpful in understanding this. Hemingway tells how he knew many details of every character in the fishing village to which the old man belonged, but he left that out. He had also seen a school of more than fifty sperm whales in the same stretch of water and he left that too.

Here we have a brief history of Hemingway's narrative technique. Artist does not have to include everything that he sees in every work. If he knows he can compress details and can also safely leave out things he knows too well. His story would acquire strength in proportion to the clever handling of comparisons and omissions.

Works Cited

William Deahn Howells, Outed in Vision of Disaster. p.10

Earnest Hemingway, The Killers in Interpreting Literature, Penguin Books 1970. P.1

Earnest Hemingway, , The Killers in Interpreting Literature, Ed Knicked Bocker. P 133

Edmund Wilson, The shores of Light. P. 577

Earnest Hemingway The Green Hills of Africa. New York, Charles Scribners sons

1952. p.96

John V Hopkin Style and meaning in Hemingway and Faulkner. P .170

Ibid. P. 170

Melvin Blackman, The matador and the Crucified in modern Fiction Oxford University Press. P140

Earnest Hemingway For Whom the Bell Tolls Jonathan and Cape. P.406

Earnest Hemingway- The Old Man and the Sea Charls Scribners. P 109

George Pimpton, An interview with Earnest Hemingway and his Critics. P 24

FREEDOM AT MIDNIGHT: DISRUPTIVE SPATIALITY OF NORMATIVE DISJUNCTURE AND DECEPTIVE WILL OF RESISTANCE

Jesto Thankachan

Assistant Professor, Department of English

St. Peter's College, Kolenchery

ABSTRACT

Erasure of an individual's socio- psychic space can be a paradoxical predicament for him/her. The Malayalam short film directed by R J Shan critically attempts to enunciate the expressive angst of a confined feminine will of subjectivity. Chandra's domestic space of subjective appropriations and the affective realm of familial wellness is morally assaulted by her husband's estrangement. At the end of dramatic fury and seemingly subversive verbal performances related to the critical erasures of morally familial spatiality, the feminine resistance which adopts deceptive faces of self-expression is dragged to be the victimized continuity of the masculine moral norms of institutionalized insecurity which is originally intended to be destabilized by the feminist concerns of narration.

Keywords: Affective Power, Masculine Morality and Deceptive Resistance.

• • •

Freedom at Midnight: Disruptive Spatiality of Normative Disjuncture and Deceptive Will of Resistance

Freedom at midnight is a Malayalam short film directed by R J Shan. The short film directly reveals the wounded life of the female protagonist, Chandra, with this crucial title of semantic outburst. The title bears the problematic concern of free will which is juxtaposed with critical ruptures of the image, midnight. It reminds us of the break of darkness that disconnected India as a socio-political space of cultural liberation from the shackles of colonization. The territorial spatiality is symbolically attached to the evolution of feminine free voice from the side of socio-political consciousness. It says something. To be analytical on freedom one needs to be open to the critical spatiality of collectivity.

The imaginative quests of feminine freedom become explored with this spatial dimension of collective subjectivity. Freedom finds the modes of subjectivity not essentially in a solitary chamber, but in the openness of collective identity. The feminist political strand is clearly established in a sense by the narration with the positioning of subjectivity and the idea of collectivity within the frames of the imaginative ruptures of freedom.

The opening scene is set alongside a calm water body where the protagonist talks to her friend about a possible legal separation between her and her husband which is almost impending. The quietness of water with the shapelessness of reflections and the surrounding silent greenery depicts her mindset. The sensitive calm of the protagonist is located within the symbolic layers of natural productivity offered by the greenery. The feminine subjectivity has the strength and figurative spectrum of a water body. But that well-composed subjectivity that seemingly projects the face of attacked will talk to her distant companion about the act of separation. At the same time, the subjective will of her shapeless calm is concerned about the future of her daughter after her marital separation. Freedom is not just a conceptual map of preconceived contentions here. It gradually reveals itself as an ardent voice of subjective loss which tries to discover its state of originality consistently.

Towards that context which is dominated by the shapeless feminine will the husband, Das, enters. He does not know anything about the impending act of separation. His initial response itself is related to the readability of her personal decisions in their private life. Then he shares a grievance. That is how he reveals his mode of presence. That grievance is too symbolically related to a kind of longing and disconnect. He has waited to meet her a few hours before that conversation. She too has waited for him before she has been drawn to suspend her waiting without informing him anything. The conversation on the failed symbolic longing is interrupted by other 'calls' also. They try to make their individual demands heard. But the active intrusions make the channel of mutual readability feeble.

Das again raises a grievance regarding their daughter. He easily accuses the mother of the hostility shown by the disobedient girl who has thrown a phone to a bowl of 'Sambar', the popular Malayali dish when she has not been given permission to use the phone according to her wish. Her father taught her to use the phone. But to him when she crosses the border of the normative discipline of that cyber utilitarian culture her act deserves to be attacked. Even when she makes the act of transgression which has a strong attachment to her ties with her father, her mother is conveniently accused. The real and instrumental value of utilitarian performance is owned to be taught by the father figure. The distortion of that utilitarian order caused by the 'unauthorized' response of the individual is owned to be given by the mother by birth. Moral fixity organized by masculinity and performative distortion of femininity can be read in this fragment of grievance. Interestingly the familiar face of the dish, Sambar, too signifies the dominant culinary drives of the Malayali social psyche. The phone with a feminine attack on utilitarian will fall into the familiar taste of Malayali masculine appetite.

Chandra, the name of the protagonist with its semantic roots in Malayalam can indirectly be elevated to the completeness/ incompleteness of the moon. That tenderly cultural romantic image illuminates the private spatiality of the night to which the radical question of freedom is attached. Das the name of her husband semantically addresses the brokenness of a hierarchical relationship when we locate the word in the milieu of Malayali culture. The protagonist asks her husband for a free ride initially on their bike and later in the car. Her wish is simply rejected. The bike ride is her first option. The romantic openness of the bike ride is given up easily owing to the husband's dislike for rain which is inevitably another image of romantic order of alterity. A cab with the space of secure closure is also not taken as he finds other serious commitments at that time. The rejections made by the husband are appropriated and sharpened by the codes of authentic needs of normative order. Rain, the chaotic other, which is attacked by the husband as a romantic rebellion of time enters into the scene with dramatic pace to be the facelessness of the abandoned subversive drives of Chandra's free space. Another referential remark can be spotted at this point in time. The husband who easily marks his wife as the representative of the disrupted and destabilized utilitarian order of life in a call offers a free space to his female colleague. But that offer is also an extension of the masculine moral malleability.

As Chandra abandons herself in rain her husband breaks into that solitary space that contains the psychic stillness of feminine face. He takes her away from the rain. Das tries to be someone who stands for the wellness of his wife when he raises a grievance against her affinity towards rain, the rebellious order of being, which can make her sick. When they enter into the house, the domestic space of familial regularity, a caged bird appears as the contextual presence. A delicate piece of musical facelessness that represents a romantically feeble paternal presence too emerges to irritate Das.

Chandra and Das get into a dialogue then. She talks about her patterns of affection towards their familial bond and her subjective needs related to that. She wants him within that legible domestic space of being where her romantic layers of individuality to are logically acceptable. The feminine affinity encloses the rhythms of attachment within the realm of her individuality.

The subjective space of difference in her husband's life is masked utilitarian wellness which does not have sensible edges of perceptual clarity. She tries to attack her husband's image which encapsulates feminine love in bottled wine. Wine is the erasure of the moment of psychic singularity. But she indirectly supports the critical tenderness of subjective confinement when she identifies feminine affinity as an emotional reality which becomes elevated primarily in domestic regularity. She attempts to delineate the volatile pain of closure which is experienced by the caged bird within the framework of the cage.

The central quest of the film is fixed in this crucial context of ambiguity which is drawn by the acceptable masculine patterns of closeness and feminine model of affective certainty. Chandra expresses her perception of the internal erosion of masculine affinity then. To her, men do love primarily in a utilitarian manner before the network of relationships is appropriated socially. But women do love more after the closure of social regularity is fixed with critical openness of mind. Affinity is not free and subversive in masculine and feminine frameworks of social performance here. Chandra reads masculine focus of affinity as a utilitarian preface to the internal stability of institutionalized feminine affection. From this context of a socially organized code of affection, Chandra prepares her demands to frame the measurability of her familial (not subjective) wellness. The love before the activation of familial structure and the affective power after the appropriation of domestic space come together in feminine rhetoric which tries to talk about the highly problematic aspect of self-satisfaction. Here the idea of self critically is lost as a conceptually free terrain of subjective openness.

The familiar feminist concern is quickly raised by the protagonist. She asserts her performative power in the domestic space when she reads her own subject position socio-politically as cleaner, cook, teacher etc. It's an act of self-recognition which is related to the measurability of her affective power. Position of self and desire becomes a crucial point of argument. The feminine voice of subjectivity demarcates its own structural regulations when she talks about the critical ownership of masculine/ feminine sexual freedom. Typically aggressive approaches from the man become faceless. With her potential moral ruptures, she demands sexual liberty. This gradually is identified as a deceptively instrumental strategy of affective power. The performative affirmation of bodily spatiality comes from the side of the woman when she tries to do the arrangements to dry the washed clothes. With the potential emergence of this sensual quest of identity masculine paradigms of moral power fall noticeably.

The woman states dramatically about the inadequacy of bodily free will which gets performed within the familial circuit of power. At this point, the tale finds its centre. Her seemingly ambiguous and internally distorted voice of subjectivity in an imaginative way depicts before her husband a sensual context of fantasy verbally. It slightly shocks the husband. The expressed demand for sexual freedom seems to be terribly subversive. But there the narrative begins to fall.

She does not have her own tools and images to embody her own subjective needs politically and poetically as the central sexual fantasy to is taken aggressively from the psychic space of the masked masculinity. The cause for this lies in the initial stage of her disappointment. She steals the hidden emotional life of her husband from his own phone when it is caught accidentally by her daughter. The tale of restlessness begins again from the rootless utilitarian combination between their daughter and the phone. The husband accepts the other side of his emotional life with another married woman as an act of fantasy. Chandra simply transplants that institutional inadequacy to her scheme of resistance. The opening of this morally ambiguous affective frustration begins proceeds and breaks with masculine templates of masked utilitarian desire.

The quest for radically free sexual will is revealed as an adopted instrumental image of desire which originates from the masked grounds of her husband's masculine desire. The power structure of affective morality from the side of the woman becomes in a sense just a mirror in which the normative morality of masculine desire gets a slightly sharpened reflection. The subjectivity of woman truly is located outside when we closely read this schematic resistance shown by Chandra who uses the utilitarian fantasy of internal disconnect and institutionalized alienation owned by the masculine morality. When she expresses her seemingly subversive feminine desire she is completely engaged in domestic chores. Her real driving force is not the subtlety of feminine sexual freedom but an emotionally moral frustration that is fuelled by the paradigm of familiar effective power within the model of the familial circuit. Performative layers of deceptive sexuality depicted by Chandra in a sense weaken the radical space for feminine resistance. Chandra's manipulative strategy can portray her own existential hollowness too. This kind of performative rebellion fails even while Chandra succeeds to attack her husband emotionally. That failure comes at the point of its emancipatory aspect and originality of vision.

Sexual freedom gets confined within the effective utility of the institutionalized feminine bodily space and the playfully disruptive masculine desire. Chandra initially seems to have something to say. But her attempt to depict the layers of pain addressed by feminine identity falls when the narrative tries to narrow down these existential predicaments of women to a single extremely familiar emotional and moral conflict and borrowed (masculine) techniques. Freedom becomes a quest of the common norm of collectivity for Chandra.

In "Nietzsche, Genealogy, History" Foucault remarks that only through the destruction of the body does the subject as a 'dissociated unity' appear: "the body is the inscribed surface of events (traced by language and dissolved by ideas), the locus of a dissociated self (adopting the illusion of a substantial unity), and a volume in perpetual disintegration.". The subject appears at the expense of the body, and appearance is conditioned in inverse relation to the disappearance of the body. The subject not only effectively takes the place of the body but acts as the soul which frames and forms the body in captivity. Here the forming and framing function of that exterior soul works against the body; indeed, it might be understood as the sublimation of the body in consequence of displacement and substitution. (Butler 91)

Judith Butler critically addresses the concerns related to the social appropriation of the subject meticulously when she traces the psychic networks of power. The bodily will of feminine subjectivity suspends itself to be deceptively resistive. The true centre of Chandra's internal distortion is against the masked masculine morality. But when it comes to performative rupture Chandra's rebellion too becomes a subtly lost frame of subjective spatiality. The masculine fantasy of sensual strangeness infects the body of feminine facelessness here. That body of signification with the face of erasure becomes masked to be deceptive like the masculine morality.

Chandra as the performative site of subjection disowns her body of feminine free will and locks herself as the playfully aggressive exterior soul of masculine morality. "The soul is the effect and instrument of a political anatomy; the soul is the prison of the body" (Foucault 30) Foucault's well-known observation can be taken to conclude this argument related to the problematic loss of Chandra's feminine free will with her paradigmatic dependence on the masked quest of masculine will. The soul and body face critical distortion in different ways when they establish a critical relationship between each other to design a subject's space of performative confinement. Chandra's bodily will of sexual identity is attacked by the deceptive tool of masked (masculine) fantasy which becomes her soul's moral facelessness. The political anatomy of the soul's victimhood which also becomes the spectrum of loss for body stays at the centre of Freedom at Midnight, where freedom inevitably and ironically becomes a critical suspension of subjective will which enlivens the normative fantasy of institutionalized body.

Works cited

Foucault, Michel. Discipline and Punish: The Birth of the Prision. Vintage Books, 1995.

Butler, Judith. The Psychic Life of Power: Theories in Subjection. Stanford University Press, 1997.

DISMANTLING UTOPIA TO DYSTOPIA: THE ANTHROPOCENTRIC GREED AND ENVIRONMENTAL CATASTROPHE IN J. G. BALLARD'S THE DROUGHT

Lismin P. Samuel [1] **& Roopa Jose** [2]

Al-Azhar College, Thodupuzha,

St. Joseph's College, Moolamattom

ABSTRACT

James Graham Ballard's climate fiction The Drought opens with a dystopic world that exposes the aftermath of an environmental cataclysm marked by anthropocentric greed. J. G. Ballard is a British writer who is considered the pioneer of climate fiction or cli-fi that challenged the existing trend of Western science fiction of the 1950s. Climate fiction or cli-fi, a term coined by an American environmentalist Dan Bloom in 2007, illustrates climatic changes and ecological threats from a fictional point of view to make the people aware of the seriousness of the issue and thereby enable them to find remedies for these problems. Ballard's novel The Drought, which is also known as The Burning World, is an open ending climate fiction. It visualizes through the perspective of the protagonist Dr Charles Ransom, how a year-long drought has dried out the planet due to humankind's uncontrollable exploitation. This paper studies the relationship between literature and physical environment and how anthropocentrism leads to dystopia.

Keywords: J.G. Ballard, The Drought, Cli-fi, Ecocriticism, Anthropocentrism, Dystopia.

• • •

Dismantling Utopia to Dystopia: The Anthropocentric Greed and Environmental Catastrophe in J. G. Ballard's *The Drought*

Introduction

The literary study of ecocriticism emerges as an eco-philosophy that explores the relationships between humans, nature and the environment coexisting together and how environmental issues are represented in literary discourses. The changing conceptions of the natural systems and our roles within them are depicted and studied in ecocriticism. This mode of study can be seen in the works of the environmentalists and transcendentalists like Thoreau, Emerson, Carlson etc. Ecocriticism includes a number of approaches like Green Studies, Ecopoetics, Environmental Literary Criticism etc.

The term "eco" is derived from the Greek word "oikos" which means "house"; that is – the "criticism of the house." The word "ecocriticism" first appeared in William Rueckert's essay "Literature and Ecology: An Experiment in Ecocriticism" in 1978. It is the publication of The Environmental Reader by Cheryll Glotfelty and Harold Fromm and The Environmental Imagination by Lawrence Buell, seminal works of the mid 1990s that lead to the development of this theory. Glotfelty observes:

What then is eco-criticism? Simply put, ecocriticism is the study of the relationship between literature and the physical environment. Just as feminist criticism examines language and literature from a gender-conscious perspective, and Marxist criticism brings an awareness of modes of production and economic class to its reading of texts, ecocriticism takes an earth-centred approach to literary studies. (xviii)

Ecocriticism gained momentum in the recent years following the World Wars, with the rise of capitalism and emergence of the rampant commercialism and consumer culture. The constant need to look for technological innovation in science, medicine and gadgets have led to the devastation of the environment. This rampant savagery is the seed of anthropocentrism. The concept is centred on the belief that the moral obligation of human beings lies in their own development, irrespective of the outcome. Elements of techno-centrism are also embedded in this approach and this puts its trust in technological improvements to solve environmental problems. With the modern world so enlightened in the investments of technology and advancement, the natural habitat and the biosphere is in constant threat. Cheryl Glotfelty points out the concerns expressed by Donald Worster, the historian:

We are facing a global crisis today not because of how our ecosystems function but rather because of how our ethical systems function. Getting through the crisis requires understanding our impact on nature as precisely as possible, but even more, it requires understanding those ethical systems and using that anthropologists and philosophers cannot do the reforming of course, but they can help with the understanding. (27)

Ecocriticism, in other words, fictionalizes the dilemma of the world and it also offers the unfamiliar realities of the nature. It is not only the application of ecology and ecological principles but also the study of literature and theoretical approach to the interrelations of nature and culture. In another sense, it manifests the purity of the environment through literary texts and theoretical discourse.

Anthropocentric Greed and the Emergence of Dystopian Society

Anthropocentrism is the belief that humans are superior to nature. This belief emerged from Western philosophy and religion that allowed humans the lawful right to exploit nature and its resources for their selfish betterment. The Christian notion of "Creation of mankind" implies that humans are created in the image of God to "control" earth and have "command over all" other living beings. However, this belief is criticized by environmentalists. Anthropocentrism focuses on the negative impacts of environmental degradation caused by man-made interventions. Such interventions impact all spheres of human life and biodiversity. Human beings tend to forget that biological diversities can only be maintained through the co-existing of all species. This is the only means through which the environment can be safe, keeping us alive. Through continuous depletion and oppression by humans, nature is treated as the "other." The anthropocentric greed of humanity always provides for self-abundance and glory, ignoring the cataclysm that is bound to happen if we do not shift our approach.

Environmental Apocalypse in The Drought

"What was wrong with these people? How could they live like this? Didn't they realize there was a natural world out there?"

- T. C. Boyle, A Friend of the Earth

Writers of all time have been very vigilant about nature and the environment they lived in. Nature and its elements always provide true inspiration, imagination and insight for them. It moves the creative minds and generates an appropriate background for the conception of masterpieces. The lines quoted above, is an example for it. T. C. Boyle, the American novelist and short-story writer, provides some sort of warning to his readers. Like him, J. G. Ballard also cautions the readers by providing a weird picture of the future world through his climate fiction The Drought. When his wild imaginations combined with the hidden realities of the present world, he could clearly depict the formless lands of the future.

The Drought unfolds through the eyes of the protagonist Dr. Ransom. Chapter one of the saga illustrates Ransom's voyage through the banks of "Lake Constant". For Ransom, the river seems to have lost its "spirit". Along with the spiritless river, the author also portrays the indifferent attitude of modern man, especially the youth, through Quilter, "the idiot son of the old woman" (3). Quilter's impassiveness shakes the feelings of Ransom when he happens to see him "smiling at the dead birds floating in the water below his feet" (3).

Ransom's announcement on the river that it has "lost its spirit" can be interpreted differently: firstly, this "lost" may be due to the drought, secondly, it may be due to dumping of garbage or pollutants from nearby factories, and finally, it might have been caused by the unending exploitation of humans. Also, Ballard informs his readers that the drought is not a new thing and such repeated falls affected the mentality of the natives like Quilter. Ransom says: "The continued fall of the river, sustained through the spring and summer drought, gave him a kind of warped pleasure, even if he and his mother had been the first to suffer" (1). Ballard uses a number of phrases like 'draining creeks', 'mudflats', and 'humps of damp mud' to convey the intensity of the drought.

Basically, in the first chapter itself, Ballard tries to reveal the reality of the modern world and how reality affects the emotions of human beings. Also, subtle narrations are used to explain how the earth's greenhouse has been affected by the heavy pollutions of vehicles, and it is evident in his description of traffic – ". . . the windows of thousands of cars and trucks flashing like jewelled lances as they set off along the coast road to the south" (Ballard, 1). The image of ". . . the slopes of mud, covered with the bodies of dead birds and fish, stretched above him like the shores of a dream (1)" deepens the aridity.

Ballard is brilliant enough to paint the current scenario and it is evident when he says, "Ransom surveyed the silent banks of the river as they wound westwards to the city of Mount Royal five miles away" (1). Here, Ballard uses the word "wound" purposefully to denote the existing situation. The river is wounded due to the misdeeds of men. Ballard plays with words like "recollection" to acknowledge to his readers the long-term sufferings of the native people due to water scarcity. The exclamation "Rain!" itself tells a lot about the drought:

Rain! — At the recollection of what the term had once meant, Ransom looked up at the brilliant sky. Unmasked by clouds or vapour, the sun hung over his head like an inferno. The cracked fields and roads adjoining the river were covered with the same unvarying light, a glazed motionless canopy that embalmed everything in its heat. (2)

For humans, rain has become a memory and they even had partially forgotten its meaning too. Even the sun does not show any kindness and the land becomes a 'motionless canopy'. Ransom notes that due to the long absence of rain, the 'raintraps' eventually transforms into dusty 'garbage scoops'. Ballard has studied each of his characters very well and he weaves vivid images of every one of them through his simple narrative techniques. His characters occupy their own spaces in the plot. Quilter and his mother Mrs. Quilter have their own mannerisms and even their slightest of emotions are drawn by Ballard. Another thing to point out is that his long character descriptions are effortlessly merged with the novel's scenario. Quilter's vague, unpleasant and ambiguous smiles and his mother's indifference make the tale more realistic. Also, Ballard purposefully presents Catherine Austen in a "white beach robe" with enough descriptions, mental as well as physical, to illustrate the routines of the people affected by drought.

Through the thoughts of Ransom, the readers learn that she is one among the last people to remain in the "abandoned town". Also, through her, Ballard portrays the sad condition of the river. Only a little water is left in the river and the woman needs to bathe due to the hot weather. Once again Ballard makes his ideas obvious that the never-ending hot weather, unavailability of water, and the pollutions from the factories emptied that thickly populated land.

The inhabitants also have a role in making the land a waste. The local purification methods of the polluted river water are also explained carefully by the author through the depiction of Catherine: "She lifted the bucket from the water, then decanted the dark fluid carefully into the river. The inside of the bucket was cloaked by a black oily veil" (22). Eventually, through Catherine, Ballard shares his philosophy and his plot in a nutshell, "It's an interesting period ". . . Nothing moves, but so much is happening" (4).

For the natives, lack of water is a major problem. However, it is the least of their problems. Ransom, tries to make Catherine aware that, "There's barely enough time to hunt for water (4)", and she faces the advice bravely. Ballard's long narrations often quote his own philosophies. For instance, long conversations with Ransom and Catherine reveal the thoughts of Ballard.

The extreme pollution of the river has been revealed with the introduction of Philip Jordan, a boy in a "faded khaki shirt and trousers (4)". He has been described as the "foster-child of the river (4)" and the "friend of the water-birds (4)". For Ransom, he is "part waif and water elf (4)". Philip, irrespective of other humans, creates his own "world out of the scraps and refuse of the twentieth century (4)". Like the world, Philip has also been surrounded by many enigmas. He appears along with "a large nest of wet mattress floc, covered with oil and cotton waste, lay in a parcel of the damp newspaper" (4). Ballard has keenly portrayed the characteristics of Philip, like his "wide eyes", "small gruff voice", his "strange changes of costumes (4)" etc. An important symbol used by Ballard to denote the suffocation of human beings is a 'snake-like swan which suffers amidst the mud and oil. Philip's request – "Can you save it, doctor? (4)", reflects humans' own helplessness. However, Ransom does genuine efforts to protect the swan. The toxic nature of the river and the upcoming threats to human lives has been presented by describing the extremely bad condition of the poor swan. The oil had matted the feathers into a heavy carapace and choked its mouth and respiratory passages.

Through the swan's agony, Ballard expounds on the future of the natives. Anyone in the future may face a situation just as that happened to the swan. So Ballard warns the generations to be careful while dealing with nature. Ballard keenly chooses words to describe the destructive setting. He says, "The river was no more a natural environment than a handful of pebbles and waterweed in an aquarium" (9). He uses a number of similes and metaphors to transfer his notions of heavy drought to his readers. He consciously makes use of such figurative language to warn his generation against a hectic future.

In chapter two - "The Coming of the Desert" - Ballard expounds how the cities like "Larchmont" becomes deserts due to the lack of rain. In Ballard's novels, images speak louder than words. The cities were enveloped in dust due to the decrease in rainfall. Also, the pavements are strewn with scraps of paper and garbage. Ransom on his journey to his hometown narrates each and every change that had taken place there. He becomes emotional when he goes through his home city:

Most of the houses were empty, windows boarded and nailed up, swimming pools emptied of their last reserves of water. Lines of abandoned cars were parked under the withering plane trees, and the road was littered with discarded cans and cartons. The bright flint-like dust lay in drifts against the blistered fences. Refuse fires smouldered unattended on the burnt-out lawns, their smoke wandering over the roofs. (12)

Ballard also portrays the artisans of the countryside. The peasants lost thousands of their cattle and for them, the drought seems like the "end of the world (7)". People's life faded and now they are living out of their "fantasies of death and destruction (7)." Ballard also narrates the sights of abandoned houses. The images of leftovers like "melted butter", "limp salad", "sour milk", "bad meat", "ample stock of canned food and cereals (8)", all intensify the darkness of isolated houses. Also through these pictures, Ballard gives a note on the lifestyles of the modern man.

Ballard uses the strategies of "news reporting" and "radio broadcasting" to indirectly acknowledge to his readers the progressing terrors of the drought. The references like decreased water levels of "Nile", "Amazon Rainforest", "Atlantic and Pacific Coasts" etc mean that "there was no rain" and " there were no clouds (11)". Just as the lakes and all other water bodies, oceans also get contaminated due to "millions of tons of highly reactive industrial wastes, unwanted petroleum fractions, contaminated catalysts, and solvents" and the "wastes of atomic power stations and sewage schemes (15)".

In chapter three "The Fire Sermon", the priest Johnstone uses "chapter IV, verse 8, of the Book of Jonah" as he compares "Jonah's wish for the destruction of Nineveh with mankind's unconscious hopes for the end of their present world (18)". The withering of Jonah was Lord's decision; like that humanity should welcome the destruction of their own lands and homes. Johnstone's sermon has an optimistic tone and he exhorts his believers to trust in Jesus Christ. He also believes that "God's grace would come to them only through his final purging fire (18)". So, this chapter's title itself illustrates the very situation in Mount Royal and that in Johnstone's sermon.

The next chapter "The Drowned Aquarium" shows the miserable conditions of a zoo and Ransom's attempts to feed the animals. Most of the "cages were as dry and arid as desert caves (14)". The image of a "dead camel" which lay on the floor and the aquarium that was crowded with the corpses of hundreds of dead fish deepened the gloominess of the zoo. The fish was "poisoned by their own wastes, they hung weightlessly in the gloomy water, their blank eyes glowing like phosphors, mouths agape . . . Gazing at them, Ransom had a sudden vision of the sea by the coastal beaches, as clouded and corpse-strewn as the water in the tanks, the faces of the drowned eddying past each other" (28). Ransom's meeting with Jonas and a group of fishermen during their 'quest for a lost river' offers the novel a different angle.

Ballard's detailing of each and every little thing is interesting. It makes his plot complete and realistic. His novel has a natural flow and continuity which is congruous with the after effects of the drying earth. He showcases each happening in the backdrop of a shattered land. He creates meaningful connections. Ballard has never diverted from his very subject matter and throughout the saga, he effectively maintains the core theme of the novel. Most of his vivid imageries, word pictures, figurative languages, distinct comparisons etc assist him in achieving this effectiveness.

Chapter 5, namely "The Burning Altar", is a manifestation of extreme "numbness and uncertainty (20)". It depicts the varying attitudes of people like Lomax, his sister Miranda, and Quilter. Ballard compares Miranda to "Ophelia" and Quilter to "Caliban." The later chapters like "Journey to the Coast" express Ransom's voyage to the coastal region in search of water. The sea has retreated and it is now nothing but a "white desert" and a dune of dried salt. However, his change in behaviour becomes evident when he says he desires to "cut off all continuity with his past life (22)."

Ballard introduces Philip Jordan's foster father in this episode and just as the rest of his characters, Ballard gives a detailed study of that unnamed blind man who is in his late middle ages. Through this character, Ballard explains the utter starvation caused due to the drought. Also, he narrates the compassion between the son and his foster father. Eventually, for the first time, Ballard offers a positive note to humanity. Also a change in character occurs in Quilter and his mother Mrs Quilter. Quilter's character transformation has been shown through the release of a "black swan".

The seventh chapter is named "The Bitter Sea" and it depicts the battle for a new land that happened between the "early conquerors" and Ransom's team – including Catherine Austen, Mrs Quilter, Philip Jordan and his blind foster father. With the narration of this particular section, the novel showcases a new variant of the selfish behaviours of humankind. The never-ending drought has increased the humans' selfish nature and the after effects of this change can be seen in this episode. People fight against themselves for a newly founded sea coast. Instead of facing the drought with utmost harmony, they clash among themselves and fire at each other hoping for their own safety.

Part II of The Drought is further divided into three chapters –"Dune Limbo", "The Stranded Neptune", and "The Sign of the Crab." These chapters expound the happenings after ten long years. Apart from the previous chapters, Ballard visualises the future of the past events in part II. To remove his plot from all types of artificialities, to make his novel much more natural, he ardently specifies each minute aspect that has already happened in the existing world – the Tsunami, for instance. He illustrates a world where "life" can only be seen on the sea coasts. The men who have survived all the threatening calamities came together under the same umbrella - the sea coast, to lead a life by refining the seawater.

Ballard's surrealist tastes are more evident in the final five chapters. He heightens his wild imaginations, absurdities and fantasies to newer levels without losing all sorts of realities. The

Drought and other climate fiction, in general, gives the readers a pre-experience about the dangers that await them in the future.

Conclusion

Literature plays a very significant role in the conservation of the environment. It analyzes the real-life interactions of human beings in different socio-cultural contexts. A cli-fi novel gives us an ecocritical insight through literary narratives and exhorts us to preserve the green earth. J. G. Ballard through this apocalyptic narrative The Drought is putting forth a quasi-scientific literary speculation of what will happen if human beings continue the anthropocentric patterns of thought. The novel is an eye-opener to the entire human world.

Works Cited

Ballard, J. G. The Drought. Penguin Books, 1968.

Boyle, T. Coraghessan. A Friend of the Earth. Bloomsbury Publishing, 2019.

Firsching, L. J. & P. R. M. "J.G. Ballard's Ambiguous Apocalypse". Science

Fiction Studies, 12 (3), (1985). 297-310

Glotfelty, Cheryll & Fromm, Harold. (1996). The Ecocriticism Reader: Landmarks in Literary Ecology. The University of Georgia Press, Athens.

Worster, Donald. The Wealth of Nature: Environmental History and the Ecological Imagination. New York: Oxford University Press, 1993.

Boi-Note:

Lismin P Samuel is currently working as a Guest Lecturer of English at Al Azhar College of Arts and Science, Thodupuzha, Kerala. Her research areas include Film Studies, Science Fiction, Gender Studies and subaltern literature. She has published a few book chapters and also presented papers in various national and international seminars.

Roopa Jose is an Assistant Professor of English at St. Joseph's College, Moolamattom, Kerala. Her areas of interest include Women Studies, Green Criticism, Queer Studies, and children's

Literature. She has done research on the influence of psychoactive superheroes on postmodern adolescents and has publications in this and related areas.

NARRATOLOGY, ITS FEATURES: A STUDY BASED ON INDIAN NARRATOLOGY

Ramdas V. H.

Assistant Professor & Research Scholar

Department of English, Ilahia College of Arts and Science

Research Scholar in Sree Sankara University of Sanskrit

ABSTRACT

Narratology represents the narrative techniques. In another word, it represents the human's perspectives. Differences in narrative techniques also mean the different viewpoints of human beings. Indian narratology is a wide area that covered so much literature. India has an l0ong tradition of the storytelling process. If the style of narration is different, the primary aim of narration is to describe the story and its content to the readers. Different art forms and literature forms have their own style of narration. Indian tradition considered the audience/readers as the primary object. 'Sahrudaya' is the Sanskrit word that depicts the capacity of the audience. Several works like Puranas, Ithihasas, myths, Fairy Tales, folk literature etc have their own narrating style. Each one is famous for its narrative techniques. Some are verbal while others are written narratives. For example, folk tales and folk literature are mainly oral. Indian style of narration influenced foreign literature also. The old generation's narrative style is another example of oral tradition. Because the narrating techniques of old people to communicate moral values to the younger generations are also depict the Indian tradition of storytelling. Authors of India have a beautiful narrating style for embracing the readers. Kalidasa, commonly known as Indian Shakespeare, has proven that he is the master of narrative techniques. Through this paper, I wish to point the elements of Indian narratology.

Keywords: Narratology, Indian Narratology, Indian Tradition, Myths, Oral Tradition.

• • •

Narratology, Its Features: A Study Based on Indian Narratology

Introduction

Narratology denotes a recent concern with narrative in general. It deals especially with the identification of structural elements and their diverse modes of combination with current narrative devices and with the analysis of the kind of discourse by which a narrative gets told. Narration is a story, whether in prose or verse, involving events, characters and what the characters say and do. This theory picks up and elaborates upon many topics in traditional treatments of fictional narratives1. Narratology describes the techniques of narratives in oral as well as written. The best example of the written narrative is our epics that are the Ramayana and the Mahabharata. Indian narrative techniques have worldwide acceptance and they influenced the writers in other nations. Indian narrative techniques have a predominant position when compared with other literature in the world. This is very difficult to calculate the origin of Indian storytelling. It originated hundreds of years ago and covered all areas of literature.

Indian narrative techniques can be seen in Short Stories, Stories, Epics, Puranas, Ithihasas, and so on. Narration is possible through oral and written styles. For example, the old generation people describe a story to the grandchildren. Their way of story description, its rhythm, structure etc is a new experience to the grandchildren. This type of narration includes mythical elements and is similar to fairy tales. These stories include sub-stories inside them. The main use of these stories is to provide moral lessons to the younger generations. Folk tales and folk stories are other examples of Indian narrative techniques. These folk tales and folk stories are mainly oral in nature. They also have narrative techniques because they perform an oral descriptive style which gives an imaginative world to the listeners. Ithihasas are the works that represent India's narrative style. Ithihasas include stories and sub-stories written by many authors. In one story, there include so many stories and each story includes again sub-stories. Through this paper, I wish to point out the elements of Indian narratology.

Indian Narratology: an Overview

For embracing the readers, an author can choose so many writing methods. The Indian way of storytelling is based on these concepts. The readers in India were treated as an important part and they are commonly known as Saturday and Pratibha. Pratibha is commonly used to denote the person who has the ability to analyse the things which he/she enjoys. That word has so many meanings. Indian Epics, Puranas, Ithihasas, Akhyayikas, Novels, Mural Paintings, Classical Dance forms, temple art forms like Kathakali, Koodiyattam, Kooththu etc are providing a wide range of narrative techniques.

Folk literature, especially folk music indicates the elements of narrative techniques. Folk tales convey messages to the public through their style of narration. The main story contains many sub-stories just like the layer of a flower. The narrator can include his own ideas and imaginations in the story which can impress the audience. The time period or the origin of Indian narrative techniques can't be mentioned. It has been taken a long period since the method of storytelling began. It originated hundreds of years ago and has undergone serious changes .that means the early period of narratology is far different from the present scenario.

The changes in the culture, ideologies and taste of the audience influenced the changes in narrative techniques. The Puranas, especially mythical stories indicate India's narrative techniques because the mythical stories create a world, an imaginary world, in the mind of readers. These stories sometimes take the stories of kings, ghosts, Indian Goddesses, serpents, and other warriors and so on . These stories are again recreated by the author with his/her own imagination and convey it to the audience. Here the two or three-level transformation of the story has happened. The story from the first narrator is passed through another narrator, who has his own freedom to recreate the story, and finally reached the audience in another way. These all happened in the case of folk literature and oral literature also.

The chain narrative system is another important area of Indian narratology. Chain narrative means many stories are combined to form a new story. Jathaka Kadhakal and Panchathanthra Kadhakal are the best examples of chain narratives. Panchatantra Kadhakal includes the stories of animals. The author wants to tell the moral values of life to the audience. For that, he includes animals as the characters so that the audience, especially children, can enjoy the story. These stories contain some extraordinary imaginative elements and are structured as fantasy type stories. There was no specific study in the early period about Indian narratology. But in later many theoreticians like k. Ayyappa Panicker wrote books in the field of Narratology. In the early period poetry (kavya) gets a more important position in literature. Works of ancient, medieval periods and Tamil, Sanskrit, and Pali languages have been picturized the narrative elements of India. K. Ayyappapanicker, in his famous work 'Indian Narratatology' classifieds the narrative techniques into ten major headings. They are:

1. Interiorisation
2. Serialisation
3. Fantasisation
4. Cyclicalisation
5. Allegorisation
6. Anonymisation
7. Elasticisation of time
8. Spatialisation
9. Stylisation
10. Improvisation (pg: 4)

This categorisation is very much important for later studies. But this study is not the last one because later theoreticians argued that the characteristics of Indian narratology are always changing. The changes in the cultural and social elements of the audience affect the structure and contents and style of the literature itself. For example, the folk tales there is no specific narrative techniques and rules. The narrator can have his/her own freedom to express their creations too. Western literature adopted the narrative techniques of India. India has a strong Puranic and Vedic culture which influenced the foreign writers and they adopted the narrative techniques in their works. So many Vedic tales and encrypted hymns are used by several writers, dramatists and so on. Our Epics like Ramayana and Mahabharata influenced common as well as intellectual writers. Kalidasa wrote his works on the basis of these Epics. The Epics in India are the first and foremost examples of Indian narrative techniques. The Ramayana is simpler than the Mahabharata in its narrative techniques when compared. The Mahabharata consist of stories and sub-stories. That means the sub-stories play an important role and it is intelligently blended with the main stories. The Vedic literature and its narrative structure influenced the Sangam literature also. Vedic encryptions are picturized in the mural paintings and art forms. The paintings of the Kerala and Tamilnadu are the best example of this.

Puranic and Vedic tales are based on the heroic deeds of Gods and their incarnations. The heroic deeds of Gods such as wars, conquest, love and separations, etc are the basic themes. These themes are adopted by eminent writers, musicians, artists, painters and so on for their works. Their narrative techniques influenced the readers, especially the critics. Indian Ithihasas, Puranas, etc are followed another type of narrative technique. For example, in Bhagavatha we can see the chain narrative system. That is the story is transferred from one person to another and that person narrates the story to others. This is a continuous process and an example of another type of narration.

Conclusion

This is very difficult to denote the narrative style and techniques of India in a few sentences. Because Indian narratology is a wide range of areas which include Puranas, Ithihasas, Epics, common man's stories and folk literature etc. In the case of folk literature, the narrative style is different. The style of oral tradition is adopted in the case of folk literature. Folk literature represents the stories of the common man while Puranas and Ithihasas are representing the stories of kings, Gods and their incarnations etc. The Indian narrative tradition is adopted by many foreign writers. In India, the readers are treated as Sahrudaya which means the person who can enjoy the aesthetic pleasure of work. Kadha and Akhyayika are the two divisions of literary forms and they have a separate styles of narrative techniques. Kadha means short story which has the influence of fantasy while Akhyayika means the story based on historical elements. Similarly, the Sangam literature, Thirukkural, Akananoor, Purananoor, etc are other examples of Indian narrative techniques.

Works Cited

Ayyappa Panicker, k. Indian Narratology, Indira Gandhi National Centre for the Arts, Janpath, New Delhi-110001

Kane P. V. (ed.) Harshacharitham of Banabhatta, Motilal Banarsidas Publishers, Delhi

Kulkarni, V.M. More Studies in Sanskrit Sahithya Sastra, Sarasvati Pustak bhandar, Ahmedabad.

CHAPTER IX

REGISTERING RESISTANCE: REPRESENTATION OF THE OTHERED DALIT WOMEN IN BABY KAMBLE'S THE PRISONS WE BROKE

Radhika Raj P.
Assistant Professor, Department of English
Baselios Poulose II Catholicose College
Piravom, Ernakulam, Kerala

ABSTRACT

When Dalit women writers began to write about their life histories, neither of their autobiographies could assimilate their concerns and aspirations. The trajectory of Dalit life was completely different and alienated from the social structure. The lives of Dalit women, in particular, are problematic to study similarly since their individual narratives were entangled within the power narratives of caste. They had to suffer double oppression. Dalit life writings are testimonies of collective struggles. The methods of collective resistance in the life of Dalit Mahar women are assessed here where the peripheral space becomes the central site of offering such resistance. This is a study of the ethnic dynamics and the power structures which are accountable for the immobilized subsistence of female Dalits in the Mahar community. Also, how they capture the stance to venture upon the circumstances and seek further advancement, by critically analysing the Dalit female account The Prisons We Broke by Baby Kamble.

Keywords: Dalit, Patriarchy, Women, Oppression and Discrimination.

• • •

Registering Resistance: Representation of the Othered Dalit Women in Baby Kamble's *The Prisons We Broke*

Dalit community is not a homogeneous community. It is a highly heterogeneous community in terms of social customs, sophistical values and literary creativities. The word Dalit can be associated with realisation rather than being a complaint of society. Their narrations disturb the complacencies entrenched in the rigid society. Such disturbance requires the mainstream to attempt a review and redetermination of the Dalit standpoint. Dalit literature represents the unique and distinct experiences that arise from the centuries-old hierarchical system. The essence of saltiness is untouchability, as they are treated as unclean and impure. Dalit literature challenges this saltiness using biographical and autobiographical methods. It portrays the authentic Dalit experiences, describing the minutest details of their daily life in a language that is crude and impolite, contrary to the refined and polite language of elite literature.

This is a constructive enterprise in the process of creating their authentic representations. It primarily protests literature against upper-class literature. Its objective is to create a counter-culture and a separate identity for the Dalits in society. The mainstream literature is based on aesthetics, whereas Dalit literature presents the intense pain that makes all definitions of aesthetics meaningless. This assertion through literature seeks to bring about a social change through revolution and it would destroy the social and cultural order. It would then reconstruct the social reality assuring human dignity. The purpose of the work The prisons We broke by Baby Kamble is to make the Dalits aware of their past and to create Dalit consciousness in them.

Dalit womens' life writings differ from the usual feminist writings, making their visibility known, their identity as a Dalit woman was been acknowledged and the vocabulary to speak against repressive social forces were sanctioned. To this extent, several scholars have called for the imperative to invoke a new literary genre for Dalit women because they have so far been neglected from the literature seen as a result of their systematic domination. There have been feminist movements of liberation that emerged in the 1960s and 70s, particularly Dalit liberation movements. But these movements were not able to provide a visible space to Dalit women in order to foreground their issues clearly. Dalit activists like Sharmila Rege, Gopal Guru etc. had suggested that the Dalit women need a different vocabulary to be historically located in the real struggles of marginalised women. Bama's autobiography Karukku is also a fine example of the struggle of existence that has been exploited and suppressed for centuries. It expresses the saga of suffering inflicted upon Dalits and her struggle to liberate the Dalit community from the clutches of caste.

Baby Kamble's autobiography brings to light the social, economic and cultural aspects of the Dalit community where women were always a subject of marginalization under the Indian patriarchal society. Dalit women had to overcome the taboos of their gender discrimination and caste. She deliberately portrays the issues like subjugation of women, where they are subjected to subaltern state. The text also highlights the influence of Babasaheb Ambedkar on Dalit women to bring them socially. This autobiography by Baby Kamble represents the voice of the subdued and distressed women in the Dalit community. Brahminical hierarchy and patriarchal sovereignty are challenged through this novel. The work had been published only 20 years after she had finished it because the writing was not meant for Dalit women. She had hidden her writings even from her husband and son.

The Dalits as a collective community who belonged to the subaltern caste are not only historically placed in the marginal space, but also are denied the way to the mainstream. Nevertheless, boundaries have been pushed back constantly and the dominant culture has been challenged in centuries. The young generation Dalits are resisting the politics of exclusion. If resistance is there, there would be some kind of discrimination. Discrimination is not a thing of the past. The kind of resistance that we were having in the 19th century has changed coming to the third generation. So along with resistance, comes the celebration. They are celebrating adulthood. The third generation Dalits have changed their strategies. They are not ashamed of their identity. There was a time when Dalits were camouflaging their identity. They used surnames that would not declare their identity. In contemporary Dalit activism, they brought about some changes in their retaliation. There was a kind of upper caste hegemony that existed in the mainstream.

Baby Kamble speaks for the marginal space. She begins her book with the description of her locality called Maharwada, a place in Maharashtra. Ambedkar took up the Dalit causes as he himself belonged to the Mahar community to which Baby Kamble also belonged and Ambedkar has been a hugely influential figure in uplifting the Dalits economically, socially and spiritually. He introduced education to the Mahar children and thereby it brought a radical change in Mahars where they realised their own self. Society treated Dalits as subhumans. An untouchable was required to wear a black thread whether on his neck or on his wrist for the purpose of ready identification. This was the status of Dalits in pre-independent India until Ambedkar become their cause. Kamle used writing as a powerful weapon to challenge the hegemony of casteism.

Maharwada became the space for free and unhindered movements. That space became the space for Mahar debates, arguments and counterarguments to discuss the deliberations of Babasaheb Ambedkar which brought an apocalyptic change in the consciousness of the Mahar community. Kamble talks about the miserable conditions of women in the 1940s and traces their transformation to self-sufficient agents of resistance. The text is a sort of manifesto for the Mahar community, especially its women where she advocates the preference to bring about radical changes of their destinies. The transformation of the elementary level of life can be realised by the women as the community was promulgated by Ambedkar. Women are traditionally considered to be more associated with the basic instincts of life. Also for the fact that women and children in association with men constitute the basic family, which forms the structure of any community. Hence Kamble points out how Ambedkar had encouraged the women in the households to bring about social changes.

Baby Kamble provides an insight into the oppressive caste system. She describes the subhuman treatment of the upper caste where she narrates the incident of a Dalit woman when she brought things from a shopkeeper. She had kept a distance from him and begged him to sell her the things she wanted. He took advantage of the situation and taught his children about how to treat a dalit. Kamble realised that the powerful tool to fight against injustice, exploitation and oppression is the unity of the oppressed.

This text can be read in terms of collective consciousness instead of recording individual life history. It talked about the limited mobilization of the Mahar womens' circle. The ordinary incidents that Kamble writes about indicate the building up of the public territory of Maharwada. The subordinate caste first of all longs to speak and to subsequently question the mistreatment that they had been enduring. The interconnectedness of class and caste complicates the understanding of the Dalit condition.

This work originally written in Marathi titled 'Jina Amachin' was translated into English by Maya pandit. Its English translation would be 'Our Miserable Lives'. But Maya Pandit had given the title The Prisons We Broke as the novel portrays the aggression of the entire Mahar community and their struggles to attain self-esteem and self-respect. The mental agonies of Dalit women in a patriarchal society are described from collective and personal spaces. Their collective resistance is registered in order to mould a reconstructed society. It is a rebellious magnum opus as it not only addressed the predicaments of the Mahar women, but also extended the cause for the eradication of the caste system. Kamble, through this work, exposes the three main problems of Mahar women, their caste, gender, and the oppression of patriarchal society.

They had to receive callous treatment from society even though they are not responsible. They had to put up with psychological, emotional and physical torments. The first half of the work discusses the egoistic domination of the brahminical class who crushed the Mahar community as a whole. Mahar women became the victims of brahminical upper-caste along with Dalit patriarchy. Next half deals with the revival of the whole Mahar community under the the guidance of Ambedkar which challenged the caste system with a firm attitude. The term Dalit can be considered as an umbrella term for the people who are not considered as high caste. Kamble herself had to face burdensome experiences at her school, as teachers too promoted the caste system where they favoured brahmin students blatantly. While going through the narrative, it is mentioned that in schools, Mahar girls are ill-treated by the upper caste girls. She says:

We, the daughters of the activists in the movement, were enrolled in school for girls. It was basically a school for Brahmin girls, with a few girls from other high castes. There were some ten or twelve Mahar girls spread over in various classes. So each class had only a sprinkling of the polluting Mahars. All the girls in the class had benches to sit on except us, Mahar girls. We had to sit on the floor in one corner of the classroom like diseased puppies... We were like fiery god flies burning for vengeance. (Kamble, 62)

It is to be noted that even though Dalit men were also marginalised in society, Dalit women were marginalised twice, ie. by the brahminical upper caste and by their own Mahar men. She unravels the brutality of Mahar men towards their women. Even, she herself was a sufferer of her husband's patriarchal turn of mind. She quotes in the novel, " Once we went to Mumbai to attend a meeting, we travelled in a general compartment that was very crowded and some young men happened to stare at me. My husband immediately suspected me and hit me so hard that my nose started bleeding profusely... The same evening we returned and he was so angry that he kept hitting me on the train.".(155)

The newly married young girls are supposed to prepare bhakris to manifest their cooking skills, if not they will be ill-treated by their in-laws. In Maharwada, the women are supposed to be at home. They are caged by the unequal treatment of society. Even though higher caste women too faced gender discrimination, Mahar Dalit women are suppressed twice than them as they are from the Dalit community. A situation is narrated in the novel where a newly married young girl, totally ignorant of the custom of bowing where she neglected a high caste man. Later this man raises it as a big issue and shouts, "Who, just tell me, who the hell is that new girl? Doesn't she know that she has to bow down to the master? Shameless bitch! How dare she pass me without showing due respect? " (53)

Her mother-in-law's response to this too is to be noted as she requests, "No, no kind master! That girl is a new animal in the herd! Quite foolish and ignorant. If she has erred, I, her sarsa, fall at your feet, but please forgive us for this crime"(53). Kamble also mentions the superstitions that prevailed in the community. In the month of 'Aakhad', women will be possessed by the spirits. She is treated and worshipped like a goddess and there she receives great respect. But when the day is over, the very next day she is treated as ever. Mahar women were considered inanimate beings. Young girls of 8 to 10 years were made to marry and they were subjugated both by men and women in their community. They were tortured brutally. Father also would give advice to their sons to be like a man and to suppress their wives by punishing them. For instance:

You are a man. You must behave like one! You must be proud and firm. You must walk tall. Twirl your moustache and show us that you are a man. Never mind, if you have to go to prison for six months! You must chop off your wife's nose and present it to her brother and father. They mustn't have any respect left to sit with the members of the panch. (100-01)

Some of the women had to suffer the pain of their chopped nose, which is bleeding heavily. They will cut their nose and ears so that they will look ugly. The sorts of inhuman practices were there till the 1940s. This was the plight of Mahar women. Kamble's work not only depicts the unfortunate lives of Mahar women, or their agonies, but also it portrays their determination to gain self-identity beyond the patriarchal dominance. Even the condition of women at the time of delivery is pointed in the novel. "Many new mothers had to hungry. They would lie down, pining for a few morsels while hunger gnawed their insides. Most women suffered this fate. Labour pains, mishandling by the midwife, wounds inflicted by onlookers' nails, ever gnawing hunger, infected bones with pus oozing out, hot water baths, hot coals, profuse sweating- everything caused the new mothers' condition to worsen and she would end up getting a burning fever." (60)

Mahar women were treated just like reproducing machines that gave birth to children until menopause. They were the victims of caste consciousness and patriarchal domination who lived like slaves. So many Mahar women passed away in childbirth. Even though after the delivery, they needed soft grains, they were not accessible. Even sexual violence against Dalit Mahar women was also common. They will be used as mere sex objects. Dalit women were not only being sexually exploited by non-dalit men but also were subjugated by their own men. They had to face double patriarchy.

The Mahar women will collect firewoods and it would be bundled to sell to the brahmin women where they would get only half price. They had to shield their faces when they went to sell the firewoods. They were not supposed to use the roads that the upper caste used. If anyone who belonged to the upper caste came in front, they should withdraw immediately. The brahmin women were more concerned about whether they would get polluted. Kamble writes:

When Mahar women labour in the fields, the corn gets wet with the sweat. The same corn goes to make your pure, rich dishes. And you feast them with such evident relish. Your palaces are built with the soil soaked with the sweat and blood of Mahars. But does it rot your skin? You drink their blood and sleep comfortably in the bed of their misery. Does it pollute you then? Just as the farmer pierces his bullock's nose and inserts a string through the nostrils to control it, you have pierced the Mahars nose with a string of ignorance. And you have been flogging us with the whip pollution. (56)

The story won't demand the readers to pity the condition of the Dalit women but urge us to react against the political agenda that prevailed during the times. Dalit women were not only oppressed by society but also they are victimized within their own community. The text brings a graphic perception into the patriarchal doctrines of society. This work is the first among the entire gamut of Dalit literature of its kind. It describes the struggle of everyday life of the Mahar community, especially the Mahar women in Maharashtra. Baby Kamble claims that if the Dalit community is marginalized as 'the other' by the elite Hindu community, Dalit women are suppressed as 'the other' by their own Mahar community. Baby Kamble mentions the influence of Ambedkar. Kamble, influenced by Ambedkarite ideologies have inspired most of the Dalit activists to come to the forefront for their rights. In the Ambedkarite movement, Mahar womens' engagement was significant and this is clearly stated by Kamble with a strong voice. Influenced by him, she opened a grocery store with the help of her husband where she found time to read and to reflect her feelings.

Even though the book is an autobiography, it can be seen as the biography of the Mahar community as it wraps the real-life situation of Mahars from the pre-colonial to the post-colonial period. Critique is pointed not only on the upper caste brahmins but also Kamble points the patriarchal behaviour within the Mahar community as such, who suppresses the Mahar women. This autobiography helped Kamble to regain her self identity and to bring out the nasty experiences of women who had undergone the aftermath of gender politics and social hierarchies. The work can be considered as a breakthrough in the whole Dalit autobiographies which questioned the oppression of women by male patriarchy.

Works Cited

Abrams, M H. A Glossary of Literary Terms. New Delhi, Harcourt India,1999.

Bama, Karukku.Translated by Lakshmi Holmstrom, Chennai, Macmillan India Limited, 2000.

Barker, Chris. Cultural Studies:Theory and Practice. London, Sage, 2000.

Barry, Peter. Beginning Theory: An Introduction to Literary and Cultural Theory. Manchester,

Manchester UP,1995.

Fanon, Frantz. The Wretched of the Earth. London, Penguin, 2001.

Kamble, Baby. The Prisons We Broke. Translated by Maya Pandit. 4th ed., Orient Blackswan.

2014.

Limbale, Sharankumar. The Outcaste. Translated by Santhosh Bhoomkar, New Delhi, Oxford

University Press, 2008.

Rege, Sharmila. Writing Caste/Writing Gender: Reading Dalit Women's Testimonies. New

Delhi, Zubaan, 2006.

Sarkar, Tanika. Hindu Wife Hindu Nation: Community, Religion and Cultural Nationalism.

New Delhi, Permanent Black, 2001.

Valmiki, Omprakash. Joothan. Translated by Arun Prabha Mukherjee, Kolkata, Samya, 2007.

• • •

JOB STRESS OF COLLEGE TEACHERS ESPECIALLY AFTER COVID-19 PANDEMIC

Sanil Thomas

Commerce Department, Yeldo Mar Baselios College
Puthuppady,Kothamangalam, Ernakulam,Kerala

ABSTRACT

Teaching is the most blessed profession because teachers help to inculcate culture, basic values and ethics in the future citizens. In other words, they are the people who mould the future citizens. Stress is inevitable in everyone's life, especially in a teacher's life. How do people know that they are stressed ?. The body responds to stress negatively. Many biological changes take place like Head / Neck Ache, Dry mouth sweats ..etc.There are many mental symptoms also for stress like mood swings, loss of interest in work etc The teacher's stress negatively affects their performance that in turn affects negatively the students as well as the institution. The more serious the stress is, the greater the negative impact is. Covid -19 makes the situation more miserable. Since the entire academia has been changed to online mode, the teachers are under stress. Managing these stressors effectively will help a lot in the teaching profession and the generation also. The study is concluded by providing stress management guidelines for reducing the stress level of teachers

Keywords: teacher's stress, stressors, symptoms, strategies to overcome stress.

Job Stress of College Teachers Especially After Covid-19 Pandemic

Introduction

Many of us have heard the word stress. This word used on many occasions is sometimes used to describe others and sometimes even for ourselves. The word 'stress 'evokes a negative feeling in everyone. Our body responds to stress negatively. The more serious the stress is, the greater the negative impact. Reasons for the stress may be psychological or physical. How can we identify stress? Many biological changes take place which includes the following but are not limited.

Dry mouth, Sweat, Aches, a feeling of heart beating raising, trouble in sleeping, muscle tension, stomach or digestive problem ....etc

Usually, these are the changes that happen in the human body when one is under stress. If this occurs it causes health problems frequently. Just like other professionals, teachers also experience stress. When covid-19 hit the world, it did not spare the educational field as well. In this pandemic situation, there is a drastic shift in teaching from off-line mode to on-line mode. Many of the educators were in stress because they could not cope with these changes. In the online era, many educators are not able to handle work and family life simultaneously and hence not good in an online session.

Literature Review:

The word 'stress' is derived from the Latin word ' stringere 'which means the experience of torture, pain, starvation and physical hardship is difficult to define since it is perception based and the level of stress changes according to individuals. This concept was first introduced in 1936 by Selye Hans and he defined stress as '' the non – specific response of the body to any demand placed upon it '' (Salye Hans, 1956). Stephen Robbins (1999) defines stress as '' a dynamic condition in which an individual is confronted with an opportunity. constraint or demand related to what he/she desires and for which the outcome is perceived to be both uncertain and important. Upadhyay and Singh (1999) conducted a comparative study on work stress by taking into consideration 20 executive-level officers and 2 college teachers. From their study, it is inferred that teachers exhibited many significant levels of stress when compares with executive-level people. Chand and Monga (2007) have conducted a study on stress and Burnout among faculty members of two different universities.

In their study, they say that faculty members with an internal locus of control, high communal hold and high attachment experience less stress. Further to this, the study also points out that signify the significant level of stress has been reported in the case of professors and a lower level of stress was experienced by an assistant professor. From the above literature, it can be observed that there are many research works carried out on the topic of stress management

Objectives of Research:

To study symptoms of the stress of teachers

To study the reasons for the stress

To study the strategies to overcome stress

Potential stress can become actual stress under 2 conditions ;

1) when one is not sure about the result of an event.

2) When the result of an event is important

The individuals who experience stress the most are those who are not sure about whether they would win or lose. On the other hand, those who know that they would surely win or surely lose experience stress the least. Meanwhile, there is no stress at all when the result is irrelevant

What is Teachers Stress?

Teaching is the most blessed profession as teachers make men and women better by inculcating in the citizen's culture, basic values and ethics. They are the people who create the next valuable generation. But still, considering the above-mentioned points there is a question, Are the teachers facing stress or not ?. To an outsider, the answer would be perhaps a big 'NO' because they perceive it as a relaxed job. But in reality, many of the teacher's are in stress because of many stressors (factors) like overall student development, Relationships with colleagues, superiors, students etc...At the workplace, these stressors already exist and covid -19 has added more stressors in the teaching profession like changes in the technology, shift in the teaching mode (off-line to on-line mode), handling students by sitting at home in front of a laptop/ mobile..etc .. . There is a big transformation that has taken place in academia because of covid -19

Symptoms of Stress

- Head Ache & Neck Ache
- Absenteeism, arriving late, leaving early
- Sweating, overreacting, arguing, anxiety
- Improper eating habits, sleeplessness
- Loss of interest in work, mood swing

Sources / Causes of Stress

The factors leading to stress among individuals are called stressors. Some of the stressors of teachers are as follows

- Role ambiguity
- Salary structure
- Result oriented appraisal
- Lack of recreational facilities
- Lack of appreciation
- Anxiety about a career because of a new model of teaching
- Role conflict
- Work-life balance
- Not getting enough '' me time ''
- Strict rules and regulation goal conflicts
- Less promotional opportunities

Management of Stress

As the definition puts it, stress management is a "set of techniques and programs intended to help people deal more effectively with stress in their lives by analyzing the specific stressors and taking positive actions to minimize their effects" (Gale Encyclopaedia of Medicine, 2008). Stress is relative in nature. Stress and its impact depend on how one handles the situation. If we perceive the situation in a negative way, then the situation will be stressful and vice versa Stressors are events or conditions in our surroundings that may trigger stress. There are many factors that trigger stress like job security, injury, depression, anxiety, workload etc. Handling the stress differs from individual to individual

For example, sometimes if a teacher gets an additional subject to be taught, he/she considers this situation as a challenging or thrilling opportunity. But another teacher can be under stress in such a situation even if he/she is an experienced teacher Stress affects everyone differently. Some people are naturally good at stress management. Others may need some help. The most important thing is everyone must find positive ways to manage stressors

Strategies For Managing Stress

Stress experienced by the teachers in their job has a negative impact on their health, performance and their behaviour in institutions as well as at home. so stress has to be managed wisely to avoid the harm

Strategies For Managing Stress

• The institution must have effective hiring and orientation procedure.

• The faculties must be given feedback on how well they are heading towards these goals.

• The institution must have fair incentives and a salary structure.

•The faculties should make a "To-Do" list daily prioritize acts in the list and plan the acts accordingly. By effective time management, faculties can do their work time and avoid stress.

•Encourage a healthy lifestyle like regular sleep, drinking plenty of water and healthy eating habits.

•Promote relaxing techniques such as yoga, listening to music and meditation.

•Faculty counselling is a good strategy to overcome stress.

Conclusion

Wolf & Goodwell (1968) defined stress as a dynamic state within an organism in response to a demand for adaptation. Stress and stress management are directly related to personal well being. The objective of the study is to find out the symptoms and factors causing stress among teachers. From this study, we can understand the factors causing stress and strategies to overcome the stress. We also get a clear picture of the physical symptoms like Headache, Neck ache and mental symptoms like frequent mood swings. For institutional and individual development and efficiency management, an individual has to adopt stress management strategies

Works Cited

Selye , H (1956). The Stress of Life . New York , McGraw Hill

Stephen , R (1999). Organizational Behaviour (8th Edition) . New Delhi , Prentice Hall of India

Upadhyay , B.K and Singh , B, (1999) '' Experience of stress : Difference between college teachers and executives '' psy. Stu . 44 (3) ,

Chand , P. and Monga , O.p (2007) ''Correlates of job stress and burnout '', J.Com . Gui.Res 24 (3)

www. Google .com

NATURE AND CULTURE; A JOURNEY INTO THE WILD IN SEAN PENN'S FILM INTO THE WILD

Ms. Sarah Santhosh

Assistant Professor, Department of English

The Cochin College, Kochi, Kerala.

ABSTRACT

Nature is not always seen with eyes but felt with the heart. It is like a living poem that has got infinite and often controversial interpretations. However, humanity's attempt to define nature has consistently resulted in nature's tendency to slip away and evade definition, a reality that has led Raymond Williams to claim that nature "is perhaps the most complex word in the language". There arise numerous questions once we try to define nature, and recently movies also started addressing humanity's relationship with nature. The way and authenticity of representation of the environment in movies is a vital concern of environmentalists. This paper attempts to explore how the nature-culture dichotomy is represented in Sean Penn's Into the Wild. It also attempts to bring out the existential crisis experienced by the hero Chris pursuant to his rejection of the modern American dream and his attempts to find his true identity in the wilderness as he feels nature is the right place to experience life in all its true essence.

Keywords: nature-culture Dichotomy, Wilderness, Representation

Sean Penn's Into the Wild portrays the 'true story of Chris McCandless, a young American adult hiker who set out for Alaska in the early 1990s. He was a twenty-four-year-old college graduate turned vagabond, went alone into the backcountry of Alaska in April 1992 and died there 113 days later. Into the Wild (2007) is director Sean Penn's film interpretation of Jon Krakauer's (1995) well-researched book with the same title. Penn's engaging direction provides a glimpse of what Chris McCandless found so seductive in the vast expanses of nature and the open road. He was particularly fascinated by Alaska and had long planned an Alaskan odyssey as a form of physical and spiritual proving ground where he would test himself by "living off the land" for a period of time.

The film is told in a disjointed fashion and is structured much like a classic American road trip narrative in which the protagonist while journeying to discover himself meets interesting characters along the way who influence and discuss the protagonist's motives. McCandless was not particularly unique in this vision. Many young men have similarly romanticised views of Alaska and have undertaken similar journeys. What seems to make Chris McCandless's story so well known is his death and what we know of his travels prior to going to Alaska.

The film depicts Chris's relationship with his parents as broken and that is the reason for Chris's decision to destroy every trace of his identity in the human world, give up all his material possessions including his name and adopt the name Alexander Supertramp, and trek across America to Alaska. McCandless has struggled to find food, may have accidentally ingested poisonous plants, and died soon thereafter.

Two years later his decomposing body was discovered by a hunter in a bus. The reason for his death was starvation. In the movie, Emile Hirsch stars as Christopher McCandless, the hero, and Marcia Gay Harden and William Hurt as the parents of Chris. The film also features Jena Malone, Catherine Keener, Vince Vaughn, Kristen Stewart and Hal Holbrook. The film was released on September 21, 2007, and it was an international success. Penn says "What moved me about the story was I felt this kid had furnished himself with a very full life in a short time. He lived all the chapters, in a way that very few people do" (New York Edition 21).

Nature as Destiny in Into the Wild.

Nature is the central theme of the film. On Chris's exploration in the wild, he learns the secrets of nature and finally succumbs to her and encounters a tragic death. "To experience life, you should go into the wild" (Into the Wild). The film begins with a quote from Lord Byron's Childe Harold's Pilgrimage,

There is pleasure in the pathless woods,

There is a rapture on the lonely shore,

There is society, where none intrudes,

By the deep sea, and music in its roar:

I love not to man the less, but Nature more.

The quote at the very beginning of the film guides the viewer to think about nature and the solitude found in it. The quote could also be seen functioning as a connector between physical natures on the one hand and nature as a non-physical concept giving the spectator an indication of the link between nature and transcendentalist spirituality found in it presented in the film.

One of the first striking and significant images of nature occurs at the beginning of the film in which in an extreme long- shot, looks across a snowy vista of white. The title of the film appears then on the screen. There is no sky in the shot; the landscape seems oppressive, which suggests that; once you enter into the landscape there is no real chance of escape. From the outer nature, Chris voyages into the inner nature where he aspires to find spiritual beauty.

Chris goes into the wild to experience true life, considerably different from the life in modern society. It is only later in the film Chris speaks passionately about his planned Alaskan trip: "Alaska, Alaska. I'm gonna be all the way out there. All the way fuckin out there, just on my own... you know big mountains, rivers, sky, and game. Just be out there in it, you know. In the wild." When Chris entered the Alaskan forest, he was full of positive enthusiasm, considering himself as an explorer of the wild. At the time of going into the Alaskan wild, the river he had crossed was calm, quiet and romantic and the woods attracted him towards the interior.

But the Alaskan forest was not a perfect habitat for a modern gipsy. Chris was warned about the harsh realities of Alaska by the natives of Alaska. But his aspiration towards exploring Alaska was deep-rooted in him that no one was able to stop him from his journey. In the final phase, Chris was ill-prepared as he approached to live in nature. He spent only a little time studying how to lead a life in harmony with nature in the Alaskan region. This young man was ignorant of the inner spirit of nature. He walked into the wild without having any precautions with the hope of conquering the wild easily. But Chris failed to understand the true identity of the woods. He led a primitive man's life. He considered his whole life as an adventurous sport. It was his love for risk which killed him.

The two months of solitary life in the woods taught him the real power of nature. Not just the power of nature, but he had also learned the importance of sharing happiness within a social circle from the solitary life at the woods. Chris's ideologies when he stepped into the woods had undergone tremendous changes within a short span of time. He scribbled down in his diary "happiness is only real when shared" (Into the Wild). In his attempt to survive in the wilderness Chris relied too much upon books. He started to eat potatoes which were poisonous. This eventually leads to his death. Chris went to the woods with a great deal of romantic and idealistic notions but in his attempt to find himself in the wilderness he failed pathetically. He was unable to understand the pulse and nature of the wild. It was his destiny to die in nature isolated from humanity.

Chris attempts to bridge the divide between humanity and nature or language and nature. Chris tries to define his environment, sits by a fire that he had made in the bus's furnace, eats berries, roots and shrubs he had picked during the day. The camera focuses on a written list of the plants he had identified in his environment, with the "wild potato root."The scene also speaks of Chris's desire to convert nature into something quantifiable. This comes as a result of Chris's loss of control over nature. In trying to use language to define nature for the purpose of survival it seems that Chris makes the assumption that there exists the potential for language to lose its anthropomorphic depiction of nature and eliminate the divide between language and nature.

Chris wakes up the next morning in a confused state. He tries to swallow water but seems unable to hold it down. It is clear that he is sick. He looks across his bed and we are able to identify the Priscilla Russell Kari book, Tanaina Plantlore: An Ethnobotany of the Dena'ina Indians of South-central Alaska. As Chris pages through the book, we are given a close up of the page in which the inedible wild sweet pea is described. After this, there is a contrasting close up of the edible wild potato. Turning back to the page in which the wild sweet pea is featured, Chris reads the description of the inedible plant and we are able to read that the wild sweet pea possesses "lateral veins" and is "poisonous." Indeed, when Chris picks a sample of the plant from a bag, he observes that the wild sweet pea has said lateral veins. As Chris picks another plant sample from his bag, this time, we assume, a leaf of the wild potato, the words "plants resemble each other" may be read as it pans across the screen.

The suggestion that Penn is attempting to make here is that Chris mistook the inedible and fatal wild sweet pea for the edible wild potato. This mistake eventually leads to Chris's death. Penn shows that language cannot represent nature with accuracy. Thus, Penn seems to be making the point that language alone cannot be used, firstly, as an adequate and accurate representation of nature, and secondly, as a means of surviving in nature. Penn states that Chris's death was due to an inability of language to grasp all of nature, making the point that the kind of deep interconnection Chris attempted to establish with nature was doomed to fail.

Culture also uses nature to provide a sense of morality. Thus, all cultures develop an anthropomorphic understanding of nature in order to gain a sense of right and wrong. An Eco-critic rejects the notion that everything is socially and or linguistically constructed. Chris is highly influenced by the anthropomorphic mixing of morality and nature. Chris's journey into the wild was weighted significantly by a deep-seated sense of morality. One of the best examples of Thoreau's sentiments on the relationship between morality and nature is exemplified when he writes that "all good things are wild and free".

Nature and Culture

Chris uses culturally determined tools and constructs to come to the conclusion that, culture poisons the purity of nature. In the end, Chris wrote a note which read: "happiness is only real when shared" (Into the Wild). This annotation shows that whatever kind of happiness one may derive from nature must be happy that is accompanied by some degree of anthropocentrism as it must be happiness in which others are invited to partake. Chris represents everyman, who themselves escape into the wild and run away from material comfort. Everyone looks into a life where no one judges, none imitates no questions and no answers. Only to live one with nature, to enjoy the full essence of nature and tastes its complete beauty. But men cannot completely throw their inner passions out. Humanness always haunts them.

That is why they cannot completely enjoy real. Wilderness is nature untouched by humans. Chris becomes a tramp, Alexander Supertramp in the wilderness. Chris's real intention can be seen in his words; Two years he walks the earth. No phone, no pool, no pets, no cigarette. Ultimate freedom. An extremist. Anaesthetic voyager, whose home is the road, escaped from Atlanta. Thou shall not return, because the west is the best. And now after two rambling years, comes the final and greatest adventure. The climactic battle to kill the false being within and victoriously concludes the spiritual pilgrimage. Ten days and nights of freight trains and hitchhiking bring him to the Great White North. No longer to be poisoned by civilization he flees and walks alone upon the land to become lost in the wild (Into the Wild).

Chris wants to free himself from material bonds. Ultimately the journey proved to be too difficult. He was unable to take the ultimate test of survival in the wilderness. Chris's vision of nature was created by the books he read. This served as an inspiration for his treks. Chris imitates the romantic notion of life following his passions without social and cultural restrictions, a life completely free of bonds and bondages. Chris preferred the fictitious characters more than men in society. Those characters became his soul companions. His journey away from society was in search of a unique identity, an identity not moulded by the urban society, but an identity acquired by Thoreau in Walden and Buck in The Call of the Wild.

Unravelling the Frames in Into the Wild

"The auteur writes with a camera as the writer writes with a pen." (Alesandre Astruc 107)

Into the Wild works as a hero's journey as Chris is called to and embarks upon a spiritual quest. Scenes in the film speak about Chris's intimacy with nature, what he achieved from his voyage and the various stages of his life where nature is either presented as a friend or a foe. Watching a film is much like reading a book. The scenes are divided into "chapters" with subtitles and dates, often lending the impression that we are reading Chris's own words as he enacts the activities he describes. Penn includes a shot of Chris's reading a poem to his sister in a scene that both reinforces the film's textuality as well as shows what is to come. When Chris comes to the line "you're going to do bad things to children," we become aware of a dark shadow lurking within the otherwise seemingly normal McCandless family.

Penn uses the technique of voice-over effectively, which allows Carine (Chris's sister) to explain the family's background and the psychodynamics of the relationship between their overbearing father who bullies them and their mother. In this way, Carine also describes how the parents forced her and Chris to watch them and even to take sides during a discussion of divorce, which they never actually end up getting. Carine tells, "I understood what he was doing. That he had spent four years, fulfilling the absurd and tedious duty of graduating from college, and now he was emancipated from that world of abstraction, false security, parents and material excess, the things that cut Chris off from the truth of his existence." (Into the Wild). Such "witnessed violence" is bad enough, but even worse is the discovery during an earlier trip to California by Chris that he and Carine are technically illegitimate, having been born before their father was divorced from his first wife. Carine reveals what she calls the "ugly truth that redefined Chris and me as... bastard children of a fraudulent marriage" (Into the Wild).

There are two aesthetics set up in the film that outline the social aesthetic which people attempt to create within the society and the raw aesthetics of the wild. The former aesthetics is exemplified by his parents and the way they live their lives according to how nice their house looks, how expensive their car etc. The material possessions that Chris's parents use to create the aesthetics of their life are deceitful aesthetics. The aesthetics of the wild provide a kind of truth for Chris. Chris is able to see that the aesthetics represent the true nature of the wild. All of the aesthetics in the wild represent exactly what they are. At the end of the film, he dies from an aesthetically deceptive plant. Aesthetic deception is the very thing that Chris's parents have set up and fabricated all around them and exactly what Chris wants to leave behind. The false beauty of a falsely happy suburban life has no truth in its aesthetics for life.

In Chris's character, we see a complicated collection of complexes that make him seem more anti-hero than a hero. While the stuff of many myths, heroes are unsupported by contemporary society, which cannot encourage its individual members to become too independent. Indeed, society imposes strict sanctions on those who dare to buck the system: individuation comes at a high cost. In many ways, Chris's journey may be seen as a peripatetic purification. Feeling unclean after discovering the truth about the circumstances of his birth, Chris sets his sights on Alaska to "purify." Chris's chastity is portrayed most notably by his eschewing of love interests.

Contained in Chris's pursuit of purification is his quest for truth since part of his scene of defilement is based upon the elaborate lie foisted upon him by his parents about his childhood, which made him feel " his whole world turn and made his childhood feel like fiction," (Into the Wild). Consequently, truth takes on monumental importance for Chris, which is why he can't bring himself to forgive his parents for their duplicity. After spending several years on the road, making friends along the way, Chris discovers that separation from his parents alone is not enough to soothe the savage beast within. His meanderings around the continental U.S. fail to assuage the utter disdain Chris continues to feel toward his parents and all they represent to him, especially what he sees as their hypocrisy and dis-ingenuousness. However, it is not just his parents Chris is at odds with; he is rebelling against a society that seems to encourage materialistic greed. He has nothing but contempt for material possessions and money.

Chris relates to his newfound friends on the road, he finds their presence a hindrance to his presence to himself. Consequently, he becomes attracted by asceticism, simplicity, and naturalness. Chris understands he must finally do what he has been talking about for two years: go to Alaska. Chris chooses the deep woods as his final destination underscores the symbolic significance of the wilderness forest, which is not simply a miscellany of trees; it is enchanted. In other words, a forest is a place where the spirit is infused throughout and the psyche's work of transformation becomes possible, as we see in Chris's encounters with the moose and the bear.

Chris commits a cardinal sin against the nature goddess. He assumes he is sufficiently prepared for his confrontation with her, but he is not. When Chris finds his moose covered in maggots much earlier than his hunter friend had predicted and before he has had the opportunity to finish curing it, he is devastated. It is one of four critical mistakes Chris makes that leads to his downfall, the others being his choice to go to Alaska in May when hunting and gathering is especially difficult, his failure to take into account the increase in water level in the river during the summer which makes it impassable, and his failing to understand that the potato seeds he thought were safe to eat become toxic in the summer.

Chris paradoxically is transformed by his experience; the predator becomes the prey. Chris's journey comes full- circle when he arrives in Alaska. Convinced when he heads out that he must lose everything that connects him to his past, he apparently undergoes a change of heart while there and arrives finally at a sort of decision to go back. Evidence found with him in the old Fairbanks transit bus he inhabited during his months in the wilderness includes a marked-up copy of Doctor Zhivago in which he indicates his apparent readiness to return to civilisation. At the top of the page he has printed nature/purity, and the illuminating words "happiness is only real when shared".

The irony is that by the time he is ready to return to civilisation, Chris is too incapacitated from starvation to walk out of the wilderness- a potent image of the spiritual pull going too far. Such paradox is the essence of the heroin that he can cope with the greatest perils, yet, in the end, something relatively insignificant is his undoing. It is at this point in the film that Penn presents what is perhaps his most magical personification of nature. Chris is standing motionless, undoubtedly frightened but not outwardly so, as a massive Alaskan brown bear wanders by, its hulking body just inches away. Chris attempts to discover himself through nature. It is a certain kind of nature that characterizes Christ's quest for the character.

Into the Wild exemplifies cinematically how wilderness works as a metaphor for the unconscious. The final message of Chris written on a piece of paper and attached to the bus seems almost upbeat, considering the circumstances: "I have had a happy life and thank the lord; goodbye and may God bless all" (Into the Wild). We see Chris's journey as something to which he has been called, in the words of Carine, "everything he is doing has to be done" (Into the Wild). Through Chris, we become visually intimate with the search for self and depth. It is a journey that can take place only by going "Into the Wild". We recognise in ourselves a sense of adventure, of independence, a desire to leave the arbitrary rules of society behind us and reject the culture of our accumulation nation, to live in the world "as God and nature intended." Chris was able to take the risks we wish we were able to take or wish we had taken.

Representation of nature

This paper discusses how nature is represented in film in contrast to the written text and how representing nature in film modified existing ecocritical premises. It analyses whether the film influences anthropomorphism or anthropocentrism. Any definition of nature is culturally determined. Thus, in the process of providing a definition of nature, each culture does so by negotiating its placement on the nature-human continuum. It is assumed that nature and humans fall on opposite ends of the same scale. Nature is culturally determined comes mainly from the fact that every culture views nature in a different way.

Penn is critical of eco aesthetic sentiments. Penn also manages to use this eco aesthetics to criticise Chris McCandless. Chris in addition to being influenced by romantic artists such as Emerson and Thoreau is also influenced by Russian realists such as Tolstoy and Pasternak. Penn is critical of the ways in which Chris seemed to internalise the director's sentiments. Penn manages to utilize the kind of eco aesthetics to convey this criticism and highlights the danger of eco-aesthetics in the life of Chris. Wilderness itself is part of Chris's life.

The appearance of nature on film may be more potently anthropocentric when compared to its appearance in written text as the moving images give the impression of being more convincing and realistic. Because the thing is being depicted in the film is similar to the way in which we may view it in real life. The consequence of this is that the viewer may be more inclined to believe that he or she has exercised full control over nature, that she has captured the essence of nature. Thus, issues such as anthropocentrism and anthropomorphism are apparent in filmic texts. Thus, due to the inevitability of anthropocentrism, to place a value judgment only on the act of depicting nature through the vein of anthropocentrism would prove futile. It is therefore the manner in which these depictions take place, and the context in which they are situated proves useful in the analysis of the work of Sean Penn.

Ecocriticism praises positive representations of nature in written texts, but reading only this quality in texts, written or film, does a disservice both to the text being studied and the theory used to analyze that text. When giving an ecocritical reading of a written text, one observes the manner in which the environment is portrayed, to what degree the characters and the author exhibit anthropocentric characteristics, how human characters act up on and react to the environment, how the characters and authors use place and space to what degree nature is anthropomorphised. These are the same qualities that ought to be observed when giving an ecocritical reading of a film.

Into the Wild unravels a layer of fear within the heart of every man who hankered for Mother Nature's soft embrace. Penn shows the core of wilderness, its dreadful beauty, and its unforgiving ruggedness. In doing so he created a modern classic of travel literature that sparkles perilously with man's craving for adventure and his self-destructive instincts.

Sean Penn implies that our understanding of the connection between language and nature is quite literally a matter of life and death. Chris's views on the issue of language and nature are inspired by the literature he has read. Chris is attempting to bypass the anthropomorphic quality of language and use language as a tool for identifying and describing nature correctly. He believes that if he is to survive he must translate nature's purity, through nature's language. There are certainly several repercussions that arise when assigning a particular and idiosyncratic definition to nature Penn is successful in presenting nature as a character.

Penn successfully comes to a valid conclusion that to achieve the kind of immersion into nature pursued by Chris is an act that requires a degree of knowledge of nature that is simply impossible to achieve, at least for modern humans. Penn shows the earth as an elusive and mysterious figure and also the unexpected dangers that lie in nature. Unable to understand the pulse and nature of the wild, Chris is trapped in the labyrinth of the wild. It is clear that the film tries to portray the hero's attitudes towards nature and his attempts to explore the land and his mind through the aesthetics of nature.

Works Cited

Astruc, Alesandre. "Art of Cinema: Aesthetic sense and Ideology". Public Space and Creativity. Ed. Shaji Jacob. Kannur: Kairali Books, 2014. 107-156. Print.

Barry, Peter. An introduction to Literary and Cultural Theory. Manchester: Manchester University Press, 2008. Print.

Berman, Tzeporah. "The Rape of Mother Nature: Women in the Language of Environmental Discourse." The Ecolinguistics Reader: Language, Ecology and Environment. Eds. Fill, Alwin and Peter Muhlhausler. London: Continuum, 2001.

Biography.com Editors. Sean Penn. The Biograph.com website. A&E Television Networks, n.d.web.25 June.2020.

Buell, Lawrence. The Future of Environmental Criticism: Environmental Crisis and Literary Imagination. Malden: Blackwell Publishing, 2005.

Debord, Guy. "Cinema Theatre and Public Space". Public space and Creativity. Ed. Shaji Jacob. Kannur: Kairali Books, 2014.107-156.

Goodbody, Axel. Nature, Technology and Cultural Change in Twentieth-Century German Literature: The Challenge of Ecocriticism. Newyork: Palgrave Macmillan, 2007.

Greenberg, Joy. Rev of Into the Wild, by Sean Penn, Newyork, Mar.2010: 281- 290.

Hazlitt, William. Sketches and Essays. London: John Templeman, 1839.

Howarth, William. "Some Principles of Ecocriticism." The Ecocriticism Reader: Landmark In Literary Ecology. Eds. Glotfelty, Cheryll and Harold Fromm. Athens: The University of Georgia Press, 1996.

Ivakhiv, Adrian. "Green Film Criticism and its Futures." ISLE 15.2, 2008:1-28.

Lefebvre, Martin. "Between setting and Landscape in the Cinema." Landscape and Film. Newyork: Routledge, 2005.

McGrath, Charles. "Mother Nature's Restless Sons." New York Times 16 Sep 2007: 21.

Naess, Arne. Ecology, Community and Lifestyle: Outline of an Ecosophy. Cambridge University Press, 1989.

Penn, Sean. Dir. Into the Wild. Perf. Hirsch, Emile. 2007. Paramount Home Entertainment, 2008. DVD.

Rueckert, William. "Literature and Ecology: An Experiment in Ecocriticism." The Ecocriticism Reader: Landmark in Literary Ecology. Ed. Glotfelty, Cheryl. Vol.9.1: The University of Georgia Press, 1996. Print.

Williams, Raymond. Keywords: A Vocabulary of Culture and Society. London: Croom Helm, 1983. Print.

Bio-Note

Sarah Santhosh is an Assistant Professor with seven years of teaching experience. She specializes in English Language Teaching and Film Studies.

CHAPTER XII

ONTOLOGICAL EXISTENCE OF TRANSWOMEN: A STUDY ON A REVATHY'S TRUTH ABOUT ME: A HIJRA LIFE STORY

Shahina N.

Assistant professor

Safa college of arts and science

ABSTRACT

A Transwoman is a male to female transgender or the transsexual person who was an assigned male at birth but identifies as female. The term and its synonym male to female transsexual are often used for individuals who have not been physically transferred but many prefer the simple word 'women' after the process is complete. But do they consider women while addressing them? If they are considered as 'women' by the hetronormative society, why do they still don't possess the 'pronoun' to address them? Pronouns are basically how we identify ourselves apart from our name. In the case of assigned gender, we use 'he' for a man and 'she' for a woman. But when this hetronormative society is not ready to take transwomen as a woman how can we address them by using the pronoun 'she'. My paper questions the perplexing dilemma of the situation in which how we can address transwomen by using a particular pronoun without hurting their emotions.

The question does not rest on the use of the pronoun but it points out their ontological existence. whatever things possess the existence, have ontological meaning but a transgender who doesn't have an existence only has epistemological existence. This paper traces the problems encountered by transwomen while addressing them by the hetronormative society using the old pronoun (he), which was shed by Revathy when changed into a complete woman mentally and physically.

Keywords: Ontological existence, transwomen, pronouns, epistemology.

Ontological Existence of Transwomen: A Study on A Revathy's Truth About Me: A Hijra Life Story

Introduction

Transgender is an umbrella term that does not fit into the heteronormative society, whose gender or expression may not match with the sex assigned at birth. A transgender person may identify as a woman despite having been born with male genitalia. A Transwoman is a male to female transgender or the transsexual person who was an assigned male at birth but identifies as female. The term and its synonym male to female transsexual are often used for individuals who have not been physically transferred but many prefer the simple word 'women' after the process is complete. But this kind of transformation is taken as a defect by the heteronormative society.

It describes how heterosexuality is normalized by certain social norms and practices, it is considered as an only legitimate form of sexuality. In this paper, I am focusing on the struggles of transwomen while searching for an ontological existence in this heteronormative society where everything binary to it taken as something deviated or deceased. They view gender as something binary and fixed at birth other sexual identities are considered unnatural and sometimes even illegally prohibited. This so-called 'unnatural' struggle to maintain a space for them in the world and this paper am pursuing my study on the lack of pronouns to address this unnatural and the way we can give them equal status as human beings. My study focuses on the A Revathy: Truth About me a hijra life story. Hijras, who include transgender and intersex people dressed in glittering attire, faces heavily coated in cheap makeup, wander through crowded cities knocking on car windows and offering blessings. They dance at the temples, crash fancy weddings and birth ceremonies, sing bawdy songs, and leave with a fistful of rupees. Within Indian LGBT culture they own their subculture.

In India, the hijra community is marginalized geographically economically, and socio-politically. It is difficult for them to get employment, protection from various laws and judiciary, official recognition. They were leading a life of parallel hierarchical familiar society in their subculture. They indulge in sex work and begging and blessing on rare occasions, to employ themselves. This paper proposes the ontological existence of a hijra who portrays her travail of life which she shares to give an account of her life which was filled with struggles endured by a hijra in a heteronormative society. A Revathy begins her book with a prologue in which she opens up her intention to write such an autobiography of a hijra as it is the first of its kind.

"As a hijra, I get pushed to the fringes of society. yet I have dared to share my innermost life with you – about being a hijra and also about doing sex work. My story is not meant to offend, accuse or hurt anyone's sentiments. I aim to introduce to the readers the lives of hijras, their distinct culture, and their dreams and desires".(Revathy v-vi)

Revathy is a hijra and an activist working for the rights of sexual minorities in India. As a hijra, she underwent a lot of struggles from the heteronormative society as they were never tried to accept her newfound identity. even the law and judiciary system had shown its dark face towards her. Her activism made her write this autobiographical book A Revathy: Truth About Me A Hijra Life Story. In which she hydrogenizes the struggles of hijras while trying to make a space for them in this earth where binaries are taken as deceased or unnatural. Revathy published her first book in Tamil Unarvum Uruvavum as a part of research on hijras which was given to her by Sangam. It made her brave enough to write and dictate the struggles of hijras, perhaps it may bring the attention of people towards their treatment with them. She expected a sweep of change after the book A Revathy Truth About Me: A Hijra Life Story.

Tracing the ontological existence of transwoman

Born as the youngest male sibling in the family where three brothers and one sister with their parents reside. A Revathy was initially baptized as Doraisamy. Now while addressing her by using the pronoun, one may find it in a perplexing situation to choose the correct pronoun, whether to use he/she or his/ her. The moment we choose the correct pronoun which satisfies the existence of her makes us the persons who deviate from the heteronormative society. By giving a suitable pronoun to refer to her we are accepting their ontological existence in this world. And this absence of ontological existence is one of the main reasons for them to be ostracised or colonized from this heteronormative society. "look! I am not a man, don't call me 'dai'. My name is Revathy and that's what you should call me from now" (Revathy 90) 'dai' is a pronoun used by them to refer to Doraisamy but after she changed her identity, she preferred them to call her by her name as it was important for her to mention her name Revathy because it makes her an acceptance in the heteronormative society.

The story opens in a small village in Tamil Nadu where Doraisamy was born into a pheasant family. right from her /his childhood, he experienced violence in her school and family due to her feminine ways. He/she was not interested to play with boys but preferred to play with girls and often tried to wear his mom's clothes. From childhood itself, he felt trapped in the wrong body. He was going through mental turmoil over his gender identity. As he grows it was harder for him to hide his feelings and desires like a woman and he felt trapped in the wrong body. In a house everything was punished in the manner of violence especially by his younger brother, it was not resting on his identity but his safety was important too. During her school trip, she met with a group of people from kothi community and he heard about the things which happening inside of him and decided to run away from his hometown to Delhi with them to be true to her identity. she/ he always wanted to maintain a family of her own by marrying a man and having kids with him. But it remained as a dream for her because for transwomen it was never possible to attain completeness as a woman. From there she started to live with the hijra community and underwent a sex-change operation and before that she christened herself as Revathy and all was she dreamt of a married life with kids.

There she had to undergo physical and mental assault from the heteronormative society coupled with economic hardship. She tried to make her living by dancing, begging, and sex work. After being fed up with life in Delhi she returned to her home but she was never welcomed. She went to Bangalore and there she got a job in Sangam, an initiative for the rights of minorities which gave her strength enough to realize her potential and the need her to work for the marginalized hijra community. While started as a peon in Sangam and ended up as a director. Doraisamy being born of a male body was expected like a man by the heteronormative society. But his male body nurtured the desires of the female and her mind yearns to complete her identity by transforming into a complete woman. In that process, she underwent a series of physical and mental torture by this heteronormative society that consider it unnatural and deceased.

To create an existence of her first need to be true to her identity. But the world which sees the binary as deviant never accepted her existence. Transwomen, once they changed their gender to women, are not accepted as women by the heteronormative society. The question is with their identity. Whether they could be addressed as he or she. This fine line of confusion exploits their existence. If we can't consider them as a woman on the ground of their inability to become mothers, it is not justified because there are so many women are there who can't be a mother through natural gestation. So, this statement can be ruled out when it comes to transwomen. Why their existence can't be treated as normal? For the convenience of addressing, certain words are coined and it is the same for transgenders too. The famous British Transgender activist Stephen Whittle mentioned in his prologue to the Transgender Reader "cultural spaces and historiographies are constantly reframing the community, the identities, culture, and language. We see new languages being developed constantly; for example 'per' as a pronoun developed by the UK community members with nonexistent gender identities, and similarly the US term 'hir' for those who have both" (The Transgender Reader xi-xii)

Revathy in the autobiography narrates multiple incidents in which she shattered after addressing her by using the pronoun 'dai' which she has shed herself when turned into a complete woman. "when they addressed me as 'Doraisamy I entreated them to call me Revathy" (Revathy 94). After returning to her home as Revathy she endured physical and mental turmoil from her relatives and villagers. While she exposed herself in Infront of her brother and mother they got agitated and started to beat and curse her for the 'flaw' that she had made. Though she is a 'pottai' among them she can pass off as a woman in Infront of those who don't know her. Her sister accepted her as a woman and made her kids call her 'aunty. The villagers have taken her as someone deceased in their mind and showcased it as a peculiar thing. stared at her in a way that something odd standing in front of them. They teased her and hurt her feelings by using her former pronoun.

Pronouns are one of how we portray our identities. When someone asks to use their correct pronoun which ensures to accept their gender identity. When someone refers to the other person with the wrong pronoun it can cause them to break their feelings and disrespect their identity. It is a common fact that heteronormative society address transgenders as it, he-she, number 9, to hurt their feelings. "Look just because you decide to change like this in the middle of your life, you can't expect us to forget what we used to call you! I am used to calling you Doraisamy and that's what my tongue finds easy." (Revathy 134)

Those people who were orthodox have the problem of accepting the identity of transgender people due to their lack of realization of the changes happening in the heteronormative society. For them, a male body is not expected to behave in a feminine way and they were not supposed to change their identity in the middle of life, for them this transformation is a form of deviation from the heterosexuals. Pronouns are basically how we identify ourselves apart from our name. In the case of assigned gender, we use 'he' for a man and 'she' for a woman. But when this heteronormative society is not ready to take transwomen as a woman how can we address them by using the pronoun 'she'. My paper questions the perplexing dilemma of the situation in which how we can address transwomen by using a particular pronoun without hurting their emotions. the gender-neutral language which challenges the traditional use of the pronoun man-he and woman-she. Gender-neutrality wishes to be inclusive of people who belong to the non-binary.

Gender-neutral is the thought that policies, language, and other social institutions should avoid distinguishing roles according to people's sex or gender. A gender-neutral language is a form of linguistic prescriptivism that aims to eliminate reference to gender in terms that describes people. In the English language, while selecting a pronoun for a person whose gender is unknown, he/she is replaced with 'they'. Those who do not identify as either male/female may use a gender-neutral pronoun to refer to themselves or others. In 2012 gender-neutral pronoun 'hen' was proposed by Sweden and in 2014 it was announced that the pronoun would be included in the Swedish academy glossary. Swedish became the first language to introduce a gender-neutral pronoun by an authoritative institution. 'hen' can be used to describe anyone regardless of their gender identity. It doesn't have widespread usage outside the LGBTQ communities. LGBTQ activists suggest that the pronouns he/she and his/her linguistically enforce a normative two-sex system that falls into either male or female. It will hurt the feelings of persons who don't fit into the binaries. There is a growing variety of gender-neutral pronouns it may include sie, hir, hirs, hirsel, and also include z or p.

Transwomen in general and Revathy in particular years to identify as a woman in the society. She wants others to address her by calling Revathy. She had transformed her male body in the process of becoming a woman. On her travail to be a woman she endured physical and mental tortures. She became a member of the hijra community where she did sex work to fulfil her sexual desires as a woman. It does not rest on the dilemma of choosing the correct pronoun or whether they address her as a woman. It questions her identity or existence in this heteronormative society.in Indian culture, people observe hijra as a mixed feeling of fear and laughter.

" hijras play the dholak, sing, and dance, and this is called Doli-baddai. they do this at weddings and during childbirth. People give them what they can afford – rice, wheat, a sari. Hijras find out where there's been a birth and send word to the family, saying that they would arrive on such and such day to bless the newborn and they must be given baddai. Similarly, hijras go to marriage halls and sing and dance, teasing the groom and bride, which pleases them, and they too give money." (Revathy 47)

The people may easily question the existence of such a living in which hijras pursue their lives by begging and doing sex works. The bitter truth is that hijras are never allowed to enter into the mainstream economy. such as our social stigma is that hijra can never be accommodated into the economy in which they could maintain their economic independence. The heteronormative society is perpetuating its hegemonic discourse over the hijras. We have never seen a hijra owning her/his shop or involved in another profession that was controlled by the heteronormative society. The bitter confusion is that in every application form we have male or female. Though they were not allowed to enter into the mainstream of society how they could ask for a space of their own. Here the hegemonic power structure enforces their laws and judiciaries over these marginalized hijras, which prevent them to obtain an ontological existence in this world where everything 'unnatural ' seems as deceased or punishable.

Here hijras only have an epistemological existence as their existence is inside a question mark. A heteronormative society where everything other seems peculiar invites the question of the existence of hijra in particular transwomen. Here my study proposes that transwomen don't have an ontological existence rather they possess an epistemological existence. Ontology means knowing the reality while epistemology is how we perceive the reality and it constitutes our knowledge of the reality. it is a philosophical thought when compared to ontology. Here my paper questions the existence of transwomen based on the reality that does she is real in this heteronormative society if it is yes then why Revathy endure all forms of tortures on her travail? What defines womanhood is that those who possess an ovary are considered a woman. In the case of trans women, their reality of existence is in question that they were hidden from the mainstream of society socially, economically, and politically. Transwomen don't obtain a space in the heteronormative society while they live in a perplexing dilemma of addressing their name. Revathy frequently demands others to call her as Revathy shows how she is trying to assert her identity in the heteronormative society which has taken her as a staring piece. "I heard someone say " come pick a flower. nothing wrong with that, you are like us, you are like a goddess, unblemished unlike us who have done wrong. Go ahead". (Revathy 136)

These words are uttered by the same persons who laughed and stared at her after she transformed into the identity of Revathy. In Indian mythology, the hijra is considered equal to the goddess and has a special place among the gods. But still, why do they were teased, and tortured by the same hegemonic power as something which is a deceased one. This dichotomy of the viewpoint of people makes it clear that their existence is there but the hegemonic discourse of heteronormative society is not ready to accept their existence.

conclusion

My study on the existence of transwomen proposes that we have to realize the reality in which they exist and their ontological existence is an acknowledgeable fact and their epistemological existence is the product of a heteronormative society in so far. Revathy raised her voice to get justice from society. Are these transwomen getting benefits like women? The answer is 'no'. they have to treat like women. And should get proper education and job. This is progressive thinking. Revathy has written this autobiography for her community as it is her weapon to change the treatment of people towards the hijra community. Let it be an eye-opener to society.

Works Cited

Galani Kanta. "Being Hijra; A Stigma A Perusal to A Revathy: The Truth About Me: A Hijra Life Story". International Journal Of Research In Humanities, Arts and Literature. Vol 6. issue 11. 2018. Pp 75-80.

Revathy A. A Truth About Me: A Hijra Life Story. Trans. V. Geetha. New Delhi: Penguin Books India Pvt.Ltd 2014 .print

Samanta Antanu. "Gender Discrimination In A Revathi's Autobiography The Truth About Me: A Hijra Life Story". International Journal of English Language, Literature and Translation Studies. 4.1.2017 pp 220-223.

Summersell Jason. "Transwomen are Real Woman: A Critical Intersectional Response to Pilgrim". Journal of Critical Realism vol 17. Issue 3. 2018. pp 329-336

TRACING THE THINGS' FALLEN APART: A CASE OF IGBO CULTURAL IDENTITY REFLECTED IN THE COMEDY SERIES MARK ANGEL COMEDY

Sindhu Thomas

Assistant Professor, Department of English

Baselios Poulose II Catholicos College

Piravom. Ernakulam, Kerala.

ABSTRACT

The contemporary Igbo life and culture reflected in literary as well as media representations, when placed against Achebe's exposition of Igbo culture in his *Things Fall Apart*, gives a panoramic vision of the distortions and changes inflicted on the traditional Nigerian Igbo cultural identity. The episodes of the Nigerian comedy short videos 'Mark Angel Comedy' open up to the ordinary rustic life of the present-day Igbo people. This paper is an attempt to trace the changes in the self-sufficing notion of African cultural identity in the pre and post-colonial Igbo society and to see if the changes brought in by colonialism were catastrophic and whether it resulted in the distortion of cultural identity among the African communities especially the Nigerian Igbo life. The study is conducted by analysing the factors that transformed their cultural identity as Chinua Achebe portrays them in *Things Fall Apart* and the portrayal of the present-day Igbo culture in select episodes of the YouTube comedy shorts, 'Mark Angel Comedy.

Keywords: Cultural identity, Igbo ethnic identity, cultural symbols, language, tradition, colonialism, Christianity.

• • •

Tracing the Things' Fallen Apart: A Case of Igbo Cultural Identity Reflected in the Comedy Series Mark Angel Comedy

The past, present and future of the African cultures have been a topic of debate for decades. The colonial expansion followed by the Christian missionaries, the internal conflicts among the communities and lately the globalisation policies and the advent of information communication technologies have resulted in the breaking down of the African traditions. "Colonialism resulted in disarticulation, dislodgement and destruction of African culture and the natural economy through co-option, force and imposition of alien ways of life. Through colonial policies, Africans became alienated from their land- their primary source of subsistence" (Coleman 35). The Nigerian Igbo culture is one among those African cultures influenced by colonial oppression, reflections of which can be traced in literary as well media representations.

The writings of Chinua Achebe, the Nigerian writer whose childhood straddled the worlds of Igbo traditional culture and postcolonial Christianity, occupy a pivotal place in African Literature. Chinua Achebe's things Fall Apart published in 1958 provides an insight into the traditions of Igbo society right before the white missionaries' invasion of the Igbo land and pictures the starting point of the post-colonial oppression of the Igbo culture. Things Fall Apart is all about the "collapse, breaking into pieces, chaos and confusion" (Alimi 121) of traditional Igbo culture that suffers at the hand of the white man's arrival in Umuofia along with his religion.

The contemporary Igbo life and culture reflected in literary as well as media representations, when placed against Achebe's exposition, gives a contrastive picture. Writings of Akwaeke Emzi, Nigerian comedy web series like 'Mark Angel Comedy', 'Emmanuella' etc provide glimpses of the present-day Igbo life in Nigeria. 'Mark Angel Comedy', a comedy series of shorts on YouTube that depict the present-day life of the Igbo people in Nigeria deliver a quick dose of humour and insight into Nigerian, specifically Igbo tradition, culture and socio-political issues. Starred by a revolving cast of real-life characters, 'Mark Angel Comedy' mirrors the present day Igbo society where a majority follow the faith, principles and value system based on Christianity, who bear English or Christian names and speak English in daily endeavours. The characters are drawn from real life, with their original names; they are just like every other Nigerian in the lower class and their background influences the plots and their choice of locations for their videos.

By tracing the shifts and changes that occurred to the Igbo community of Nigeria and the factors that transformed their cultural identity as Chinua Achebe portrays them in *Things Fall Apart* and the portrayal of the present day Igbo culture in select episodes of the YouTube comedy shorts, *Mark Angel Comedy* give scope for analysing the self-sufficing African notion of cultural identity and to see if the changes brought in by colonialism were catastrophic and whether it resulted in the distortion of cultural identity among the African communities especially the Nigerian Igbo life.

In the article titled "Self-Representation and the Construction of the Igbo World Among Igbo Students in a Public University in Nigeria" (*Cultural Analysis 14* 23-47) Chinyere Ukpokolo recalls the Igbo ethnic-based students' associations re-enacting the Igbo world through the employment of cultural symbols and ceremonials for the construction of an Igbo cultural identity within the university space in Nigeria. Her study focuses on the translocation of the local culture to the territoriality of Roseville University, located in southwest Nigeria. For the construction of a distinctive cultural identity in a heterogeneous community like the university cultural forms and ceremonials were employed to re-enact *uwa Ndi-Igbo* (the Igbo world) and to confer the *Igwe* (the traditional leader). Wearing traditional Igbo attire, the use of the Igbo language and the annual Igbo Cultural Week on the University campus are suggestive of the implications on the sustenance of Igbo cultural identity in a globalizing world (Ukpokolo 24).

The word 'Igbo' has multilayered significance. According to Uchendu, it is used in three senses: The Igbo homeland/territory: the native speakers of the language, and as a language group. The fear of threats to the Igbo language and culture is anxiety shared by various scholars and academicians of Igbo cultural studies. A look at reports emanating from both theoretically and empirically based research, and international organizations such as UNESCO, suggests that Igbo language and culture is at risk of going into extinction in the near future if nothing is done to check the current trend (Ejiofor). As E. Tylor asserts, "culture is that complex whole which includes knowledge, belief, arts, morals, customs, laws and other capabilities which are learned, shared by men as members of society and transmitted from one generation to another" (Tylor). Hence any laxity negligence and hostility exhibited by the custodians of culture would result in rapid erosion and disappearance of the uniqueness of the people and their culture. In the case of Igbo culture, which has already suffered grave damage at the hands of white masters and missionaries, the preservation of its riches and potentialities is at stake with the basic transformative nature of culture in general and the multifaceted influence on the material and non-material aspects of culture in the globalizing world.

The Igbo language is a unifying factor of the Igbo culture and has proved an efficient and useful tool for the dissemination of the Igbo culture from generation to generation. Ukpokolo observes that even though the practice of speaking the Igbo language was promoted by the Igbo students' ethnic organizations in the university, one thing that remained challenging was the inability of the students to consistently communicate in the Igbo language (Ukpokolo 40).

Achebe in *Things Fall Apart* portrays speech as highly stylized in Igbo culture, with specific rules on how to addresses a neighbour, superior, ancestral spirits, and the gods. While the dialogue is usually direct in its meaning, speakers often adorn conversations with proverbs or references to folktales, which play a profound role in shaping Igbo beliefs. The white man's arrival into the Igbo land

and the quick abandonment of the Igbo language for English led to the eradication of the Igbo speech traditions. Fanon states in *Black Skin White Masks,* "a man who has a language consequently possesses the world expressed and implied by that language" (Fanon 18). In the comedy web series 'Mark Angel Comedy' the characters, representatives of the contemporary world seldom use the Igbo language. Both adults and children including Mark Angel, his niece, Emmanuella, cousin Success and other characters of the neighbourhood Denilson Igwe, K. Brown etc use English in their day to day life. In all walks of life from the marketplace to the church, in schools and in domestic affairs English is used for communication though with a Nigerian accent. The use of Igbo words in their speech is a rare occurrence; used only to express surprise or as a spontaneous reaction when startles or for cursing people.

In Episode 73, Emmanuella and her friends engage in a pleasurable play to test their intellectual knowledge and family hierarchy and Mr Nelson who is reading a newspaper sitting near finds it a disturbance and warns them to keep quiet. Despite his warnings, they continue their noisy game which infuriates Mr Nelson and use the Igbo language to curse them ("Cho Cho Cho" 1:15). In "Holiday Lesson", Episode 293, the teacher occasionally uses Igbo tongue when some casual remarks are made with the character Success ("Holiday Lesson" 1:12). English is the primary language used as the medium of instruction in schools that conditions the children of the present generation to use the English language in their daily life. The clash between two generations regarding the proper use of the English language is seen in a number of episodes which are titled "Speak English" that appears in four parts. The plots are constructed with a coating of humour and are about the children Emmanuella and Success critiquing the adults' wrong usage of English. They say, "If you don't know how to speak English, leave it" ("Speak English" 1:23).

English language which was used by the colonial masters as the tool for dominating the African culture has now become a major cause for the extinction of a language and culture. According to McLeod, "language is more than simply a means of communication; it constitutes our world view by cutting up and ordering reality into meaningful units" (McLeod 21). He argues that for attaining freedom from colonialism people from all sides need to refuse the use of dominant languages of power that have divided them into master and slave, the ruler and the ruled. Ekwuru rightly notes that "the use of a foreign language affected a paradigm shift in the mental perception and conceptualization of the Igbo cultural reality" (Ekwuru 53).

The Igbo religion consists of three major categories of belief: the worship of the great public deities, the cult of personal gods, and the worship of the ancestors. Achebe, at various points throughout the novel, presents the concepts of the Supreme God – *Chukwu*, the Personal God – *Chi*, and the spirits of ancestors, *egwugwu*, which shape the world-view, moral code and ethics of the characters in *Things Fall Apart*. The whites, when brought in Christianity to the Igbo land, were not offering salvation, instead, it was the breaking down of their culture. The advent of Christianity brought most of the Gods and their worship to an end.

Achebe presents the white missionaries as aliens to the Igbo because their origins are not known. The missionaries who believed themselves to be the long-awaited answer for the problems of Igbo, the so-called primitives who are to be civilized, were in fact cunning in wanting to take control of Igbo land and the land resources by coming to Umuofia under the false pretence of their true intentions which was to rule over the Igbo. The first converts, who agitated against the evil practices in the Igbo system such as child sacrifice, abandoning of newborn twins and mutilation of dead infants (Achebe xxxvi) became passionate followers of Christianity because in "God's eyes they are equals to everyone else" (Rhoads 69). One of the fundamental conflicts explored by Achebe in *Things Fall Apart* is that of tradition versus change. Many people not previously held in high esteem by the Igbo gain prestige by converting to Christianity.

In the contemporary Igbo states, most of the people, almost ninety percent of them follow the protestant faith. Ukpokolo observes that most of the members of the ethnic student's associations in the Roseville University are Christians yet they conduct masquerade performances as an invocation to the Gods of traditional Igbo belief through which they cherish their ancestral roots, a practice which remains within the parameters of a mere performance (Ukpokolo 32).

The characters that appear in the episodes of 'Mark Angel Comedy' belong to protestant Christians and Jehovah's Witnesses. Most of them bear Christian or English names except for a few characters like Chukwuemeka, Nwanyiocha Denilson Igwe and Success Madubuike. One can study the social, religious, historical and political issues in the Igbo society through Igbo names, which must be understood within the context of the Igbo worldview and the symbolic functioning of such names (Ukpokolo 20). "In *Morning Yet on Creation Day,* Chinua Achebe has extended this significance to the names a man gives to his children and advised: "If you want to know how life has treated an Igbo man, a good place to go is the names his children bear" (Ukpokolo 23).

In 'Mark Angel Comedy' the characters' world views, communal bonds, morals and values are governed by the principles of Christianity. The traditional Igbo language often adorned with proverbs or references to folktales, which play a profound role in shaping Igbo beliefs, has now been replaced by the language of the missionaries which is condensed with biblical references and instances. The concept of being 'born-again', the role of the 'pastor' in one's life, giving away the 'tithe' etc are cherished profoundly in some episodes. In the episode titled "Born Again", Mark angel is planning to question a person who had insulted his girlfriend. Despite Denilson's warnings he reaches his doorsteps and calls him out. But on realising the fact that the person is an army officer Mark Angel resorts to preaching the gospel saying that he is a born again Christian, who reads Bible always and so he wants to hug the army officer. ("Born Again" 2:28). In the "Who is Your Pastor" series we find the pastor influencing the personal life of people. The people in the church congregation find refuge from the stress and problems in life by consulting their pastor. In another episode, Denilson is seen proclaiming the gospel in the streets and speaking in tongues calling out to the youth to follow Jesus to attain salvation ("Who is Your Pastor Part 3" 0:12)

In the comedy series, however, there are instances where the follies of the church, the materialistic way of life led by the church leaders, speaking in tongues are criticised though wrapped by humour. K. Brown, the pastor is asking Emmanuella the amount she gave as offering and wonders why the people of that church are reluctant in giving offerings and later preaches about the importance of tithe. He makes some of his allegiance to pronounce false testimonies to persuade the members of the church to give away big amounts as offerings and tithe. ("The Assistant Pastor Part 4" 2:20-8:50). In another episode, Denilson is pleased to receive a big sum from a rich man as tithe and makes a tremendous prayer for him ignoring those who brought smaller amounts as tithe ("God Bless You" 1:18).

Achebe, in *Things Fall Apart*, deals with the clash of cultures and the violent transitions in life and values brought about by the onset of British colonialism in Nigeria at the end of the nineteenth century. The sanctity of old traditions and rituals which were the agencies of cultural integrity which include the cultural practices such as age-grade system, *Umunna* (patrilineage) grouping, masquerade institution, kola nut rituals, the vigour of Igbo music and dance movements, Igbo cuisines, traditional attire art designs such as *Uli*(body painting) and pottery designs have been destroyed by the new policies of consumerism and the change in food habits.

Through the activities of the Igbo students associations at Roseville University, the Igbo culture is translocalised and the (re)creation of the Igbo cultural identity is done through the (re)production of the Igbo world in diverse ways. In recent years the conferment of the *Igwe*, the "traditional leader" has become one of the ways of translocalising the cultural patterns of Igbo and a way of defining their cultural peculiarity. Igbo Cultural Day is marked with various competitions related to Igbo cultural practices. However, despite the efforts taken for the recreation of Igbo ethnic identity, not just for the sake of cultural nostalgia but also for self-preservation and prevention of homogenisation, for the 'cultural outsiders,' it appeals as a mere 'performance' and they are pleased to look at the *Igwe* for the Igbo attire, whom they would like to take a snap with (Upkopolo 37).

Globalisation is designed to advance the culture of stronger nations at the expense of weaker ones. Cultural globalisation involves the constellation and interconnectedness of different values, norms and knowledge of different peoples. In this interaction dominant culture dislodges recessive culture. In the globalising world, African lifestyles and attitudes have drastically changed. Western foods such as MacDonald's, Coca-Cola, Starbucks, and Dominos have replaced the core Igbo delicacies. An increase in appetite for Arabian and Asian food has replaced Ogiri, Uziza, Utazi Abacha etc from the Igbo cuisines. The unfolding dynamics of the consumer culture influence the lifestyles of the Igbo people through the establishment of chain supermarkets, the influx of cosmetics companies and the use of international consumables which accentuate the novel modes of behaviour and a new identity. Even the notions of beauty standards are reshaped by the western perspective, the portrayal of which can be witnessed in the 'Mark Angel Comedy' episodes, "Slim People", "Nice Legs", and "Again" etc.

Every culture has a dual tendency, a tendency towards stability and a tendency towards change. Before the arrival of the white man, the Nigerian Igbo culture had its own unique ways of balancing the harmony of it people's life with its systems of law and justice, religion, tradition and rituals. The effects of western tradition on African culture instilled a social, religious and military mentality into indigenous peoples and different ethnic behaviours changed in accordance with colonial agendas. Anuradha Ghosh opines, as cited in Mala Pandurang edited *Chinua Achebe: An Anthology of Recent*

Criticism, that the ambivalent modernity that the post-colonial nations experience makes the exercise of cultural re-writings of histories an exploration into the myriad complexities that enmesh societies trying to live on their own terms.

The cultural identity of a people is closely related to the pace with which they accept or reject the demands of modern industrial or commercial operations. The rise of global empires under the aegis of one or the other imperial power makes the question of cultural sovereignty a near impossibility. Hence the question of identity, whether it is the individual's identity or the community's identity, becomes more problematic. The shifts and changes that occurred to the Igbo society from the time of *Things Fall Apart* to the present make us realize and convince us that 'identity is a construct; it changes over time and space.

Works Cited

"Again." *YouTube*, Uploaded by MarkAngelComedy, 15 July 2016, https://youtu.be/SPBuhk7hPGg

"Born Again." *YouTube*, Uploaded by MarkAngelComedy, 25 September 2015, https://youtu.be/8xRFZEc1-DY

"Cho Cho Cho." *YouTube*, Uploaded by MarkAngelComedy, 3 June 2016, https://youtu.be/35oRa33UlYY

"God Bless You." *YouTube*, Uploaded by MarkAngelComedy, 27 November 2015, https://youtu.be/l-VDp_uBKbM

"Holiday Lesson." *YouTube*, Uploaded by MarkAngelComedy, 1 January 2021, https://youtu.be/YSfiwxQOyvA

"Nice Legs." *YouTube*, Uploaded by MarkAngelComedy, 7 December 2018, https://youtu.be/0y5Uic0-7qo

"Slim People." *YouTube*, Uploaded by MarkAngelComedy, 21 December 2018, https://youtu.be/agvYwToO0_4

"Speak English." *YouTube*, Uploaded by MarkAngelComedy, 5 October 2018, https://youtu.be/-hX89noO_2U

"The Assistant Pastor Part 4." *YouTube*, Uploaded by MarkAngelComedy, 13 August 2021, https://youtu.be/-J6PRyvUX-0

"Who is Your Pastor Part 3." *YouTube*, Uploaded by MarkAngelComedy, 8 June 2018, https://youtu.be/b0Q0thPEnwM

Achebe, Chinua. *Things Fall Apart*. New York: Fawcett Crest, 1959.

Afigbo, A.E.. 'Prolegomena to the study of the cultural history of the Igbo-Speaking Peoples of Nigeria', *Igbo Language and Culture*, Oxford University Press, 1975.

Akers Rhoads, Diana. "Culture in Chinua Achebe's Things Fall Apart." *African Studies Review* 36/2: 61-22.

Alimi, A. S. "AStudy of the Use of Proverbs as a Literary Device in Achebe's Things Fall Apart and Arrow of God." *International Journal of Academic Research in Business and Social Sciences* 2/3: 121-127.

Bhabha, H.K. The Location of Culture. New York: Routledge, 1994.

Coleman, J. Nigeria: Background to Nationalism. London: Longman, 1959.

Ejiofo, Peta. "Oche Ndi Igbo Bunyere Asusu Igbo." Lecture Delivered at a Meeting of Anambra State Association (ASA-USA), Dallas, Texas, October 14, 2011.

Ekwuru, Emeka George. *The Pangs of an African Culture in Travail: Uwa Ndi Igbo Yaghara Ayagha (The Igbo world in Disarray)*. Abuja: Totan Publishers, 1999.

Fanon, Frantz. *Black Skin, White Masks*. New York: Grove Press, 1952.

Harnett-Sievers, Axel. *Constructions of Belonging: Igbo Communities and the Nigerian State in the Twentieth Century*. NED - New edition ed., Boydell & Brewer, 2006. *JSTOR*, www.jstor.org/stable/10.7722/j.ctt1bh2m5f. Accessed 12 Oct. 2021.

Innes, C. L. and Bernth Lindfors eds. *Critical Perspectives on Chinua Achebe*. Washington, DC: Three Continents Press, 1978.

Lindfors, Bernth ed. *Approaches to Teaching Achebe's Things Fall Apart*. New York: MLA, 1991.

McLeod, John. *Beginning Postcolonialism*. Manchester, U.K: Manchester University Press, 2000.

Pandurang, Mala. Ed. *Chinua Achebe: An Anthology of Recent Criticism*. Delhi: Pencraft International, 2006.

Rhoads, Diana Akers. "Culture in Chinua Achebe's Things Fall Apart." *African Studies Review*, vol. 36, no. 2, 1993, pp. 61–72. *JSTOR*, www.jstor.org/stable/524733. Accessed 12 Oct. 2021.

Tylor, E. *Culture*. New York: Signet, 1871.

Uchendu, V.C. *The Igbo of Southeastern Nigeria*. London: Holt Rinehart and Winston, 1965.

Ukpokolo, Chinyere. "Self-Representation and the Construction of the Igbo World among Igbo Students in a Public University of Nigeria." *Cultural Analysis* 14:23-47.

CHAPTER XIV

FROM DESIRES TO THE BECOMING: ANALYSING SEXUAL PREJUDICE AND HYPOCRISY IN JEANETTE WINTERSON'S ORANGES ARE NOT THE ONLY FRUIT

Sneha K.

Assistant Professor, PG Department of English
Yuvakshetra Institute of Management Studies
Mundur, Palakkad, Kerala.

ABSTRACT

The bildungsroman novel Oranges are Not the Only Fruit by Jeanette Winterson discusses the growth of the protagonist Jeanette. As she grows up she realises the desires of her body, which according to society is unnatural. Along with depicting the girl's perseverance in continuing her life the way she likes, the writer brings forth the hypocritical society which bounds her. The article focuses on the protagonist's realisation of her inner self and the acceptance she later achieves. The treatment of the heterosexual society towards lesbians is also evident from the different instances in the novel.

Keywords: Lesbian, sexual community, the quest for the self, oppression, hypocrisy, power structures, dictates of the society, hegemony.

• • •

From Desires to The Becoming: Analysing Sexual Prejudice and Hypocrisy in Jeanette Winterson's *Oranges are Not the Only Fruit*

Lesbianism, as we know is defined as the sexual relationship between women. While defining it in this way we forget to point out the fact that lesbians are women who struggle to realise their inner self and live accordingly. But at the same time, they face social ostracism in the course of asserting their sexuality. Gayle. S. Rubin in her seminal essay Thinking Sex: Notes for a Radical Theory of the Politics of Sexuality discusses her ideas about the formation of sexual communities. She mentions that various sexual groups are in various states of community formation and identity acquisition. "The realm of sexuality also has its own internal politics, inequities, and modes of oppression". She also put forwards the notion of the erotic pyramid which is a visual representation of the hierarchy of sexual value. It presupposes that society undertakes a process of mapping to identify and categorise all available sex practises within the diverse sexual cultures. The heterosexual communities occupied the highest positions in the pyramid, whereas the bottom of the pyramid was occupied by the sexual casts which were despised by the society. It included lesbian and gay couples, transsexuals, sex workers etc. These individuals are perceived to be mentally ill, of less repute, criminal instincts, lack of institutional support and economic sanctions.

Oranges are Not the Only Fruit by Jeanette Winterson is a semi-autobiographical, post-Modern lesbian bildungsroman novel that intermingles fairy tales, Biblical allegories, dream fantasies etc. The novel revolves around the transformation of the protagonist Jeanette, from the so-called binary of normal, natural, heterosexual surroundings to lesbian identity. The novel also depicts the reactions of society towards the changes that happen to a girl as she grows up. It deals with Winterson's experience while she grows up. The writer denies calling the novel a lesbian since almost all the readers can relate to the incidents in the novel.

When it was published in 1985, Jeanette Winterson's first novel was unanimously regarded as a realistic and heavily autobiographical comedy of coming out, in which structural elements derived from the bildungsroman tradition expressed in the heroine's quest for individualization, as much as a feminist gesture of self-assertion, deployed in a hostile Pentecostal

Evangelist environment. (The Guardian)

The novel is divided into eight chapters, all with titles taken from the Bible. There is a connection between the actions that take place in the life of Jeanette and the story of the Bible. Sometimes the incidents in Jeanette's life resemble the actions in the Bible whereas, sometimes there is a deviation of her thought and actions from the Bible. In the first chapter of the novel titled "Genesis", Jeanette talks about her family and their Sunday routine. Jeanette is the adopted daughter of her parents. Her mother, a hypocritical woman wanted a baby without having sexual intercourse. But Jeanette never felt that she is not 'special' to her parents. Though this chapter deals with the childhood of Jeanette, it foreshadows the events that take place in the latter part of the novel. One day when Jeanette and her mother went outside, a gipsy woman by studying her hand told that she will never marry.

The Mother is a person who always categorises things into good and evil. She never sees things from a mixed or an open point of view. She takes Jeanette away from the gipsy woman. This shows the mother's attitude of fleeing away from the situations that challenge her belief. In another instance, when one of the two women who run the paper store offers Jeanette a 'banana bar' and invites her to the beach, the mother never lets her go. Also, she doesn't even allow Jeanette to inform them about it. Later Jeanette hears her mother talking to Mrs White that "they dealt in unnatural passions" (Winterson 20). But as she grows up, Jeanette learns that 'there is a demon in each of us and it is that demon makes us different from others. This conflict in ideas between the mother and the daughter is later reflected in the act of expelling Jeanette from the house when the mother comes to know about her lesbian relationships. Jeanette exists in the grey space, which, according to her mother's ignorance and belief does not exist at all. Like the Christ, for the mother, Jeanette wants to change the world. She changes the world, but not the way which is expected and followed by the accepted moral, social and religious norms.

Being a lesbian, Jeanette feels that she is a stranger in her own land which is bounded by heterosexual territory. While living in a society that is controlled and ruled by heterosexual, patriarchal representatives, one must look inward to understand and identify the desires of the body. The opening of the second chapter 'Exodus' shows that Jeanette may not always keep with her mother's ideas. The ideological separation of Jeanette from her mother is evident from Jeanette's first day of school. It is Elsie Norris, who always forcefully begs Jeanette to listen to her internal self as well as see the external world. It is through Elsie, Jeanette learns about a world beyond the Bible. ...Knew the importance of numbers and the great effect of the imagination of the world. What looks like one thing may well be another. If you think about something for long enough more than likely, that thing will happen. It is all in the mind (Winterson20).

This contradicts Jeanette with her mother's saying that "if you prayed for something long enough it happened" (Winterson 21). Her mother always wanted to make her a servant of God. The hypocritical nature of the mother and the church authorities is apparent from many situations of the novel. The mother, who is more devoted to the church fails to take care of Jeanette while she is admitted to the hospital. Similarly, while realising the homosexual relationship of Jeanette, she rejects her in the future also. The safety and sanctity Jeanette felt in the first chapter begins to change as new emotions become unveiled. The mother actually enjoys singing hymns to irritate the next-door neighbours. She finds pleasure in hearing the fight of the next-door neighbours by keeping the wine glass on the wall along with Mrs White. When the church authorities come to know about the unnatural passions of Jeanette, they ask the mother to lock her in a room for thirty-six hours without providing her with food.

Though Jeanette confesses about her 'sin' due to her hunger, she continues to live in her own desired world even after. It is later that she realises Miss Jewsbury is also a lesbian who is torn between the two contradictory worlds; the world of lesbians and the religious world. But Jeanette doesn't like her because of her lack of courage to reveal her true identity to the external world. Miss Jewsbury is like the Humpty Dumpty in the nursery rhyme. She lives on the border, managing both her desires and also religion. This again is an example of the hypocrisy of society. One can lead life the way in which one wants without openly confessing the identity, without revealing the internal desires and passions. The problem arises when a person tries to be open before the external world. She always uses stories to explain or understand her own existence.

In the novel, the notion of romance has been slowly brewing. Using the stream of consciousness technique, the writer shows the growth of Jeanette and her deviation from the normalised heterosexual society to lesbian. She fights many battles in the novel. But she triumphs in the end because she understands and accepts her own homosexuality. Her persecution broadly testifies to the prejudicial treatment that homosexuals frequently suffer in society. She frequently sees dreams and tries to interpret them the way she wants. The walls in her dreams stand as a metaphor for the social forces that distort her. She has the intelligence and balance to set things right. Widespread and irrational prejudice against homosexuals is elaborated in the novel.

The pastor's belief that women are biologically inferior to men and his findings of Jeanette's deviation from the normal society that she behaves so because she has plenty of works and charges which a man can manage easily reveals the attitude of the patriarchal society towards women and their methods of implementing them. Everybody, including the mother, says that Jeanette has no love for God and that's why she runs behind these kinds of unnatural passions. But through the voice of Jeanette the writer questions the fact that why can't a homosexual believe in and love God. She is cast out from the church and even from home though she possesses a pure love for God. The writer repeatedly asserts and makes the readers realise the fact that we are born into adhering to a biological binary that is constructed by society. Whereas for the writer, there is not a clear biological role for men and women and gender is socially constructed. Jeanette never wanted the acceptance and protection of society because along with the acceptance comes the confinement also. She proves with her life that the power of creating self lies in each individual's hands. Her life can be compared to Perceval; both lose the comfort they had and undergoes a transformation in their quest. She, like Ruth, becomes the victim of the prejudices of society. But the victory in this quest leads her to attain the accepted life she wanted. She thinks that she is a prophet and is never going to follow the rules and laws of the priest but to write them.

In the chapter 'Numbers' we see that the mother rewrites the ending of Jane Eyre so that Jeanette will think that Jane will marry St John and not Rochester. Instead of narrating things as they are and later trying to convey the morals, the mother always alters situations that are favourable for her and in-lieu with her beliefs. She tries to mould Jeanette according to her conservative beliefs. All these realisations, though silly, makes Jeanette understand that the mother is only partially true with her. Though there is ample evidence of homosexual relations in many historical texts, our society is still reluctant to accept it as a natural human tendency. Many religious sects still consider such relations as blasphemy. Many nations around the world are still opposed to decriminalising such assertions of sexuality. Such relations are looked down on as taboo and evil. It is only during recent years that the various struggles and movements by LGBTQ and associated communities have gained momentum and worldwide attention. Only a few nations have legally sanctioned marriages between people hailing from these communities.

These people are revolutionary in their questioning of the blind adherence to the rules laid by the majoritarian sect of the society. The stigma surrounding the existence of such sexual communities is rooted in the religious taboo that was based on the formation and of kinship. They were despised for the inability to provide kin and offsprings for the continuation of birthing. At the end of the novel, the realisation dawns upon the mother in the novel that oranges are not the only fruit, symbolically signifying that there exists many OTHER.

Works Cited

Mullan, John. True Stories. The Guardian. 27 Oct 2007. Web

Rubin. S. Gayle. Thinking Sex: Notes for a Radical Theory of the Politics of Sexuality. Deviations Gayle Rubin Reader, Gayle S. Rubin, Duke University Press. 2011, 137-11.

Winterson, Jeanette. Oranges are not the Only Fruit. New York: Grove Press, 1985.

Bio-Note

Ms Sneha K., currently working as the Assistant Professor in the PG Department of English, Yuvakshetra Institute of Management Studies, Mundur, Palakkad, Kerala. Completed degree from Mercy College, Palakkad and PG from NSS College, Ottappalam.

.

CHAPTER XV

MAPPING POPULAR SCIENCE NARRATIVES: A READING OF V.S.RAMACHANDRAN'S THE TELL–TALE BRAIN

Urmila K.

Assistant Professor of English

University College, Thiruvananthapuram

ABSTRACT

Science communication attempts to popularize scientific knowledge, scientific temper, scientific methods of enquiry and scientific culture among the masses and tries to understand how science and society interact. Popular science writing is an emerging genre within science communication that provides an interpretation of science for a general audience. Obviously, the subject matter is complex and conceptually difficult, and the unreadability stems from its content, structure and use of language. Communication studies have identified the potentials of narrative structure in communicating science to a wider audience. The narrative format helps to easily structure, store and retrieve human knowledge. It plays a crucial role in knowledge construction because of its ability to supply the context necessary to interpret facts. This paper tries to explore popular science writings as a genre of nonfiction within science communication and through an analysis of V. S. Ramachandran's The Tell-Tale Brain attempts to introduce specific steps that successful science narratives follow.

Keywords: Science communication, popular science, nonfiction, narratives

• • •

Mapping Popular Science Narratives: A Reading of V. S. Ramachandran's *The Tell-Tale Brain*

Science communication is a significant area of research in Communication studies that aims to popularize scientific knowledge, scientific temper, scientific methods of enquiry and scientific culture among the masses. It includes various modes of communication such as television documentaries, books, science magazines, science articles, journals, coverage of science in newspapers and more recently science websites and blogs. Since its aim is to inform the public by way of popularising scientific findings and thereby filling in the gaps in public knowledge, it becomes imperative for these works to get into the readers. Unlike literary and creative writings, these works get limited readership partly due to the fact that the subject treated is not capable of giving them aesthetic pleasure, delight or wonder. This is one of the greatest challenges faced by popular science writers, science communicators and researchers working in this field. There is no simple alternative to this as the gap between literary and scientific writings cannot be so easily levelled. The only way out is by gaining more literary characteristics through the process of popularisation.

This paper is an attempt to identify popular science writings as a genre within science communication and to explore the features of such writings through an analysis of V. S. Ramachandran's The Tell-Tale Brain. It is a work of a neuroscientist that takes us on a journey into the human brain, through various case studies. The work becomes significant for this study primarily due to two reasons. The topic discussed in this book resists all sorts of simplification and hence to maintain an essential distance between popular science writing and academic science writing becomes a challenge to the author. The study also seeks to understand how the narrative structure of the text has been instrumental in creating 'a popular framework'. Theories on narratives from communication and media studies have been used to understand the feasibility of the narrative structure. A synthesis of the popular and the narrative framework has made the text more accessible to the readers.

Popular and Science are two contrary terms and when yoked together 'Popular Science' becomes more of an oxymoron. Attempts have been made to define this genre by communication theorists. "Popular science writing refers to all written forms of science popularization. Popular science texts are published in books and in a range of shorter genres, including newspaper and magazine articles and essays, and on online forums, such as scienceblogs.com. By 'science popularization' I mean science-related communication directed at no specialist audiences" (Sarah Perrault xiii). Peter Broks in his Understanding Popular Science cites Topham and Secord's categorisation of it as an 'unworkable analytical category'. The aim of the popular science discourse is the popularization of scientific information and its mass dissemination. It differs from other counterparts in its purpose, treatment of the subject matter, content, nature of the recipient and to whom they are addressed. Thus, the distinctive features of popular science discourse are educational, cognitive, entertaining, exploratory, illustrative, expressive and informative.

Popular Science helps us to make sense of the developments that are taking place in the field of science.

It links academic scientific literature as a professional medium of scientific research, and the realms of popular, political and cultural discourse. Obviously, its subject matter is complex and conceptually difficult, and the unreadability stems from its structure, use of jargon, scientific and technical vocabulary that makes the readers task much difficult. Every writer is blessed with the enormous resources of language and the choices we make create the style. There is no such thing as the correct way of expressing ideas, facts and opinions. Each writer selects a form and arrangement of words that he or she thinks will best express the sense and tone necessary to produce the desired response from readers.

Popular science narratives may range from personal narratives describing why one became a scientist; explanatory narratives dealing with a particular scientific concept; narratives of discovery;

to grand narratives which includes historical and evolutionary narratives on the origin of life and the cosmos. The first category may include a first person or third person narratives that speak of the various events in the life of the individual in question. Narratives of discovery tell stories of how a scientist or a group of scientists come up with new ideas, concepts, or have serendipitous findings. As third-person narratives, the narratives of discovery convey not only the experiences of making discoveries but also interject the authors' view and evaluation of the scientific discipline described and his/her attitudes and evaluations of the discovery. All these are predominantly narratives about people. However, in other forms of science communication, they are rarely presented as personal experience stories even though they do describe the attitudes and experiences of the scientists involved.

Communication studies have identified the potentials of narratives and hence science communication, philosophy of science, and popular science have been paying increased attention to narratives and their ability to transfer complex scientific concepts to lay audiences. They have traditionally been a popular format for cultural and knowledge transmission, entertainment and to create shared perspectives. "Narrative, have an inherent power to provide unification... to connect all narratives and the whole of reality in a cognitive sweep which makes a unified sense of the whole" (García Landa). The Tell-Tale Brain connects the various chapters through the authorial voice. A neurologist's presence is felt throughout the book and the readers become one with whom he shares his experience with the patients. In the chapter "Beauty and the Brain: The Emergence of Aesthetics" he becomes a scientist putting forth his rational arguments to validate his findings.

Scholars like Schank and Gjedde suggest that narrative is the preferred method for humans to acquire and process new information. "Narratives are often associated with the increased recall, ease of comprehension, and shorter reading times (Pilkington)". Human knowledge which is structured, stored and related in the form of narrative will be easier to retrieve and hence it is possible that narratives play such a crucial role in knowledge construction because of their ability to supply the context necessary to interpret facts. "A narrative includes interpreted information," and this eliminates the need to draw conclusions between the events presented. Turney surveys the kinds of narratives employed in popular science and suggests that they all serve one purpose--to explain or "translate" science into laymen's terms. (Gjedde, 1998).

This view of narrative usually predominates in discussions of popular science texts. One can read and understand Mirror neurons and Phantom Limbs as one's personal experience. V. S. Ramachandran relates with great ease how the scientist in him has arrived at the idea of Phantom limbs from experiences of amputated patients."Sophie Moirand argues that popularisation is not a linear process from scientist to public, but a circuit. It involves communicative as well as cognitive dimensions, and it is not written on a blank slate of public ignorance, but enters into an interdiscursive memory bank" (Myers). So is the case with The Tell-Tale Brain. It forms a circuit, between the scientists, the readers, the existing knowledge base of the readers, their interest in a subject like neuroscience, language ability and a number of other aspects. No information can be processed in isolation, and hence it put greater pressure on the readers. Any missing link in the circuit, any difficulty connecting to the other will impede the understanding of the text.

Even while enjoying the progress science has attained in terms of inventions and discoveries, it is not appealing to laymen. Reading is a leisure time activity for the majority of the readers. As these readers have access to many other forms of entertainment, it is a great challenge to catch their attention. This "hooking the reader," adopts various techniques such as using a quotation to begin a chapter, adopting a conversational tone, using descriptive details to make the readers feel they are in the action, relating personal events and anecdotes or sharing a common experience, ask intriguing questions and so on. Structural analysis of V.S.Ramachandran's The

Tell-Tale Brain would reveal the role of narrative structure in making a purely academic work one of the most sought after popular science texts.

The title of a book is the first linguistic element one notices. With a subtitle like "Unlocking the mystery of Human Nature" and a title like The Tell-Tale Brain, the author has achieved the twin purpose of inducing curiosity in the readers and at the same time hinting at the topic of discussion. All the chapters of this text bear such short and pithy titles. No mere Ape, The Power of Babble, Beauty and the Brain, Loud Colours and Hot Babes: Synaesthesia. Reader's curiosity is sustained through various questions the author asks:

How do we perceive the world? What is the so-called mind-body connection? What determines your sexual identity? What is consciousness? What goes wrong with autism? How can we account for all those mysterious faculties that are so quintessentially human, such as art, language, metaphor, creativity, self-awareness, and even religious sensibilities? Is man an ape or an angel? Are we merely chimps with a software upgrade? (2)

Once these questions are raised the author starts expanding on it. The use of interrogatives, hortatory sentences and a personalised manner of narration, helps the writer to involve the reader in the process of thinking and initiate discussions. Slang, idioms and colloquial lexicon also contribute to a personalised narrative method diminishing the elements of formality between the author and the reader. V. S. Ramachandran has used it naturally and effectively." It is difficult to talk about the brain without waxing lyrical" (3). Personal or topic-centred narratives can be very effective tools for communicating technical and dry data. The inherent persuasiveness of narratives offers science communicators a means of conveying information to resistant audiences. The Tell-Tale Brain, describes several neurological case studies that illustrate how people see, speak, conceive beauty and perceive themselves and their bodies in three-dimensional space. Its narrative structure seeks connections through cause and effect to provide meaning to facts. This work unearthed many of the findings of V. S. Ramachandran while working with people who have interesting or strange brain injuries and disabilities. The narrative structure employed here is that of relating the experience of many of his patients and through such stories he links the events into a cause-and-effect relationships making the conclusion of the narrative seem inevitable even though many possibilities could have happened.

Simplification of scientific facts without compromising with accuracy is very essential to this genre since the readers are not specialists in the area. But the intelligence of the reader needs to be respected. Popular science writings as a genre that distinguishes itself from its other counterparts like academic science writings and scientific prose, attempts to inform and convince scientific outsiders of the significance of data and conclusions and to celebrate the results. Some level of distortion and oversimplification happens in such writings even with politically neutral scientific topics. Scientific articles are defined by clarity, logical representation, specialised vocabulary and lack of emotional signification. The core of any science article is the use of scientific and technological terminologies or jargon, the defining purpose of which are aspirations for unambiguity, absence of emotional signification, and easy and precise expression of certain notions. Jargon is often attacked as being pompous and unnecessary, used deliberately to exclude laymen from understanding scientific discourse. In his article titled "Why Academic Writing Stinks", Steven Pinker claims that the result of unreadable academic writing filled with jargon and unnecessarily technical language "is a cognitive blind spot called the Curse of Knowledge: a difficulty in imagining what it is like for someone else not to know something that you know."

A text like The Tell-Tale Brain that deals with neuroscience cannot progress without the use of jargon. Terms relating to the different regions of the brain are used and are explained using diagrammatic representations. Thus, we hear of synapses, hippocampus, Wernicke's region, Brocca's region, occipital, temporal, parietal and frontal lobes of the cerebral cortex, phantom limbs and the list goes on but this becomes inevitable to convey the topic discussed. Success in communicating information is not solely a matter of choosing a suitable style. In judging the effectiveness of communication, it is necessary to take into account not only the language but also some other factors like readers familiarity with the subject, his attitude to the subject, to the writer and to the text, and the writers organisation of his content. The Tell-Tale Brain deals with cognitive neuroscience and there are concepts and ideas only a medical student can understand in its fullest sense. However, his findings were simplified and the most significant information is provided in a subjective manner. In his preface to The Tell-Tale Brain, V.S.Ramachandran himself makes it clear that this is one of the defining features of Popular Science Writing.

The Tell-Tale Brain is written in a conversational style for a general audience.... I hope this book proves instructive and inspiring to students of all levels and backgrounds, to colleagues in other disciplines, and to lay readers with no personal or professional stake in these topics. Thus, in writing this book I faced the standard challenge of popularization, which is to tread the fine line between simplification and accuracy. Oversimplification can draw ire from hard-nosed colleagues and, worse, can make readers feel like they are being talked down to. On the other hand, too much detail can be off-putting to non-specialists. The casual reader wants a thought-provoking guided tour of an unfamiliar subject- not a treatise, not a tome. I have done my best to strike the right balance. (Ramachandran xix)

While speaking about science communication, Alan Paige Lightman, an American Physicist and writer, declares that a real scientist isn't a real scientist if he can't explain his theory to a common barman in order for the latter to understand it. This is what popular science writing is meant to do- giving access to the essence of things not resorting to the high complexity of scientific texts.

To conclude, Science which has been a specialised field of knowledge and enquiry from which layman was excluded became accessible to the public with the emergence of popular science communication. It is a fact that the narrative structure of the popular science discourses has increased the public engagement in science-related topics, this, in turn, had an adverse impact upon the veracity of facts claimed in such texts. Attitudes towards the authority of scientific facts are shaped in part by the discourse in which it is encountered. Narrative discourse has a bad reputation in this regard and hence this genre is being interrogated for epistemological relevance of the contents being conveyed.

Works Cited

Broks, Peter. Understanding Popular Science. Open University Press, 2006.

García Landa, José Angel. The Story behind any Story: Evolution, Historicity and Narrative Mapping, January 2017. DOI:10.1515/9783110555158-026 accessed on 26-10-21.

Gjedde, L. "Narrative, Genre and Context in Popular Science". Paper presented at the seminar" Public Fact and Private Fiction? – Borderlines of Genre", University of Tampere, Department of Journalism and Mass Communication, Feb 5-6, 1999.

Gjedde, L. "Making Sense of Science: Experience as Cognition through the Use of Narrative in Popular Science". Paper presented at IAMCR, University of Glasgow. 1998.

Myers, Greg. "Discourse Studies of Scientific Popularization: Questioning the Boundaries"

Discourse Studies, Linguistics and Modern English Language Lancaster University,2003.

Perrault, Sarah Tinker. Communicating Popular Science from Deficit to Democracy. Palgrave Macmillan, 2013.

Pilkington, Olga A. "Structural complexity of popular science narratives of discovery as an indicator of reader-awareness: A labov-inspired approach." Linguistic and Philosophical Investigations, vol. 16, annual 2017, pp. 7+. Gale Academic OneFile, link.gale.com/apps/doc/A503274713/

AONE?u=anon~38d8870d&sid=googleScholar&xid=9bedb1a7. Accessed 24 Oct. 2021.

Ramachandran, V.S. The Tell-Tale Brain. Penguin Random House, 2011.

Russell, Nicholas. Communicating Science Professional, Popular, Literary. Cambridge University Press, 2010.

Secord, A. (1994). 'Science in the pub: Artisan botanists in early 19th century

Lancashire.' History of Science 32: 269-315.

• • •

CHAPTER XVI

INFRINGEMENT OF RUDIMENTARY RIGHTS: AN ANALYSIS OF KHALED HOSSEINI'S A THOUSAND SPLENDID SUNS

Anakha Saji

Department of English and Centre for Research

Sacred Heart College (Autonomous), Cochin

ABSTRACT

This paper is an attempt to portray the miserable situation that prevailed in Afghan society owing to the violation of human rights. Almost all the characters depicted in A Thousand Splendid Suns, experience tribulation in the enjoyment of radical rights. The women and children have silenced victims all throughout the plot of the story. The study analyzes those circumstances that breach the universal laws made to ensure security of human dignity, inflicting pain on the citizens. The lives of women characters, Nana, Mariam and Laila are viewed in the limelight of infringement of global women rights. The child characters Mariam, Laila and Aziza, with their innumerable traumatic experiences are analyzed in the wide perspective of child rights. Also, the concept of Crimes Against Humanity, as encountered by the Afghan inhabitants under the absolutism of Taliban are surveyed, pointing out the inhumanity to which the characters were subjected to. The children were deprived of education, health facilities, whereas the women were forbidden a public exposure. The lives of Aziza, Mariam and Laila gets excessively affected with the political turmoil in a principally religious and patriarchal society like Afghanistan. The existence of an individual in a politically unstable country results in a disheartened clouded in anguish with none of rights being fulfilled.

Keywords: violation, violence, discrimination, inequality, torture, perversive, subjugation, illiteracy, political turmoil.

• • •

Infringement Of Rudimentary Rights: An Analysis Of Khaled Hosseini's A Thousand Splendid Suns

"To deny people their human rights is to challenge their very humanity", once stated Nelson Mandela, capturing in his words the unavoidable necessity for the implementation of human rights. Despite many attempts made to smoothen the enforcement of laws and to ensure the fulfilment of individualistic rights all throughout the history of the human rights movement, nothing had much changed in countries like Afghanistan. According to the UN Assistance Mission in Afghanistan, the toll of civilian deaths in the year 2020 was forty-five per cent under the attack of Taliban forces. Of all the casualties, 44 per cent were men and women, the report suggests. With a sound population of the world experiencing the trauma of basic human right violation, with an existence often below human, it is right time to evoke the attention to the miseries of Afghan populace, assessing the Afghan-based story of the novel A Thousand Splendid Suns. Human rights are entitled to an individual for the sole reason that he/she exists as a human. Such rights are not granted by any state, rather inherent to each one, regardless of nationality, gender, religion, or any status.

The objective of this paper is to pinpoint those instances in Khaled Hosseini's A Thousand Splendid Suns where the author consciously portrays the violation of human rights. From the very beginning of the novel to the end, the reader finds that each of the characters faces a violation of basic human rights in one way or the other. Ranging from children to women the intensity of the issue varies. The major focus of the study will be on women rights, child rights and crimes against humanity. The novelist successfully imprints those images of torments his characters underwent due to the patriarchal set-up of the Afghan culture clubbed together with the tottering political leadership. The discussion on violation of human rights becomes inevitable during the current scenario when Taliban has shockingly captured control over Afghanistan leaving the population in despair with an uncertain future. The upliftment of Afghan women and children through education to resist the forces of oppression and the social norms is the need of the hour.

Literature through all the narratives in some way or the other discusses the very concept of human rights. The Afghan novelist Khaled Hosseini while depicting the story of Afghan community in his second novel, A Thousand Splendid Suns, published in 2007, unraveled the extend of human rights violation in Afghanistan, unimaginable for a modern reader. Even after a decade and more of its publication, the currently Taliban ruled Afghanistan undergoes a much similar situation that Hosseini wrote down in his work. The pages of the novel open a Pandora's box of human rights violation. Each and every character in the novel suffers some sort of indifference, as the novel develops. Looking at the lives of Mariam, Nana, Laila, Aziza and Tariq, they have endorsed various hardships from very childhood. Mariam as a child and a married woman was always silenced in her protests to grant her rights. The situation with Laila was not different. After the accidental loss of her family, she found all her rights being curtailed by the male counterpart Rasheed, who made an unexpected entry into her life. Aziza, daughter of Laila, as a young child faces deep-rooted discrimination from her father Rasheed. There are also circumstances in the novel when the Taliban rule changes the whole life of men and women, questioning their rights. The basic rights are not enjoyed by the citizens of the country owing to the political unrest.

The contemplation and discussion on the area of human rights is not just a movement of the present. The aftereffects of two world wars ignited the human rights movement. Dating back to the Magna Carta that came in 1215 and through writings of philosophers like John Locke, Jean Jacques Rousseau, Thomas Paine, Immanuel Kant the significant nature of basic human rights as an inevitable part of human existence got cemented. With the American Declaration of Independence in 1776, followed by the French Declaration in 1789, and later the Versailles Peace Treaty of 1919 a backdrop was provided for the birth United Nations. In 1939, when H.G. Wells the British author wrote to The Times suggesting the need for a serious discussion on war aims and appending a declaration of Rights, which was later included in his 1940 publication entitled The Rights of Man: Or What Are we fighting for?, the whole world turned its eyes to the matter with utmost care. The torment of two world wars and the horror inflicting holocaust made the countries determined to prevent any future catastrophe. As a revolutionary move, the UN General Assembly adopted the Universal Declaration of Human Rights in 1948. The very first Article of the 1948 Declaration proclaims "All human beings are born free and equal in dignity and rights" (Universal Declaration of Human Rights). The Universal Declaration has had a great influence in spreading the concern behind defending human rights and preventing violations to an extent.

When viewed in this perspective, the women in the novel lacks every sort of their rights, facing discrimination, torture and sexual assault. Under the convention of Elimination of All Forms of Discrimination Against Women which entered into force in 1981 states are obliged to modify the patterns in the society, eradicating all prejudices "based on the idea of the inferiority or the superiority of either of the sexes" (Clapham 50). In a predominantly patriarchal society like Afghanistan, the access of women to education and opportunities in the public sphere are negligible. The seizure of the nation by Taliban forces in August 2021 now repeats the patterns of human rights violations. Michelle Bachelet, the UN High Commissioner for Human Rights, in her report remarks about the subordination of womenfolk, their denial of movement and access to the educational system, manifests the gravity of such study.

Viewed from the principles of the 1981 treaty, the characters Nana, Mariam, Laila and Aziza, the four-generation of women never ever accomplished a dignity of their own. No women character enjoys a standard education, employment status and equality in marital life. The representative of the first generation of women, Nana, Mariam's mother was regarded as a "harami" by society. Being impregnated by wealthy Jalil at a young age, Nana was cornered and devastated psychologically by society. She was denied a right to lead a life of her own and lived under the mercy and scrutiny of Jalil.

Mariam, who adored her father, faced the perils of inequality when she was ignored by him and later when she was married off to Rasheed. The marital life turned out to be disastrous when Mariam faced six miscarriages. Rasheed was a man who believed in the principle that a man should control his wife. In the very beginning of their married life, Mariam is gifted a burqa by Rasheed with the statement "a woman's face is her husband's business only" (Hosseini 69). Having never worn a burqa in her lifetime Mariam is bewildered to wear it. "The loss of peripheral vision was unnerving" (Hosseini 71). The decision was already made that she was supposed to hide herself behind a burqa in public. While the male partner roams around with his face visible to society a woman was forced to conceal her identity. The fate of Laila was the same when she married Rasheed.

The character Rasheed could be regarded as a specimen of perversive Afghan masculinity. Mariam discovers the sex magazines flooded with nude images and realizes that her husband fantasies a sexual life. The copulation was never pleasured given to her and left a mental trauma that never disappeared. The continuous miscarriages earned her Rasheed's hatred. Also, Mariam suffered brutal and savage torture from her husband. She was beaten up with a leather belt, forced to eat pebbles, thrashed and dragged.

The Declaration on the Elimination of Violence Against Women was adopted in 1993 which defines the term "violence against women" as "any act of gender-based violence that results in... physical, sexual or psychological harm or suffering to women..." (Declaration on the Elimination of Violence Against Women). Mariam was forced to chew pebbles on the accusation that the food she cooked was distasteful, which gifted her with "fragments of two broken molars". There was no resistance on her part as years passed. She hardened herself to bear the "systematic business of beating". Hosseini depicts the effect of torture on Mariam, the fear that haunted her, in the words "she shivered with fright when he was like this... It was the fear of the goat, released in the tiger's cage..." (Hosseini 234)

The predicament of Laila too was to be a victim of domestic violence. Laila is dragged and locked up in a room for several days when Rasheed comes to know about her plan to escape from Kabul. Even after all the heavy blows and punches, when he unlocks the room, Rasheed kicks Laila in the flank making her urinate blood for days. On another occasion, when she protests against his decision to send Aziza to an orphanage she is slapped. But this time Laila retaliated with a punch only to receive savage like blows from her tyrant husband. She was "lifted off her feet and slammed against the wall" (Hosseini 293).

The tyrant in Rasheed becomes all the more violent when his shop catches fire and is financially ruined, and unleashes his frustration as tortures on the whole family. "After the fire, Rasheed was home almost every day. He slapped Aziza. He kicked Mariam. He threw things. He found fault with Laila..." (Hosseini 297). At yet another instance, when Rasheed comes to know about Tariq visiting Laila on a daily basis, his anger mounted as beats on her body with his belt. He chase her and wounded her like a beast hunting its prey as the novelist goes on to describe, "He caught her, threw her up against the wall, and struck her with the belt again, the buckle slamming against her chest, her shoulder, she raised arms, her fingers, drawing blood wherever it struck."(338)

When Mariam passively succumbs herself to all the tortures without questioning the harms done to her, Laila revolts. It was Laila who planned the escape. Laila eventually succeeds to escape Kabul, only because Mariam murdered Rasheed, and shouldered the crime letting her leave the place. The misfortune that awaited Mariam was harsh. The punishment Mariam endures is a public execution under the Taliban.

The next relevant violation of rights in the novel is that of child rights. The Convention on the Rights of the Child which came into effect in 1990 defines a child as "'every human being below the age of eighteen unless under the law applicable to the child, the majority is attained earlier" (Clapham 50). The convention establishes the necessity to protect children from abuses, exploitation, gender discrimination and trafficking. The child characters in A Thousand Splendid Suns undergoes a bitter childhood. The orthodox mentality of the society along with the unpolitical leadership under the Taliban made the situation worse. Mariam, a child when the novel begins, was never sent to school. She was home tutored by a Mulla Faizullah on religious matters. The child is denied its right to basic education. Mariam's illiteracy costs her life to be buried under the shackles of a tyrant husband in future. Mariam is described as the cause of her mother's disillusionment, ill luck and despair, small "harami" as society puts it.

Mariam as a child tastes the bitterness of being an illegitimate child when she is denied access to her father's household on her fifteenth birthday. Labelled as the child of a "harami", she is looked down on by the fatherly figure. There prevails discrimination between his legitimate children and this illegitimate female progeny. Though she waits a whole day and night in front of his mansion, Jalil was never turned up. This rejection from Jalil was heartbreaking for the child Mariam. Soon after the ill-fated death of her mother, Jalil marries this fifteen-year-old Mariam to Rasheed. No prior permission was sought from the girl. She was forced to leave Herat to a six hundred kilometres distant city of Kabul only because her father married her off to a man unknown to her. Though Mariam pleads she doesn't want the marriage Jalil is timid in his decision. The predicament of Mariam is worse for she has nobody to stand for her. The aspect and belief of the institution of marriage in their culture is evident in the following words, "What are you, fifteen? That's good, solid marrying age for a girl..." (Hosseini 47). The rights of Mariam as a child is dismally violated by the acts of people surrounding her. Uneducated, lacking any knowledge about what is happening in the world, the child is left to suffer sexual assaults, violence, marital rape and eventually turns out to be a murderer. Mariam's life would have taken a different turn if she was educated and listened to.

Laila, on the other hand, in her childhood faced insult from Khadim, a neighbourhood boy. On her way back home from school, she is showered with urine on her hair. Back home, Laila washed herself rubbing her face and neck until it reddened to let go of the smell. But the imprint the incident had on her mind was everlasting. Much like Mariam, Laila is also married to Rasheed out of no choice, in a disastrous situation, at the age of fourteen. Though years have passed when Laila marries, situations remain more or less the same. Unlike Mariam, she was educated but was never able to question Rasheed for he happened to be her rescuer.

The child Aziza is also a victim of a violation of rights, facing indelible discrimination from her father Rasheed. For Rasheed, the birth of Aziza was unacceptable, for he longed for a male child. The Afghan community celebrates the birth of a male child and neglects the female child. Rasheed never pampered or nurtured Aziza with fatherly love. Later when a boy child is born to Rasheed and Laila, Aziza faces discrimination in its effect. The boy child is taken out, pampered, gifted toys and nursed well. When Aziza tries to switch on the television Rasheed has brought home, she is curtailed to do so with the explanation "This is Zalmai's TV". The girl child grows out to be a burden that Rasheed ultimately sends her to an orphanage, whereas Zalmai is never abandoned. At another instance, when the family is out shopping, with Aziza having joined the orphanage, she picks up a toy, only to return it to the shopkeeper. Rasheed gives out the explanation that it is not affordable to purchase both Aziza'a and Zalmai's toys. The girl child is denied the right to buy a toy only because she is inferior and worthless in her father's perspective. The needs of a boy are of prior significance when compared to the needs of a girl. There is no trace of equality in raising children in a society that implicitly signals female genocide.

Finally, the category of Crimes Against Humanity, which was elaborately listed by the Rome Statute of International Criminal Court that came into force in 2002, and its relevance in Taliban ruled Afghanistan. Article 7 of the statute defines 'crimes against humanity as "acts when committed as part of a widespread or systematic attack directed against any civilian population with knowledge of the attack" (Rome Statute of International Criminal Court). The list includes murder, extermination, enslavement, deportation, torture, rape, enforced prostitution, forced disappearance etc. In Hosseini's novel, the political history of Afghanistan is told parallel to the main plot. The Mujahideen take over in 1992 changed Afghanistan's name into the Islamic State of Afghanistan. The communist era and freedom were now things of the past. "Women were ordered to cover, forbade their travel without a male relative and punished adultery with stoning." (Hosseini 253). The reason why Laila and Mariam were unable to escape Kabul was that they were not accompanied by a male relative. Everything turned out against their plan when the police arrested them.

The sudden shift of power to the Taliban in 1994 narrowed their life making it even harder. People were forced to follow commands without resistance. Separate rules were formulated for men and women. Men should pray five times a day, grow beards, wear Islamic clothes, writing, singing and dancing were forbidden. For women, jewellery, cosmetics, education, employment were things of the past, forced them to stay inside the home at all times. In Hosseini's description, the situation is depicted as "Men wielding pickaxes swarmed the dilapidated Kabul Museum... The university shut down and its students were sent home... books except the Koran were burned in heaps... men were being dragged from the streets, accused of skipping namaz... Musicians were beaten and imprisoned..." (Hosseini 274). Even Laila's attempts to visit her daughter in the orphanage are futile for she was hindered by the freedom of movement by the authority. Most times she was beaten, kicked and slapped by the Talibs and returned home bleeding, without visiting Aziza.

The situation of Aziza in the orphanage is equally pathetic. It is a dilapidated building, accommodating children mostly abandoned by the parents so that they will not be hungry. They are taught to read and write with curtains pulled so that they escape the inspection of the Taliban. Aziza while describing her life in the orphanage, tells Laila that the children put the books away and pretend to knit when the Taliban inspects the place. The children of Afghanistan faced onerous existence under the Taliban. They were never sent to school, but rather faced poverty, undernourishment and illiteracy for no reason.

Men and women were no longer treated in the same hospital. The Rabia Balki Hospital to which Laila is taken for delivery lacks essential facilities. There are not enough doctors and nurses to attend to the crowded patients. The female doctor who operates Laila during pregnancy explains the situation. "They won't give me what I need... I have no X-ray either, no suction, no oxygen, not even simple antibiotics. When the NGOs offer money Taliban turn them away." (Hosseini 283). The rule of the Taliban was an era of darkness for the Afghan generation. All the basic human rights were curtailed and everyone took refuge in neighbouring countries, uprooting themselves from native culture and fleeing for life. The human rights enshrined in all the major conventions were not followed in the country. Khaled Hosseini probably succeeds in representing the turbulence that prevailed in his home town through his novel.

For the development and prosperity of any country, the citizens should lead a life, without the inherent fear of death, without discrimination and subjugation. The trajectory of Afghan's future could be made peaceful and sustainable through revisiting the aspects of human rights. In A Thousand Splendid Suns, the writer unfolds to us a society where nobody enjoys rights especially women and children. Although numerous treaties have been signed, the violation of human rights prevails all throughout the world. Even seventy decades after the Universal Declaration of

Human Rights came out, the citizens in Afghanistan are not secured by all these rights. The situation seems vulgar when the Taliban had seized control over the territory, once again, to infringe the rights of people. The novel could thus be viewed as a realistic portrayal of violation of human rights, through the lives of major characters. Hosseini could have been writing to the whole world that the situation was worse in Afghanistan for years. Peace and stability will remain a remote reality in Afghanistan if the implementation of human rights is not restored in near future. The novel concludes with an optimistic time when everything settles for time being. But in the present-day situation, the billow of clouds of despot rule has once again pervaded the territory of Afghanistan making it a barren land where violation of human rights is a daily affair.

Works Cited

Akhtar, Samina, et. al. "A Legitimate End to Illegitimate Beginning: A Critical Analysis of Mariam's Character in A Thousand Splendid Suns". English Language and Literature Studies. Doi:10.5539/ells.v7n1p113. Accessed 20 Oct. 202

Clapham, Andrew. Human Rights: A Very Short Introduction. Oxford University Press, 2007.

"Declaration on the Elimination of Violence Against Women." www.ohchr.org/en/professionalinterest/pages/ violenceagainstwomen.aspx. Accessed 12 Oct 2021.

Hosseini, Khaled. A Thousand Splendid Suns. Bloomsbury, 2013.

"Rome Statute of International Criminal Court". www.icc-cpi.int/resourcelibrary/official-journal/rome-statute.aspx. Accessed on 19 Oct. 2021.

"Universal Declaration of Human Rights". www.un.org/en/ about-us/universal-declaration-of-human-rights. Accessed 10 Oct. 2021.

• • •

CHAPTER XVII

NATION AND CINEMA: TRACING PATHS OF INTERSECTIONS BETWEEN INDIAN CINEMA AND POSTCOLONIAL INDIA

Treesa Petreena

Ph. D. Research Scholar

St. Xavier's College for Women

ABSTRACT

Indian Cinema is shaped by various political ideologies and is indeed a reflection of Indian history. Likewise, the Indian nation has benefitted a great deal by using cinema as a tool to actualise a sense of unity among the decentralised and pleural masses. During the immediate post-independent era, the national leaders of the times condemned cinema as low, vulgar and corrupting, that cinema was not even considered in the hierarchy of needs, since it was a non-essential entity in a country where even basic necessities were not met. But on the contrary, amidst all setbacks, Indian Cinema proved itself to be an effective way to propagate the idea of a unified nation that was otherwise unattainable, and it also aided in chiselling a unique space and identity for celebrating Indianness, detaching it from the Euro-centric tendencies.

This paper looks at how Indian Cinema was structured at the time of the Post- Independent India, re-routing its initial glory to a state of adjustment and adaptation, and traces how much Indian cinema has to lose and gain throughout the process of making a new nation. In Parallel, it mentions how as a means of homogenisation, the Hindi language and Bollywood film industry became the face of India, even while Indian Cinema remains as a potpourri of different regional film industries with various cultures and tastes.

Keywords: Nationalism, Indian cinema, East-West dichotomy, acculturation, western homogenisation, tradition and modernism.

• • •

Nation and Cinema: Tracing Paths of Intersections Between Indian Cinema and Postcolonial India

Introduction to Indian Cinema:

Indian cinema is widely acclaimed and exhibited across the world in about ninety countries, and has gained much popularity especially in South Asia and Middle- East, so to produce thousands of films annually in various languages. As the world's largest producer of films, the Indian film industry was able to attract foreign investors and production houses such as the 20th Century Fox, Sony Pictures, and Warner Bros (Hafeez 61). The large increase in the screening of Indian films overseas and the gradual upsurge of Indian theatres globally is due to the spread of Indian diaspora around the world who regards Indian film as the best way to connect with their identity abroad. Indian Film Industry is considered to be the union of motion pictures made in various regional languages from the states of Andhra Pradesh, Assam, Karnataka, Kerala, Maharashtra, Orissa, Punjab, Tamil Nadu and West Bengal. "According to the census of India in 1991, out of 144 regional languages of India, films are produced in about 30 languages with each of the larger languages supporting its own film industry" (Hafeez 62). Even though Bollywood (the Hindi-language based film industry) is highly disregarded as the soul of the Indian cinema in its entirety, it nourishes Indian cinema together with the regional film industries of other twenty Indian languages "whose total output makes India the largest feature film-producing country in the world" (Ganti 3). Indian cinema is backed up with different cultures, histories and linguistic multiplicity of its regional film industries, where Bollywood becomes one of the central and prominent parts of it.

Features of an Indian Commercial Film:

A well-calculated mixture of melodrama, unrealistic fight sequences, spectacular songs and gaudy dance moves comprises the basic popular components of a typical Indian commercial movie, in which reality is largely under question. Even though it is criticised for its vulgarity and irrationality, or it is blamed for its pretentious nature, its influence on the larger percentage of Indian society is shockingly undeniable rather than any other literature or art form. It is unquestionably the common man's escape from his 'damned' reality. For a regular Indian movie-goer, the theatre is a phantasmagoria where he could indulge in his suppressed emotions. The spectator deliberately forgets about his mundane life predicaments during this limited time span which results in his spiritual purgation. It is one of the reasons why parallel films do not hit the theatres as commercial films do, for which the common mass is always under criticism for their underdeveloped culture and ignorance.

Commercial films which are far distanced from authentic reality is quite influential among the popular Indian mass where "the films use dialogues instead of speech, costumes rather than clothes, sets and exotic settings, and lavish song and dance routines" (Virdi 2). It fantasises a utopian imaginary world parallel to reality where it is possible to iron out the crevices for a satiating experience of the common man. Through the popular trope of 'family', it refracts the nation's contemporary issues and deals with them "using a constellation of myths, utopias, wishes, escapism, and fantasies" (Virdi 23). Also, it acts as a dominant cultural institution that could accommodate the multitude of socio-cultural hybrids that mushroomed after independence, as a result of the recurring presence of the contradiction between 'the east' and 'the west' within the popular imaginary. Thus, independent India was a war-face where multiple discourses merged and contradicted reifying a mythical unified national identity since there were traces of both tradition and modernity, and Indian cinema was one of the influential cultural tools that reinforced it.

Detachment from Western homogenisation through commercial movies:

Indian cinema is always seen as a way in which Indian-ness is celebrated, by ruling out the Euro-centric tendencies of the West as opposed to the pre-independence position. It also bears a key role in liberating Indian cinema from the shackles of Western homogenisation by de-centring Hollywood/western cinema and exploring non-western film cultures (Virdi ix). It was indeed a celebration of Indianness, show casing its own unique features, alien to that of its western counterpart. Even though "it is aesthetically and culturally distinct from Hollywood, [it is] prolific and ubiquitous in its production and circulation of narratives and images" (Ganti 2). It stands as an alternative socio-cultural statement to Hollywood movies and today Indian cinema marks its presence all over the world wherever Indian diaspora spreads.

Comparing the formula of Indian cinema with that of its Western counterpart is irrational. When Indian cinema is condemned for its unsophisticated and unrealistic themes, one forgets about the reason that tows it down. Unlike its western counterpart, post-independent India is trapped between modernism and tradition. In independent India, the cultural intelligentsia of the country was weak enough to bring about a synthesis between the East and the West to the understanding of the common mass. The only class which was benefitted as a result of the synthesised education (which was brought about by Tagore, Nehru, and Gandhi) was the educated upper-middle class when the majority being the uneducated mass " to whom the twentieth century and its products are only a necessary evil to be lamented" (Gupta 28).

Chidanada Das Gupta, an Indian film-maker and a film historian, has scripted in his article Indian Cinema Today that, "The failure to absorb the cinema into the Indian tradition is only a part of this larger failure" (28). With the rise of 'vulgar pseudo-western pattern' due to the non-existence of a stable and reliable system, there sprouted a need for an 'entertainment formula' which could accommodate the existing social condition. Indian film then evolved as a "reference for its cultural adjustment, no matter how low the level of that culture and adjustment may be. It thus supplies a kind of cultural leadership and reinforces some of the unifying tendencies in our social and economic changes" (Gupta 28). Thus due to its extensive and effective influence, Indian cinema evolved into a prototype for the mass to look up to and mimic a unified image. Especially Bollywood film industry gave the shattered and lost generation a direction of one sort and moral stability which impacted negatively as well as positively.

Nation and Cinema:

Post-independent India was desperately in need of a unified image of a nation that was otherwise scattered in every sense. There was an insurgence within the independent nation to develop a sense of nationalism instead of nurturing regional diversities. Even though the Hindi language was used only by less than half of the population, it was constantly glorified as the national language and as a result Hindi cinema became the face of Indian cinema. Also, unlike other film industries in India, Hindi cinema does not stand for any particular regional group and this too supported it to grab a national status. The essence of nationalism was very evidently conveyed in Hindi movies, especially during the 1950s and one of the ideal examples of such movies is Theen Batti Chaar Rastha directed by V. Shantharam in the year 1953. It depicts the fearful concerns about diverse regions as well as linguistic groups in India which poses a threat to the conceptualisation of national integration. The plot revolves around a joint family headed by a wealthy Punjabi businessman with his wife hailing from Uttar Pradesh and his five daughters-in-law (Marathi, Sindhi, Gujarati, Bengali and Tamil) who are very ardent about their regional identities. In the assertion of their distinct individualities, the family gets caught up in unending troubles which are eventually resolved by the protagonist Shyama, well versed in all regional languages, who comes in as a new servant to the family. The hegemony of the Hindi language is emphasised through Shyama who tries to mend the glitches of the family with a common language. Director V. Shantharam here supports the perception of

Nehru by conveying the idea of national unity through Hindi, which eventually opposes the idea of nurturing linguistic diversities. The film here indulges in a contemporary national discourse of the time by trying to provide a utopian solution about national integration.

The concept of nation itself is a problematic and unsettled myth since it is intangible, and "yet [there are] people [who] are willing to die, fight wars, or write fiction on its behalf. Human consciousness invents a nation where such a thing does not exist" (Virdi 27). Culture fortifies the concept of nationality, where literature and art glorify it and makes it a perpetual entity, which eventually impacts individual identities. In India, the ideology of nation is a constructed one, because it didn't exist before the 19th century. The unique position of India is that it draws together the cultural, regional, and linguistic diversities under one roof of 'nation'. Being a unified nation was the only solution to overcome the colonial rule, and cinema through its visual images as well as popularity has impacted the diverse groups in India, which otherwise do not share a common platform. Due to this powerful ideological insemination, people began to think of themselves as a nation (Virdi 30). People watch a Hindi movie with national fervour imagining and believing that the whole nation is watching with them. Apart from print media, cinema was one of the means by which a coherent national identity was achieved. The fictitious idea of nation suppresses the differences and creates a common identity that could be shared among people of diverse cultural backgrounds. Now in India, nationalism stands next to religion in terms of devotion it elicits in the followers.

Burdened with contradictions, the result was a hybrid structure that supports the spirit of nationalism with a dominant elite interest and bypasses the idea of regional differences even while claiming that it opposes acculturation. Thus India acquires a unique national self, since it is a "political, contingent, developing, unfixed framework, without a forced coincidence between nation and territory or chronology, ethnicity, community and religion" (Virdi xiv). At this point of complex workings of nation-building, the role of cinema takes a key role in instructing the disoriented mass and instilling a unified national zeal within the bewildered minds. Thus independence was a dividing line for Indian cinema and from there onwards it was a fascination about the new nation. The concept of family was a constant trope used by Indian cinema to sketch the impression of a national cohesion even though the message was teeming with the number of contradictions about gender, sexuality, class, religion and various other social institutions.

The Indian film industry was never an innocent or free entity. It was always tied to the interests of ruling political parties. "Cinema has been an object of government regulation in India since the colonial period through censorship, taxation, allocation of raw materials, and control over exhibition through the licensing of theatres" (Bose 31). In post-independent India, the ruling party INC (Indian National Congress) condemned the commercial film Industry, even though "...it was the second-largest 'industry' in India in terms of capital investment, the fifth largest in the number of people employed, and the second-largest film industry in the world" (Ganti 44). Because, leaders like Jawaharlal Nehru and Mahatma Gandhi understood film as corrupting as well as "a tool of modernisation [and also] viewed cinema as 'low' and 'vulgar' entertainment, popular with the uneducated masses..." (Ganti 46). While Gandhi condemned cinema, since it was an imported technology, Nehru was concerned about its quality. Nehru hoped for better cinemas that could aid educational purposes and have some substance with social relevance. This attitude tinted with morality and internationalism by the leaders of Independent India, has played a crucial role in the development of the Indian commercial film industry and it was reflected in the form of taxation and censorship.

In contrary to the hope invested in independent India by the filmmakers, cinema was not even considered in the hierarchy of needs, since it was a non-essential entity in a country where even basic necessities were not met. There was even a ban on theatre construction following "a moratorium on "non-essential building" due to the shortage of cement and building materials", which clearly shows the state's disdain towards the film industry (Ganti 25). It was normal for any government to have an aversion towards the entertainment sector because the nation was in such a fragile state where immediate intervention was needed about heightening the food crisis, unsettling refugee issues, and beaming illiteracy. In addition to that, a sudden hike in tax and strict censorship but the Indian film industry in great distress. More than half of the profit from a film was levied by the state in the form of several taxes, and also the stringent censorship rules disapproved most films claiming it to be corrupting the purity of Indian culture. However, the film industry reclaimed its position with the increased production of nationalist and patriotic movies which facilitated the conceptualisation of national unity or 'the Indianness' to a great extent.

Indian film industry took another blow right at the reign of Indira Gandhi as the cost of raw material for film production high-rocketed, since it was an imported product. It is during this time the most popular trope of 'family' was replaced by the figure of 'angry young man' portrayed by Amitabh Bachchan through the film Zanjeer (1973) and it became a huge success. Here, the concept of the 'hero' steps out into the streets from the comforts of family and fights for a common cause. This is to be read in the context of the national crises of the time, such as poverty and unemployment. The audiences' whim is satiated as the hero tries to resolve issues that daunt them in everyday life, even though in reality their plight is the same. The failure of the law to enact justice became the talk of the time and deceitful politicians became constant villains. Another recurring narrative of the 1980s was "the lost and found genre" (Ganti 33). The theme of partition was sketched through the portrayal of reunion stories of families, whose members got separated years ago. This separation is the symbol of the harrowing experience of thousands of families who were forced to relocate due to the India-Pakistan partition.

Even while in history, the 1990s were marked with constant deliberations between the leaders of INC and the Indian Film Industry, negotiations were going parallel by BJP (Bharatiya Janata Party) as a means to establish "Hindutva Agenda" (Bose 33). They identified cinema as an effective and easy way to propagate political ideologies into illiterate masses and understood that moving image is more effective than the written word which they used for various purposes (Bose 40). This incessant monitoring chained Indian Cinema to political interests and became an ideological tool that was successfully used to safeguard certain belief systems and traditions, which included important domains such as fierce nationalism, religiosity, patriarchal norms, biased gender expressions, stringent morality etc.

However, Bharathiya Janatha Party (BJP) also aided the film industry to evolve into its current position, even though there was a proliferation of portrayals of Hindu rituals, traditions and culture. From the 1990s onwards the state started to approve Indian cinema's contribution to the nation's economic development and considered it as a national asset. In 1980, National Film Development Corporation (NFDC) was established which financed and supported films with high artistic content. In May 1998, Indian cinema got its status as an industry that is to be nurtured and supported instead of perceiving it as a vice (Ganti 50). Since Indian cinema always indulges and reflects on themes of national importance by contributing generously to the economic development of the nation, it is now considered as national pride that ensures national integration and propagates Indianness in all forms.

Conclusion

Indian commercial cinema can be identified as a hybrid entity that was channelled from its initial purpose of mere art and entertainment to that of a non- innocent political tool, to initiate and promulgate a sense of nationalism upon the scattered Indian mass. Nationalism in India is therefore a creation of dominant elite discourse that operates power and was tactically forced upon the citizens through introducing a new common language for the nation, that is Hindi, which does not share ties with any particular individual Indian state. The Bollywood film industry which was affiliated with the Hindi language was in one way encouraging the acculturation process and thereby accommodating a sense of Indianness that facilitated cultural hegemony. The social psychologist Ashis Nandy, "a proponent of an "indigenous sensibility," views Hindi cinema's peculiar hybrid nature as a deliberate refusal of "authenticity" and "realism" of the kind expected by a western audience. He reads this as a symptom of protest and resilience against an alien culture of modernization" (Virdi 4). That is, in one way it was a deliberate act of pulling out Indian polity and culture from the traces of Western homogenisation.

It is also fascinating to know how the once condemned medium of cinema then became a powerful political apparatus, which played a critical role not only in actualising the goal of the unified nation but also in generating political ideologies with utmost care and subtlety. The emergence of commercial masala movies and its unique formula of hyper-realism eased the way in which the Indian mass could be directed as well as controlled. Various political ideologies based on gender, religion, morality and nationalism were smoothly disseminated throughout the nation with accelerated speed through the medium of commercial cinema, even though it was condemned as mere kitsch. The most common theme of family was one powerful trope that was simultaneously innocent and political in nature. Recurring projections of the concepts of class-caste hierarchy, power structure, gender roles, strict morality, rituals and tradition was easily amplified through the single 'masquerade' of family, which was undoubtedly a winning theme as well as a huge success among the popular imaginary. Therefore, nation and cinema in India are concepts that must be read together, since their intersections are indeed revelations about how the reification of nationalism and cultural hegemony was successfully materialised.

Works Cited

Bose, Nandana. "Between the Godfather and the Mafia: Situating Right-Wing Interventions in the Bombay Film Industry (1992–2002)". Studies in South Asian Film and Media, vol.1, no.1, 2009, pp. 23-43. Intellect Publishers, doi: 10.1386/safm.1.1.23/1.

Ganti, Tejaswini. Bollywood: A Guidebook to Popular Hindi Cinema. Routledge, 2004.

Gupta, Chidananda Das. "Indian Cinema Today". Film Quarterly, vol. 22, no. 4, Summer 1969, pp. 27-35. JSTOR, www.jstor.org/stable/1210307.

Hafeez, Erum."History and Evolution of Indian Film Industry". Research Gate, 2016, https://www.researchgate.net/publication/332751636_History_and_Evolution_of_Indian_Film_Industry

Virdi, J. The Cinematic ImagiNation: Indian Popular Films as Social History. Rutgers University Press, 2003.

• • •

CHAPTER XVIII

AN ANONYMOUS SIGNATURE: UNDERSTANDING GUESS WHO GRAFFITI

Lakshmipriya A. S.
CMS College, Kottayam

ABSTRACT

The paper intends to make an analysis of Guess Who graffiti, which emerged anonymously in the first edition of Kochi-Muziris Biennale in 2012, in and around the premises of Kochi. The paper focuses on how graffiti is viewed as a popular art form which is capable to dismantle the forces of domination that operates through the grounds of caste, class, gender and contemporary politics. Guess Who graffiti operates against the dominating forces, and urges to bring it to the foreground with an intention to respond, by establishing itself as a form of popular culture. Guess Who is an anonymous graffiti artist known under the pseudonym of 'Indian Banksy'. It is quite salient that the identity status of Guess Who in respective to gender, habitat, religion, profession, age, and whether an individual or a group of people belonging to the same or different gender seems unaware to anyone living anywhere. By responding to social reality, with the moniker tagged as Guess Who, the artist or artists come out actively from their hibernation during biennale session, even though the artist/s who behold the improper noun occasionally appear with the work at different places in Kerala, Karnataka, Tamil Nadu, Bihar and Delhi.

• • •

An Anonymous Signature: Understanding Guess Who Graffiti

"As long as there are advertising billboards, there will be graffiti, too. Even though there could be a difference in opinion about which is legal and which is not, there should be no contest as to which is more true" – Guess Who (Dutta). Cultural Studies emerged as an interdisciplinary field of studies from Birmingham Center for Contemporary Cultural Studies in the UK in 1968, by looking into the multiple ways in which the culture is created and maintained in a particular society. Tracing the various dimensions, and forging different definitions to Cultural Studies, the field often juxtaposes with the concept of popular culture since the beginning. The concept of dominance, hegemony and cultural construction overlap to design the term popular, as Raymond Williams defined it as "well-liked by many people" (Storey 5). One distinguishing feature of popular culture has thus always been its "strict contemporaneity" (Prasad 6). The object that is called as popular today will be replaced by another popular object tomorrow and may have passed into history with less significance. Popular culture usually emerges as a form of counter-response to the dominant ideologies in society. John Fiske in Understanding Popular Culture commented: "there can be no popular dominant culture, for popular culture is formed always in reaction to, and never as part of, the forces of domination" (35).

At the global level at the point of its origin, graffiti was synonymous with the idea of vandalism, where the graffiti artists intended to extinguish the pertaining subculture with their artistic revolution. However with a positive critical response to the graffiti has subverted the notion of vandalism and elevated it from the status of crime to an artistic work, with more value and public acclaim. Graffiti thus emerged as a radical form of art that speaks out social, political, and economic issues, even though the targeted subculture has unexpectedly proliferated over the other plain. It can be read as a "conscious mimesis" (Balkin 7) of a particular society, where the art pictures a particular event or epoch, either in a direct way or in a satirical manner, as a cultural response to society. Making the use of spaces effectively, the significance of the graffiti adheres to the time in which it has created. Instead of swallowing the scribbled art form entirely as a mere representation, graffiti allows a critic to sweep its constituent elements in the background, and thus enhances the possibility of making it a substance of political discourse, at the academic level.

Art forms have succeeded in reflecting every trace of transformations the society had gone through. Guess Who created graffiti at a time when society seems to be on verge of a transformation in political and ideological dimensions. Analyzing the graffiti from its time of beginning, Guess Who is noted for the unique mode of representation through wheatpaste posters, in conveying certain political messages either as consent or dissent. The essence of matter that Guesses Who chose to paint largely reflected the backdrop of socio-political, cultural and economical ideologies of the time. It successfully plays the role of vehicle or medium which acknowledges the shifts that happened in the contemporary social scenario, with its own unique style of representation. Graffiti as an art gained its significance in Kerala since the international exhibition and art festival, The Kochi-Muziris Biennale, and it is remarkable to note its radical outbreak into the popular form from the first time of its representation in 2012. The art community in Kerala opened its hands to receive graffiti as an art form that makes stark responses to contemporary social issues and attempted to popularize it all over the state. Critically examining the political and counter-cultural movements in Kerala extending from 2012, Guess Who made a satirical portrayal of society and called the people's attention for right responses as well. Guess Who graffiti succeeded in creating a new language of responses to the transformations that society encountered within a decade.

Guess Who graffiti has emerged as a response to the ideology of Biennale regarding the interpretation of art, where art became limited only to the interpretation of intellectual people. As Kochi Biennale Foundation states, "the Kochi-Muziris Biennale seeks to be a project in appreciation of, and education about, artistic expression and its relationship with society. It seeks to be a new space and a fresh voice that protects and projects the autonomy of the artist and her pursuit to constantly reinvent the world we live in" ("Kochi-Muziris"). Guess Who graffiti flummoxed the connoisseurs with the unique and eccentric Banksy style as a popular graffiti artist in Kerala. Guess Who opines that "our exposure to the various art practices is very limited. Even today most of the art that we see are meant to produce just decorative ornaments. A medium like graffiti can play a significant role in the cultural landscape and consciousness of a city" (Dutta).

The society of Kerala arranged an elite space for the exhibition of art particularly for the intellectual people with a notion that art should be interpreted with an intellect. Biennale became a space for the intellectual connoisseurs, whose interpretations brought art into the status of the elite, which seemed incomprehensible to the common people. As a counter-response to that ideology of Biennale, Guess Who's graffiti popped up on the walls of Biennale streets with a motif of art for people, which represents the current social issues with a simple sketch of the stencil. As in a form of satire, Guess Who mixed up the elite and non-elite elements of art so that to reduce the disparity between elite and non-elite, and to diffuse the binaries of high and low as well.

Guess Who's anonymity is a response to the notion of Biennale's invention of a new space which helps in the projection of autonomy of the artist, as well as the uplifting of art into an elite space by the intellectual connoisseurs. Guess Who aims to make art in the reach of every people, without making a dichotomy of high and low or creating a space of elite. This Guess Who emerged as a popular art form that challenges the concept of the elite in the Biennale and represents the contemporary socio-political issues of Kerala. The graffiti thus stands for the common people, which can be accessed by anyone irrespective of their taste of appreciation. The graffiti artist/s says that the purpose of graffiti is "about using public spaces and subversive tactics as potent means of speaking about social realities" (Wendling). And the artist/s emphasizes the need for a "culture of graffiti" in Kerala and the need "to depart from the hierarchies and definitions imposed by the traditional art institutions" (Wendling).

The dazzling element that constitutes Guess Who graffiti as a praxis of popular culture in the Indian scenario is its blending of cultural elements. The Western and Eastern cultural elements are mixed in a humorous and contemplative manner so as to produce a melange of cultural sketches such as Guess Who's graffiti of the musical trio, pop-cultural icon Marlyn Monroe with an Indian lamp, Colonel Sanders cooking up for 'Kochi Fried Chilla', Western vesture of Vikraman and Muthu from Malayalam comic strip Mayavi, evergreen Malayalam actor Prem Nazir posing like James Bond, Michael Jackson doing Kathakali, a Bharatanatyam dancer doing Moonwalk in Michael Jackson's attire, Mr Bean posing as a 'Karanavar' and so on. By juxtaposing the modern western icons with traditional Indian images, Guess Who graffiti thus transposes the Western and Eastern cultural setting in a series of satire. "Signed by 'Guess Who' these wheat paste posters of graffiti works are done with a conscious blending of the regional and the global images and in an unmistakable 'Banksy style'" (Johny).

The notion of 'Karanavar', Kathakali, Bharatanatyam, Classical music, and image of Indian Lamp belong to the higher class or the elite people in society as the common men were not allowed to take those roles during the traditional time. Similarly, the art galleries are welcoming only to the enthusiasts and the intellectual people, with a similar notion that art should be devoured with an aesthetic and intellectual sense. The stencil of Mr Bean sitting as a 'Karanavar' or the head of a patriarchal society is Guess Who's attempt to provide a critique of the prevailed patriarchal system in Kerala. As an artist who questions the autonomy of artists, or the need to look upon the art with the prejudiced identity of the artist, Guess Who opposes the notion of art galleries as an elite space, by drawing a parallel elitism of caste and gender through the unique portrayal of Mr Bean and other popular figures in Kerala context. Guess Who made a revolutionary attempt to break the elitism of space in art galleries by painting the notions of higher class, combining with the popular icons.

The artist made use of the public space to represent the elitism of space by drawing a parallel elitism of the upper class in traditional society, in a satirical manner, to show that the society is still working within the clutches of elitism, though not with a strong ostensible force as in early times. Even though the society changed its visage from the dominant forces of class and caste, the notion of elitism still operates through haphazard places like art galleries. Art galleries make no difference to the idea of Kalamandalam or Ezhuthupalli in Kerala, where only the enthusiasts with high aesthetic and intellectual sense marked their unique presence. As Biennale celebrates the cosmopolitanism of art, Guess Who made the detective James Bond and Michael Jackson's 'Moonwalk' available to the common people in the most understandable form, where art galleries still exist as a place of incomprehension to them. Guess Who replied to the blending of Eastern and Western popular culture and imagery as "it is easy for a visual connection if you use popular imagery. If it is not intended for an art enthusiast but a common man, it has to be easily identifiable. People in Fort Kochi may not connect immediately with the imagery of the Blue Man by Matisse but would with an image of Sakuntala" (Jordens).

Guess Who marks the transformation of thought and action in considering the role of women through the gender-bending graffiti. As per the 2010 Human Development Report of India, "work participation of women in Kerala is just twenty-eight percent, compared to forty-seven per cent for all India" (Devika). Guess Who Graffiti breaks the stereotypical representation of gender, where men and women are attributed with specifically concerned roles. The notion of womanhood and patriarchy are brought forefront through the gender-bending series, by reflecting an alternative choice of gender roles. Even though the twenty-first century Kerala society was on the verge of gender dynamism, Guess Who venturesomely attempted to foreground the notion by reflecting it in the local, public space.

Regarding the graffito of a woman clad in a saree spacesuit, Guess Who says, "on the day India successfully sent a spacecraft into orbit around Mars, a tweet with a picture of female scientists celebrating was an inspiration" (Wendling). Irrespective of caste or class Guess Who foresees the future of society is secured in women's hands by providing them with equal roles as of men in every sector. As to represent a typical Kerala or Indian woman who belongs to any session of society, Guess Who managed to look into the politics of dressing, where a woman wearing a saree is a common sight in society. Guess Who tried to convey the politics that, by creating gender dynamism in the society, women belonging to any session can empower and take themselves up. The notion of gender fluidity is conspicuous in the representation of traditionally macho-looking men carrying pots, and in the man who cleans utensils.

The role of the painter to paint huge buildings which were given only to men is subverted by the notion of the painter who paints on canvas or paper, a role or soft skill that the society attributed to women. Using the portrayal of Frida Kahlo, the world-famous Mexican painter and revolutionary artist renowned for self-portraits, wearing a traditional Indian costume of saree, Guess Who subverts and destroys men's traditional role of adventurously painting the roofs of gigantic buildings and transferring it to women with a revolutionary instinct. Similarly, the woman who skates, and who rides Harley Davidson in saree shows the idea of breaking the stereotype in gender roles and empowering them by giving opportunities to learn new skills irrespective of their class, age or profession, so that to escape from the patriarchal subjugation of society. The gender bending graffiti of Guess Who is a response to the changes happening in the thoughts and actions of society, where women began to emerge themselves out of the patriarchal system with the sheer free will, and potential to conquer the space itself. This Guess Who graffiti made use of the local space to portray the changing notions of society, which is in the starting point to grant women more opportunities and professional skills in the public sector, at the same time by bending the notion of domestic jobs to be equally provided to men, so as to neutralize gender roles.

Guess Who graffiti also gives a response to some contemporary social issues that happened in Kerala and India since 2014. By bringing the cartoon characters of Shikari Shambu and Appi Hippi as well as Dakini and Kuttoossan as Wonderwoman and Superman into the context of the Kiss of Love movement which was a response to the moral policing happening in and around Kerala, Guess Who questioned the authority's need to thwart the protest under the notion of illegality. As Kiss of Love emerged as a protest to the moral policing in 2014, through the portrayal of fictional characters Guess Who mocks the double stand policy of Government regarding the fact of illegality in an effective way. Guess Who questions the severity of the issue if the same is represented by fictional characters, and awaits to know the take of the Government in considering the matter as legal or illegal. Being considering them as cartoon characters taken from children's comic strips, Dakini and Kuttoossan or Shikari Shambu and Appi Hippi exerts no pressure on the Government's policy-making in disturbing the innocence of fictional characters in an illegal background. Guess Who retaliates against the dominant idea put forth by Government, by refuting it with the popular fictional characters in the society's context.

Guess Who uses graffiti as a weapon to raise a protest against the violence inflicted by the upper-class people against the minorities under the central Government's autocratic policy of 'gau bhakti in 2017. '#NotinMyName' graffiti announces Guess Who's support to the campaign that which formed in protest to the silence of Government over the cases of lynching and killing Muslims and Dalits as the beef-eaters, as Modi Government passed The Cow Protection Bill in 2017. Guess Who responded to the illegalities taking behind the Bill, where the cow wealth and its population matters more than human wealth and population. Working on different plains of social reality, Guess Who graffiti thus critiques the existing dominant ideologies, and by marking the changes it stands on the side of the subordinate so that to establish as popular culture.

Works Cited

Balkin, J. M. "What Is a Postmodern Constitutionalism?." Michigan Law Review, vol. 90, no. 7, June 1992, JSTOR, www.jstor.org/stable/1289739. Accessed 21 Oct. 2021.

Devika, J. "Women's Labour, Patriarchy and Feminism in Twenty-first Century Kerala: Reflections on the Glocal Present." Sage Journals, 16 May 2019, www.journals.sagepub.com/doi/full/ 10.1177/0972266119845940. Accessed 20 Oct. 2021.

Dutta, Anisha. "Guess Who's making the walls talk." Business Standard, 12 Dec. 2014, www.business-standard.com/article/ current-affairs/guess-who-s-making-the-walls-talk-114121000791_1.html. Accessed 20 Oct. 2021.

Fiske, John. Understanding Popular Culture. 2nd ed., Routledge, 2012.

Johny, M. L. "Clues to Find out the Artist/s behind Guess Who in Kochi." By All Means Necessary, 15 Dec. 2014, www.johnyml.blogspot.com/2014/12/clues-to-find-out-artists-behind-guess.html. Accessed 21 Oct. 2021.

Jordan, Peter. "Street art by 'Guess Who' in Kochi (India) includes Bob Marley, Che Guevara." Repeating Islands, 13 Dec. 2014, www.repeatingislands.com/2014/12/13/street-art-by-guess-who-in-kochi-india-includes-bob-marley-che-guevara/?utm_source=pocket_mylist. Accessed 19 Oct. 2021.

"Kochi-Muziris Biennale." Biennialfoundation, 2021, www.biennialfoundation.org/biennials/kochi-muziris-biennale-india/. Accessed 21 Oct. 2021.

Prasad, M Madhava. "Popular Culture and Cultural Studies." Oxford Research Encyclopedia of Communication, Oxford University Press, 30 July 2018, Oxford, www.oxfordre.com/ communication/view/10.1093/acrefore/ 9780190228613.001.0001/acrefore-9780190228613-e-561. Accessed 18 Oct. 2021.

Storey, John. "What is Popular Culture?." Cultural Theory and Popular Culture An Introduction, 2009,

www.uniteyouthdublin.files.wordpress.com/2015/01/
john_storey_cultural_theory_and_popular_culturebookzz-org.pdf.
Accessed 18 Oct. 2021.

Wendling, Mike. "India's 'Banksy' Behind Provocative Graffiti."
BBC Trending, 12 Dec. 2014, www.bbc.com/news/blogs-
trending-30447979. Accessed 19 Oct. 2021.

Bio-Note

Lakshmipriya A. S. completed her Post-Graduation in English
from CMS College, Kottayam in 2021, and graduated from Alphonsa
college, Pala in 2019. She is an aspiring teacher in the field of
English language and literature. She published articles and poems
in both online and offline sources; also presented papers at
International Virtual Conference. Interested areas include Cultural
Studies, Gender Studies, Translation Studies, and Psychoanalytic
Studies.

CHAPTER XIX

PASTORAL POWER AND REFORM OF THE INDIAN WOMAN: A READING OF SHERWOOD'S THE AYAH AND LADY: AN INDIAN STORY

Vishnu Priya T. P.

ABSTRACT

This article analyses the reform of Indian women as conceptualised in Mary Martha Sherwood's tract fiction The Ayah and Lady: An Indian Story. The analysis studies how this particular work fits into the genre of missionary literature. To that purpose, the article identifies two key features characteristic of the genre of missionary literature and sees how this particular narrative focuses on them. One of the characteristics is the emphasis on 'everyday life' and habits in the domestic setting of colonial India. Another feature is the embodiment of a particular form of power in these narratives, which Michael Foucault terms pastoral power. The article argues that through these two features weaved into the narrative, the author constructs the image of a reformed Indian woman. The narrative also establishes a norm or an optimum to be followed, which is the Christian behaviour, to be a civilised and ethical human being. The scope of the article is to contribute to post-colonial scholarship by studying missionary literature, an area that has not received much attention.

• • •

Introduction

Mary Martha Sherwood (1775 –1851) was a prolific writer who authored many books in the genre of didactic literature. She published her first story in 1795 and authored sentimental novels like Mr Hazard of Bath and The History of Susan Grey. In 1803, she married Captain Henry Sherwood, who was stationed in the metropolitan. In 1805, they shifted to India and spent eleven years in colonial India, including cities like Kolkota, Danapur, Kanpur and Meerut. She penned many didactic tales during her stay in colonial India. Many of her works dealt with the instruction of Christian ideals and the conversion of the natives. Her most famous works include Little Henry and His Bearer, Lucy and Her Dhaye and The History of the Fairchild Family. These works enjoyed a wide range of readership across many countries in different languages. Sherwood's pedagogical pursuits were not limited to her literary career; she also taught classes to the British as well as Indian children in colonial India.

As a scholar interested in the missionary archives and the contribution of religion in the post-colonial scholarship, I came across a list of books suggested for Indian women compiled by literary evangelist John Murdoch in his book Women of India and What Can be Done for Them. Murdoch was a literary evangelist who was very keen on circulating textbooks with Christian ideals in the schools of India. The inclusion of The Ayah and Lady in the suggested curriculum points out the significance of the text in the reform agenda of the missionaries. This book was first published in 1816 and was translated into native languages for the readers. Subsequently, in the list, Murdoch had included the translations of this book in Urdu, Marathi. Tamil, Telugu and Malayalam, all published by the Christian Vernacular Educational Society.

Missionaries have always been interested in the reform of native women. However, the native women in Indian homes were not easy to access for the male missionaries. Like writers like Maria Edgeworth, who tried to reform the working class in Britain, the women who came to India as wives of officials and missionaries worked to reform and convert the natives. They were particularly interested in the native women and children as they were primarily inaccessible to male missionaries. The Ayah and Lady is a guideline to fashion the native woman in the domestic setting difficult to access for the male missionaries. It is a known fact that many evangelical denominations were active in colonial India that focused on converting the 'heathens'. Nevertheless, these activities had to be justified by depicting the deplorable condition of the natives. In one of her autobiographical writings, Sherwood claims about this particular narrative that "many of its stories, and those the most remarkable, are real histories" (415). The author claims they are realistic depictions and create the binary of the Indian woman/ European woman. The term 'lady' is a polite word used to indicate a reformed and impressive woman. The term 'ayah' denotes a woman in the capacity of a servant who attends to the lady's needs. It is noteworthy that the Europeans established a well-ordered home while stationed in the colony. This home emulated the well-ordered victorian home. Ironically, these homes were run with the help of many servants designated for specific jobs like dressing, washing, and cooking.

Civilising through Defining: the Self and the Other

The story revolves around the English lady and the ayah who works for her. The story is set in colonial India, and the events unfold at the home of the English lady. The lady embodies the Christian virtues like kindness and modesty, while the ayah is depicted as a woman with no virtues. She also represents the Indian women degraded by the vices which their respective religions could not correct. Nevertheless, the lady is very kind and patient towards her ayah. Throughout the book, the lady instructs ayah to follow the ten commandments of the Bible. In the end, the ayah is transformed and has a change of heart under the supervision of the lady. To understand the reform project, it is necessary to look at the description of the ayah at the beginning of the book. When the ayah finds faults with other women implying that they do not deserve charity, the lady keenly observes the faults of the ayah thus:

"What, Ayah," said the Lady, "do you think yourself better than all the women in the compound and the Bazar, that I should give you the cloth I bought for charity? You know, Ayah, that you have many faults: you often tell lies to me; you spend most of your time in chewing paun sleeping, and gossiping; you often use very bad language when you are talking with your companions: these things 1 know you do; and what other bail things you do, when I don't see you, your own heart can tell, and God knows. Therefore, if none but good women are to have the cloth, I think it will not be yours, for you are not good". (Sherwood 14)

This passage reiterates the many stereotypes related to colonised women. One of the most repeated stereotypes is of the native woman who idles her time through gossiping. The implication is that the native women are not industrial and are unfit to be good mothers and wives. It also implies that the native woman is the inferior other through which the superiority of the English woman is established. Other stereotypes include the image of the native woman who is not modest in her words and behaviour. Most importantly, the narrative constructs the image of the native women divided by caste and religion who treat each other with hatred.

The lady helps the ayah in structuring her everyday life and habits. These changes in the everyday life of the domestic realm are pivotal to the transformation of the ayah. Jean Comaroff and John Comaroff, in their book Of Revelation and Revolution: Christianity, Colonialism, and Consciousness in South Africa, argue that colonisation can happen at two levels. The first one is the conversion of the natives through direct influence. This can be done by giving the natives enough exposure to the 'divine truth' or an "account of the sacred narrative". The second one is through the "revolution in the habits of people" (199). The lady observes the habits of the ayah very closely and supervises her conduct. For instance, the ayah does not care about Sabbath in the beginning. However, the lady instructs her to follow the Sabbath, persuading her not to work on Sundays. The lady also observes that the ayah freely mentions the Holy name of God in conversations (Sherwood 36), which is a direct violation of one of the Biblical commandments. The idea is that the transformation should begin with a change of heart (Sherwood 23), which the lady very much desires for the ayah. This change of heart can be accomplished through daily habits like reading the scripture and prayer (Sherwood 28).

The ayah and the other servants also lived within the compound, where the lady could observe and correct them. This included developing habits like helping the poor and to avoid "using bad words, and making filthy jests" (Sherwood 66). The lady often corrects the ayah through a few morality tales and by regulating the ayah's everyday life. The ayah, in return, learns to confess her mistakes to the lady and has a change of heart. This particular image of the Indian woman aims to convince the readers about the necessity to reform. It is also evident from the above analysis that the narrative posits a norm or the optimum to be followed here, which is the Christian behaviour, to be a good human being.

Pastoral Power in The Ayah and Lady

In his series of lectures published as Security, Territory, Population: Lectures at the College De France, 1977 – 78, Michael Foucault explains different forms of power. One form of power is the "juridical", which operates through law and punishment (11). This form of power was emphasised in the social contract theories of the enlightenment time. But a new form of power emerged which focused on governing rather than ruling. As opposed to juridical sovereignty, the art of governing focused on "men in their relationships with things like customs, habits, ways of acting and thinking" (96). The state and the West inherited this art of government from the Christian church, and Foucault terms this peculiar kind of power as 'pastoral power'. When the missionaries operated in colonial India, this new form of power was employed in the domestic setting, as seen in the narrative of The Ayah and Lady.

The lady's role in the narrative is that of a shepherd who leads the flock who is lost. The ayah confesses her actions, thoughts and receives forgiveness from the lady towards the end. The morality tales which the lady narrates to her servents are very contextual and related to perceived flaws in the characters of the native women. These stories are tactics employed by the lady to manage the ayah and other servants. This method of management of the conduct of the members is a characteristic of governing rather than ruling. Thus, the power that the lady wields over the ayah is a benevolent form of power, also known as pastoral power. This benevolent form of power is exercised to ensure that the native women do not go astray from the path of salvation.

Conclusion

The Ayah and Lady: An Indian Story focuses on the 'everyday life' and habits to reform Indian women. The narrative does meet its teleology, the reformed Indian woman who follows the Biblical commandments and is trustworthy enough to take care of the next generation. The narrative also shows how the reform agenda was justified through the many stereotypes about native women. The lady created an ideal Christian home for the native servants to imitate, but ironically, that home was also sustained with the labour of the native people. However, the narrative represents this relationship as that of the shepherd and the flock. Once bequeathed to the West by the Christian church, this modern form of power later found its way into colonial India. This particular narrative was the suggested reading for educating the native women during the colonial time. The pastoral power is still present in our times in the form of governmentality, the governing mechanism of the state. However, the tactics of power employed by the modern state have their origins in the pastoral power of the Christian church. Moreover, it is through these tactics that the narrative of The Ayah and Lady: an Indian Story unravels to the reader.

Works Cited

Comaroff, Jean, and John Comaroff. Of Revelation and Revolution, Volume 1: Christianity,

Colonialism, and Consciousness in South Africa. 1st ed., vol. 1, University of Chicago Press, 1991.

Murdoch, John. The Women of India and What Can Be Done For Them. Madras, The Christian

Vernacular Education Society, 1891.

Foucault, Michel. Security, Territory, Population: Lectures at the College De France, 1977 – 78, edited by Michel Senellart, Palgrave Macmillan, 2009.

Kelly, Sophia, editor. The Life of Mrs Sherwood, Chiefly Autobiographical With Extracts

From Mr Sherwood's Journal During His Imprisonment in France and Residence in India. London, 1853.

Sherwood. The Ayah and Lady: An Indian Story. 3rd ed., Boston, 1822.

• • •

CHAPTER XX

FORTUNATE SHEPARD

J. Vetri Michael Raj
MA English Literature
Thiagarajar College, Madurai

• • •

"Next stop Michaelpuram!" conductor blows his pipe

Oh my god, I napped for 2 hours, midday sunlight bounces its grim shine to my eyes, I barely open my eyes, the cracked window revealed half to me outward, and I check my pocket to reach out the phone, its 3" o clock in the dusk. I lean down to the seat, strive to settle. I take a tic-tac from my trouser pocket and crush it.

It's been 10 years since I fled the village with my family, my father lacked a steady job to feed our family, and also he couldn't afford us to study in the convent institution, the local workshop in Michaelpuram was never auspicious for him, but at least it fed us for 12 years.

We all are anxious about leaving the village, me and my sister deserting our school friends behind, my mom blowing her church behind, she's a serious Catholic, went to church daily prime. I could remember our time in an old-fashioned church when my mother and I accompany the evening mass on Saturday evenings, she used to buy me bonbons, and I'd sat on the hallway, warm sand, under the vast pillars of the church.

My father, selling his workshop to his uncle, where he employed all his time with spanners more than he relaxed at home. We didn't have any other options, after the downfall of our elementary school, we didn't go to school for 3 months, higher executives said that they'll renew it, but my father didn't wait for their help, that's also the basis for us to leave.

My spine tears, backseats are arduous to travel, very sturdy for me to sit tight without bouncing my body, and roads are also pierced, my thoughts are hopping in my mind, as the wheels kiss deeply the pits in the road.

Later, my family has settled in Chennai, my father owns a local workshop, across the Egmore junction that rewards him well. My sister, completed her post-graduation in psychology at Madras University and she has been married to a prosperous businessman, Ravi Kumar, my uncle, he owns an auto parts store, well! He's from Chennai, worked laboriously from a young age and now he owns an auto parts store, and most importantly he's very attached to my sister. My mother finally found herself in an artistic church to glorify god.

In the beginning, City times were troublesome for us to mesh ourselves in, but after some years, we felt much pleasanter that ultimately ends in misery. Like all other people, who are lodged in a worldly area, we are disappointed by the dull manes of the centre while we enjoy ourselves with its reservoir.

Plots through the window disturb me, it hauls me to talk about it, talk about its charm that being abused by the daylight fever. There, I can see the tamarind trees, filling evenly on both sides of the road, like the pillars that lead to the castle hallway. Among the green leaves, I can see the pulp, brown in hue, like cocoa fruit, some fruits are smeared by the dry coat and some are busted of heat. I sense the water-filled in my mouth, oh! I spill the tic-tac, it drops on the steel floor. I try to take another tic-tac from my poke, here comes the last hindrance, I eject from my seat, the packet dies on the floor, and I bash my head on the seat handle of the jerk.

"Last stop Michaelpuram!" conductor toots his whistle one last time

The driver parks the bus and cools the engine, the sunlight nearly choked us all, and we all need to be chilled. I take my water bottle and take a few sips, passengers depart through the portals like the bees leaving their hives. A woman, with a basket and mop in her hand, enters the bus. Driver and conductor stretched towards the teashop, she started mopping the bus floor. I stand at once, take my bag, and exit through the back access.

God! I need a shadow to protect myself, I hop on the shadow to save my skin from searing light, the bus stop is straight opposite to the church, our church was built during the period of British rule, their sense of aesthetics in architecture, "at least they dropped these for us, only to exploit" I chuckle.

After we lodged in Chennai, we never missed arriving here for the St. Michael's festival every year, it's very special for the villagers and also for us too. It's a ceremony where all families would come over from the various districts to worship their motherland archangel.

I and my sister were only curious about the village, so we can sweep the shades and dust of our pasts, forgotten in the village, but that annual visit came to die for me. Since I got a job in Bangalore. I couldn't join my family, my sister would send me photographs and selfies of them in the village. Though I had a credible reason, I felt unfortunate for not joining them. She also sent me the photo of our old school teacher Mr. Peter, who's our English tutor, who taught us poetry, drama, fiction until the school was ripped.

Yes! That's why I'm here, after seeing those selfies with him in the church, I don't want to dissipate my time in the excess system, yeah it all started from the little thought.

I held a requisition letter and left my rented home behind, I went to my home to see my mom and dad. They are astounded to see me and then I told them about my visit, they desired to join me, but this is not a family trip! More like a mission to see my English teacher. I got myself on the bus to Madurai, then I reached Sivagangai and that's the painted part of my journey.

I walk towards the chapel, there were nearly 20 story houses, on both sides of the street, not upgraded. I see an old man and woman sitting in the passageway of their home and grinding the betel leaves. A man separated the front portion of his home into a candle store, he placed a wooden table and the yellow candle bundles were arranged precisely on it.

"Hello sir, can you tell me the way to Mr. Peter's home," I ask the candle seller

"Who" he leans front and asks

I quote "Mr. Peter, the school teacher"

"Oh, the elementary school Peter! His home is not here son. He and his wife are residing outside the village, near the coconut farm" the seller replies

I'm confused, maybe he's telling about the wrong peter, but he denoted him as an "elementary school teacher". So I ask him "can you tell me the way to his home sir"

"Did you come by bus?" he asks

"Yes sir" I reply

"Then you should walk back, the way you came by bus" he replies

Did he tell me to go back? My legs look at me pleading, I smile at him and ask "sir, that's a long way to walk, is there any shortcut?"

"No son, there's no other way. It's not much longer as you think, walk straight through the main road, after you reach the pond take right, then walk straight until you reach the coconut farm, there you can find Peter's home"

"Thank you sir" I say

He's right, there's no alternative, there's no one on the road by vehicle, even if anyone shows up, and I don't think they give a lift to me. It's me, Tar Street, and the blazing sun. I can smell the mix of melting tar and heat, "how can I smell the hotness, I know it's an illusion I say to myself.

Why he abiding outside the village, I didn't see any houses, while inside the bus. I remember he and his family lived in a rented home, next to the school street, maybe he raised his own home outside the village, to live the rest of his life in peace.

Here comes the pond, which's not a pond anymore, there's no track of water inside, just green beds of algae spread around the surface. My father never allowed me to swim in the pond, so I sat in the footsteps and saw other boys swimming and swallowing the water. The seller told me to walk straight. My legs are bothering me nor am I hurting them.

After filling 10 years in Chennai, this is very unusual for me to walk on these ways, even for the family trip, we come by car, without kenning about the deadly spikes on the terrain, dents, dirt spread all over the way.

Oh! The grace, I saw outside from the bus, tamarind trees, standing in throngs, arrayed like a sketched line. Trees are raised 2 feet distance the road. I'm sure that I'll befall to the ground if I try to bounce and pluck, I need a stick to knock it all down.

A few steps further, I see a barren stick on the road. It'll be enough to disturb the pith from its cord. I top and reach out for it, a great slip. "I can't walk farther without those jams in my mouth," I said to myself. I adjust my trouser and aim for the fruits, I hop again and raise the stick towards it, and I shut my eye because the dried leaves start to shatter. I can feel the touch, stick powerfully touch the jam rapidly. I get down on my knees.

There it drops, the fruits started kissing the tar road, its handful, to add a flavour to my mission. I fill them in my pocket and resume my walk. I split and remove the skin of the pulp and kiss it

I think I missed my way to Mr. Peter's home. I see an old man with a log in his hand and a herd of goats strolling in front of him, I run towards him.

"Sir! Sir!" I call him, I see him from the rear, He's donning a white shirt, it is tidy, and its fabrics are shredded and lost their rigidity, but well washed. And he wears a brown dhoti, it nearly sweeps the ground, he didn't wear any sandals. How can he even stand in this tract? I walk around to him and ask "do you know the way to Mr. Peter's home?" My sounds are exhaling, I think it's one of the fatigued fantasies. I close my eyelids and then open wide, yes that's him. He's my English don, Mr. Peter, who completed his degree in English literature at Madurai University.

What am I doing? I shouldn't gaze at him. I smile, mostly laugh "Sir! Hello sir, I'm Michael your student"

He shrinks his eyes and pretends to laugh that he remembers me, "Mechanic John's son! Sir" I beam.

"Michael!" he greets, "I had a feeling it was you"

I know he lies, I bow to his knees, to get his grace, while my mind is steeped in the chaos of knowing. I raise and again look at him and can't act to look at him ordinarily. But his smile holds me reopening my conversation.

"Did you come here alone, where is your family? He asks

"No sir, they are in Chennai, I'm on holiday" I reply

"Did you go to the church?" He again asks

"Yes sir, actually I was coming from there, after finishing my prayers" I laugh

"Great," he says

We stand hushed for seconds, I don't know what to say and finally, I let myself slack. We see a private bus advancing our way and the goats are wandering on the road. He raises the staff, he gives them a din, like a signal and the goats are obeying his command, and they march away from the road.

"I came here to see you, sir, the candle seller told me the way to reach your home, I'm lucky I found you before, I was frequently lost," I say

The bus catches away from us, he turns towards me and says "is it? Luckily I'm reverting to my home for lunch. Come on Michael, join with me" he smiles.

What can I reply to him other than "yes" so I say "yes sir" Along with my mentor, with a herd of goats, I extend my walk towards his palace.

He's occupied with his goats, I can revel in my thoughts now.

How he ended up a Shepard, my father once told me that our prospect is unknown in this village, maybe he's right, and the English don who taught me poetry is now a Shepard who depends on his bucks. This is why he couldn't afford a home inside the village, whom I do care for him now, I left everything behind me when I cruised away with my family, but not his literature and poetry, and I missed him during my school days in Chennai. No one can teach literature like him.

#

I can see the coconut trees, grown to the clouds. I can feel chillness inside, girdled by the trees. It's like a cold sanctuary isolated from the burning village. I raise my head and look up at the branches of the coconut trees, the trees open their flowing hand to share a squeeze with me.

"Suseela" peter shouts

I look in the direction as his loudness passes through, I see a hut, yeah, and it's his place. "I am not anymore surprised," I say to myself

I couldn't expect Mr. Peter would also disappear, just like my father. He adores his village and its reality.

"Michael, go to the house, wash your hands and legs, and settle yourself I'll be back," he says to me and leads his herd towards their barn.

I turn and walk towards the hut, dried coconuts were gathered everywhere on the field like the little mountains. Their house was girdled and bound by the logs of the forest trees, but they only used a few blocks to build their hut, front portions are for chickens and ducks. Their house was made of red bricks, but their ceiling was overlaid with a hut and a banner is covered over the hut ceiling to block the fever from the sun.

I walk towards the logs and open the bar, I see Aunt Suseela coming out of the hut.

"Suseela, look who's here! Can you identify this young man" Mr. Peter says, he walks towards me from the rear and greets me to his home, no! To his palace.

"Michael" Aunt Suseela says cheerfully

"See how big has he grown up!" Sir peter laughs

"How is your family Michael, last time when they came to the festival we were very happy, I couldn't forget those celebrations and delight, why didn't you come to the festival? It's been 5 years since you came to the village" she asks to me

As I'm ready to respond, Mr. Peter say "the young man has so many important things to do, if he's busy with this annual festival how can he achieve in his life"

See, he always holds me, he even called my father for beating me, "I'm his special learner" and now I'm his special young man.

"Come on Michael, give your bag pack to her and wash," he says

Under the neem tree, a concrete tub was filled with water, he takes a cast bowl and gives it to me. I wash my face, I can sense the fever mists from my face when I splatter the icy water and then I wash my neck, hands, and legs. After me, Mr. Peter rinses his hands and legs of mud. I don't want to scrape the water in my face, neither him. We walk to the hut and sit on the terrace. I sit on the clumsy chair and he lies down on the cot.

Aunt Suseela goes inside the shed and checks the woodpile for cooking.

"So Michael, how's your job in Bangalore, you stay there alone?" he asks

My father told him about my job, but I know that he didn't tell me everything about my work, I think to myself and say "no sir, I'm staying with my friend, he's from Coimbatore"

"Oh that's good" he smiles, "your father told me that you work in Bangalore, but I don't remember him saying about the job title," he says

I snap my lip and then exhale "I work as a content writer sir"

"Oh! Suseela, did you hear that, I told you, this boy will become a flourishing writer one day" he says to Suseela

"Yes Michael, he always talked about your writings during the school days" Suseela replies from inside

"You are blessed with your writing Michael I was very happy when your father said that you have completed a degree in English literature, So tell me Michael, how many novels have you published, I'm quite sure, you would have sold all your copies, but son listen, don't be a writer alone," he says

He mounts towards me and says "complete your higher studies, become a teacher or professor, you should share what you have received, you teach them how to write and appreciate poetry"

"Tell me Michael how many poems have you written," he asks again

"Sir?" I recall myself "No sir, It's a corporate company, which I work for, content writing means writing content for the online products, e-commerce websites, and blogs, you know like descriptions for them" I reply in a deep pitch

I see his face, he didn't get a word, I said. Of course, he's great with names like Shakespeare, George Orwell, Tolstoy, Jane Austen, but content writing?! I ask to myself

"So you operate computer" he concludes

He looks at the sky, the midday sun has virtually gone to sleep, and the eventide leaves brunette tones in our faces.

"It's good Michael, at least you got a job to live your life joyfully, look at me, 15 years back I was an English teacher in this village, but now I'm just an old Shepard," he says "What you're doing now is great for your future, you're not foolish like me" he smiles

I feel desolation around me, round the hut, in the intact surrounding and I don't want to respond, I mean what can I say to him, can I say that he's the motivation behind selecting my undergraduate in English literature. How can I? He thinks that he's a mess now!

Aunt Suseela call him to come inside, "just a second," he says and goes inside the hut

I laze on the chair, just look at the sky, zero in my mind. I can feel the void surfing around my acme.

Mr. Peter steps out of his hut, he says "Michael, I'm going to the hotel in the village, I'll be back in 15 minutes" he smiles. He gets his cycle, which is held on the back of the hut, I follow him and ask "why sir, isn't there enough food in the home?"

"No, she cooked enough food for us, but we don't want you to eat that food" he chuckles "you're a special guest, I'll just go to Pandian hotel, they have their special parota and kuruma, I'll buy those for you," he says

"What?" I exclaim

I walk towards the hut doorway and call Aunt Suseela "Aunt Do you remember, after the school was over me and my sister would run to your home to taste your food along with sir, have you forgotten that aunt?" I exclaim "how can you not serve your food for me" I look at Sir Peter

Aunt Suseela laughs "ok, don't get angry, we thought that you didn't like village recipes, wash your hands, I'll get the leaves" she smiles

"Are you sure son?" Sir peter asks again

I turn towards him "sir, park your cycle, come with me and wash your hands, let's eat!" I look at him and smile

He chuckles and joins me. While we are washing our hands, Aunt Suseela sweep the terrace with the mop and cover it with a fabric to sit

She takes a knife and evades three banana leaves from the tree, raised outside their plot, she wipes the leaves. We sit on the terrace and Aunt Suseela sets two leaves for us, then she gives a cup in our hands, then she pours water in it. She brings the urns one by one, there are three vessels, one for rice, another for curry and the last one is gravy.

I can smell the mixture of dhal and masala. I crave those old days when Aunt Suseela would cook the dry fish gravy for us, she'll make it with onion, chilly, and finally serve it with curd rice. I and my sister would end up striving for the last part of dry fish.

Aunt Suseela serves the white rice in my leaf and then for sir peter. Then she serves sambar, she pours it with her dainty hand and yes finally that's the fine dry fish gravy, oh she also added tomato in that.

I just render the sambar rice peacefully with the spicy pause of dry fish gravy. There was a saying "great times ever drifts soon" that's how I dispatch my lunch on the terrace.

I wash my hands and wait for Sir Peter to accompany me, but he didn't. I lie on the cot, under the neem tree, watching them, sir peter serving his wife rice, curry, and gravy, he sits down opposite her and gazes at her eating, and they both smile at each other.

I lie down my head on the cot, look at the tiny neem leaves that launch down the fresh breeze to my skin, I feel steep, my eyes shut their lids, and they don't want to be opened for a while.

"Michael get up! You have to sit for a while son. Your food needs to be assimilated" he says and sits on the cot near me. I mount and my set legs on the soil.

"I'm very glad for you and your family. My wife would always talk about your mother and sister, they're very sweet" he smiles

"I also feel fortunate sir" I reply

He spins towards me and listens

"We combed for 5 years to find peace and comfort and received them in Chennai, I'm not even sure that it's a real satisfaction. But after seeing you and Aunt Suseela, I think you guys have reached the pure happiness here"

He places his hand on my arm "No Michael, happiness is the same everywhere" he says

He then rests on the cot "I cheated you" he laughs

I smile at him and give him a place to dwell in the cot, I know he's exhausted, spending all his time under sunlight and in the roasted woods, he needs some sleep. I see peace in him, but there's still some catastrophe lazing in the corner of my heart.

"Sir" I call him

In a low tone, he replies "yes son"

"Do you still have the poetry works with you?" I ask in uncertainty

He lifts his head "yes! How could I cast away my works?" he laughs

"I want to see your writing sir" I request in a low tone

"It's kept above the biro, a white paper bundle fastened up with red thread, it's huge, and so be cautious with that," he says and turns over to his other side

I enter the cottage, Aunt Suseela is scrubbing the vessels on the backside of the home, and I don't want her to bother. There I see the biro, it's ancient and durable, made of wood. I lift my feet and try to look up, I see a bunch of 1000 white sheets, scrapped with dust and web. I take it in my hand and thud it, removing the dirt particles.

I settle myself in the corridor with the bundle, unfasten the knot and gradually turn every page one by one. I decided to fill my next one hour reading his works. At 5 PM I have to reach the bus stop, my last ride to Sivagangai. I only have a shorter time to spend and the catastrophe still spots my heart. I turn every page, see every line of his poetry, he also wrote a play, and it's about 200 pages. I get my mobile from my trouser pocket and capture the poetry pages. I take most utmost pictures of the poetry that I can.

Aunt Suseela gives her first-class tea, made of pure cow milk. After drinking powder milk and eating unbaked loaf, chapatti, and rice from the worldly areas, everything here is delicious.

I reach for my backpack, take out my laptop, and then post the poetry lines to my friend. I see the man resting on the cot, who taught me literature, believed in the literature that gives purpose to his life. He's great but he doesn't have enough confidence in literature now, I should restore it, I think myself. I search for Kishore's contact in my mobile and call him.

"Hello Kishore"

"Hey, Michael! Yeah tell me, man"

"Kishore, have you finalized the drafts for this month's publication?" I ask

"Yeah, we'll start the editing by this weekend" he replies

"Ok, Kishore I sent you some poetry images to your mail, it's English poetry, I need you to attach that in the monthly journal, can you do that for me?" I ask

"Yeah man, I can do that, but you have to pay the publication fees, I can arrange other things" he replies

"Thanks, man, send me the payment details, I'll send you the money and author bio"

"Ok Michael, I'll send it to you"

"Take care, bye" I hang up the call

I send the first two poems to his mail, it's about 5 pages. Kishore sent the payment details. "Publication charges: 1500 for 2 pages, 2500 for more than 2 pages" I read. I send the payment and the author bio. I almost keypunched everything about him, then I rub the mug, tea is cold, I drink it in one breath and leave the mug empty.

Time is 4:30 in the dusk, I have to get myself to the bus stop, I shut down my laptop, zip my backpack.

"Michael" I hear a voice from the direction of neem tree

"Son! Oh Suseela served her special tea" he asks with a smile

"Yes sir, it was excellent"

"You have wasted time with those papers Michael, you should have got some sleep," he said

"No sir, actually I am very glad to read the poetry and drama of yours" I reach for my wallet and take 2000 rupees from it.

"My friend Kishore, he's working as a chief editor in a private publication company sir, I sent your poetry to him and he wants your work to get published monthly in their journals, here" I pry my hand towards him with the number "2000 rupees for this month"

Aunt Suseela reaches out of the hut and peers.

"Hey Suseela darling, I told you, my literature would never disappoint me" he laughs. He rolls towards me and says "thank you, Michael, I don't know what to say"

"You don't have to thank me, sir, here take this money, each month you should send your manuscript to the journal, whether it is poetry, fiction or drama, they'll pay you 2000 monthly" I smile

I can see his face, reoccurring sensations that can't be managed, he just looks at the money in his hand, and then trouble sets in his face.

"But how can I send my writing to the publication," he asks

I take a slip and pen down my house address "here, Post your work to my address sir, I'll send it to him"

Their eyes were filled with tears, I know it won't reach down to their cheeks, they'll hold.

"It's about 4:40 sir, I have to revert to the bus stop" I lie down and touch their feet for blessings. Sir Peter raise me, hold my shoulder, he just stares at me for seconds "son, comes on I'll come with you to the stop, it'll be vague in the roadsides, wait, I wear my sandals" he says and leads

"No sir, it's a long way, I'll go myself, and I remember the way we came," I say to him

He turns at me, and smiles "are you sure?"

I smile back "yes sir, and you should come to Chennai one day," I say, walking back towards the entry "Aunty I'm going to miss your tasty gravy" they both smile at me, I abruptly turn back from them, they shouldn't see my tears, it falls on my cheeks.

Again I blow everything back, sir peter, Aunt Suseela, neem tree, goats, and my gladness. I exit through the coconut farm, it's very cold inside, and I join along the main road, supervised by tamarind trees.

Sir Peter and Aunt Suseela would at least satisfy their basic needs with that small amount, I'll be transferring them monthly.

Right now, my heart is only filled with grief, for leaving behind my master and his castle. Where that catastrophe, stained for a long time, no it won't come over, I think.

I knew he'll never receive my money if I give him for free, even though he lost his schooling career, he never asked for help from anybody, living by his muscles.

That's why I lied to him, then he accepted my money. Giving him cash isn't big, I changed his belief about literature.

"Literature is the study of life and it helps us to perceive our life every second" I take a tamarind jam and perceive it.

END

• • •

LANGUAGE OF WATER IN SEAMUS HEANEY'S POETRY

Nimmy Maria Abraham

TGT English, JNV, Karimnagar Telangana

Ph. D. in English (Submitted): Kannur University

ABSTRACT

Water has become a theme, subject and metaphor in many of Seamus Heaney's poems. The well on the poet"s family farm, the river and the sea are hailed with detailing of the ecological uniqueness. Creativity is derived from the language rooted in Gaelic culture. The mythological and biblical description of water hails it as sacred. The sacred perception of nature is inherent in the Gaelic primitivism which is the indigenous spiritual, cultural and literary tradition of Ireland. The select poems on water reveal the cultural ecology influenced by Gaelic culture as interconnected with the ecosystem of the native land. The paper discusses the poetic language revealing the cultural ecology is dependent on the ecosystem of the land. Seamus Heaney"s poems are quintessential landscape poems. Water is a prominent image as well as a metaphor in many of his poems. However, water is not treated as an independent entity. It is an interrelated part of the ecosystem of the bioregion. Water is portrayed in the form of well, river and sea in Heaney"s native land. In other words, water is the reflection of the speaker"s indigenous identity rooted in the ecology of the native land. Heaney once asserted: "For me, it [the land] was all-important. When I think back, its sensation, really, rather than intellection that returns to me. A feel for places" (Wachtel).

• • •

Language of Water in Seamus Heaney's Poetry

Irish Literary Revival influenced Heaney as a poet to focus on the Gaelic rootedness on land. Irish Literary Revival consciously chose the ecological connection between the inhabitants and the land as the context: In medieval Ireland, the borders between human and animal, culture and nature were fluid and sympathetic. Such sympathy resurfaces many times in Irish literature, most notably in landscape writing of the nineteenth century, in the reclamation of the western Ireland that marked the Irish Renaissance, and more recently in the poetry of Seamus Heaney, Paula Meehan, and Michael Longley. (Holdridge 39)The identity of Irish people is moulded by Gaelic culture. The term Gaelic became common by the eighth century for the representation of Irish indigenous culture (Connolly "Gael"). However, during the colonial period, the Gaelic order was replaced by the English system of administration. The English language was standardized over the Gaelic language during this period. As a poet from Northern Ireland which is still under the English rule, Heaney cannot ignore the violence brought by colonialism which persists even at the present era. His reaction to the unrest in the North as a poet was to trace the ecological bond of the people with the native land. Heaney"s poetry tends to shift from the English influence to Gaelic culture by manipulating the ecology of the land and beliefs of the indigenous Irish society connected with the land.

The poems discussed in the paper are "Personal Helicon" from Death of a Naturalist, "Wheels within Wheels" from Seeing Things, "Remembering Malibu" from Station Island, "The Riverbank Field" from Human Chain and "The Gravel Walks" from The Spirit Level. The poems reveal the well, the river and the sea as possessing indigenous, mythical, cultural, spiritual, and ecological identity of Northern Ireland. The poetic language of the given poems is derived from such an identity. Also, the ecological identity of the water nurture the speaker"s creativity as rooted in the native land. A culture detached from nature cannot maintain the harmony of the ecosystem. Peter Finke points out the relevance of cultural ecology in tune with the natural world: In order to protect or even restore the stability and richness of our natural ecosystems, one has to analyze, influence and change our cultural ecosystems which are responsible for their damage. That is to say, the problems of the environment are problems of the consciousness of our self and its role rather than problems of nature itself....it is our cultural ecosystems that produce our unified and uniform landscapes and destroy the wealth of our natural ecosystems. (Finke 89)

Heaney"s poems serve as such a healing agent of the cultural ecosystem by reviving the bond of culture with the natural world. Creativity, metaphorically evident in the select poems plays the role of interconnecting culture and nature. The well in "Personal Helicon" is described as a hub of an ecosystem with ferns and foxgloves. The title "Personal Helicon" suggests the speaker"s belongingness to the well. The final line "...I rhyme/ To see myself, to set the darkness echoing" (19 − 20), unlike the rest of the poem is in present tense though the former lines are set in the past tense. The shift in the tense form indicates the memory of the past as continuing at present through his creativity. The „darkness" implying the depth of the well is where the speaker finds his own voice and identity. In other words, like Lucian who became a poet by having the leaves from

Helicon (Grimm 1583), the speaker is nurtured as a poet by the ecology of the land metaphorically represented as the dark well. The language of his poetry is derived from the ecosystem of his native land. His creativity is flourished from such a language. The poem also sets a contrast between childhood and adulthood perception towards the natural world. As an adult, he cannot repeat the same act of interaction with the well since it is "beneath all adult dignity...." (19). The change in the perception shows the cultural impact on the mindscape of the speaker leading to the detachment from the ecosystem of the land. The cultural ecology is renovated through the language acquired from the past kinship with the ecosystem as a child. It is from the Gaelic culture adopted by Irish Christians that the belief of well as sacred became prevalent in Ireland. Heaney"s poetic language is influenced by the Gaelic perception of land as sacred. Heaney points out: There if you like, was the foundation for a marvelous and magical view of the world, a foundation for the diminished structure of lore and superstition and half pagan, half Christian thought and practice. Much of the flora of the place had a religious force, especially if we think of the root of the word „religion" to bind fast. (qtd. in Russel 53)

Daniel Xerry traces the spirituality of nature in the archetypal patterns of Heaney"s poems. He points out Heaney"s assertion of Shamanism found in Gaelic tradition, the practice ofcommunication between the spirits of nature and humans (5). The first person pronouns„I", „me" and „myself" throughout the poem stress the personal communication of the speaker with the well. In "Wheels within Wheels" from Seeing Things, the subject of well is repeated. The well is described as a "... hole/ with water in it with small hawthorn trees/ On one side and a muddy, dunge ooze/ On the other, all tramped through by cattle" (4 − 7). The speaker works on the well with his bicycle:

I stood its saddle and its handlebars
Into the soft bottom, I touched the tyres
To the water"s surface, then turned the pedals
Until like a mill-wheel pouring at the treadles
(But here reversed and lashing a mare"s tail)
The world - refreshing and immersed back wheel
Spun lace and dirt-suds there before my eyes
And showered me in my own regenerate clays.
For weeks I made a nimbus of old glit. (11 − 19)

In "Personal Helicon", the speaker is listening to the darkness of the well whereas in "Wheels within Wheels", the speaker is active in creation from the well, „spun lace anddirtsuds" transforming to „regenerated clays". The action of the speaker represents a cultural ecology framed by the ecosystem. The cyclical nature of the work suggests creation from the already existing ecosystem of the water and returning a „regenerated" cultural ecology. Hence, from the poem, it is inferred that the cultural ecology of the speaker is cyclical in absorbing and producing creativity from the land. The

„regenerated clay" symbolises the regenerated poetic language from the ecology of the native land. The transforming power of the water is emphasised in "Wheels within Wheels". The verbs in continuous tense in the poem, „pouring", „lashing" and „refreshing" give the sense of continuity of the cyclical process of creativity like the cyclical nature of the ecosystem. "Remembering Malibu" is a recollection of the speaker"s visit to Malibu. However the place is compared and contrasted with Northern Ireland"s coastal area around the Atlantic sea.

The ascetic" nature of the Atlantic sea suggests its divinity. Monks in medieval Ireland found the ambience of the sea perfect for their spiritual life. Similarly, the wild sea had influenced the creativity of the poet. The stamp of Skellig is not faded from the „instep" of the speaker which suggests the creation of the speaker as influenced by the uniqueness of the land. The powerful influence of the sea on the speaker"s creativity is conveyed through the sibilants in the poem."The Riverbank Field" is about the river Moyola in Northern Ireland. The speaker compares Lethe with Moyola. However, the ecology of Moyola is entirely different from that of Lethe: "Moths then on evening water/ It would have to be, not bees in sunlight,//Midge veils instead of lily beds..." (8 − 11). The speaker finds the „presence" of spirits common in the banks of Moyola as well as in the Elysian fields of Lethe. Latin mythology foregrounds the sacredness of the river Moyola. However, Gaelic spirituality in relation to the ecology of the river Moyola is conveyed through the comparison with Latin mythology. In the poem, the river becomes the home of ancestral spirits to continue the cultural ecology rooted on land from past to present and towards the future.

"The Gravel Walks" portrays the effect of a cultural ecology detached from the ecosystem of the land. The images of modernisation and its impact are vividly represented through the symbol of „motorbike" and „tractor". For the speaker and his friends as children, the river was „eternal" with its biodiversity including „roadside flowers", „green nuts", „whirlpool", „the trees",

„sandstone - bits", „minnows", „hailstone" and „mackerel". A detailed description of each and every natural aspect is given through a series of nouns typical to the particular gravel bed. It is in this exclusively natural space that motorbike accidents and tractors are introduced as violence to the ecosystem of the gravel bed. Further, the encroachment by the workers with their cement mixers symbolises an anthropocentric cultural ecology diminishing the biodiversity. The line: "The Pharaoh"s brickyards burned inside their heads" (16) suggests an acculturated anthropocentric culture. lines: "And men in dungarees, like captive shades, / Mixed concrete, loaded, wheeled, turned, wheeled..." (13-15) symbolise materialistic-modernisation turning its wheel repeatedly to invade and defeat the natural world. The verbs revealing the harsh action of the workers is in sharp contrast with the peaceful action of creation by the river: As the engines of the world prepared, green nutsDangled and clustered closer to the whirlpool. The trees dipped down. The flints and sandstone-bits worked themselves smooth and smaller in a sparkle shallow, hurrying barley-sugar water (5 - 9)The cultural ecology of the mindscape free of anthropocentrism inherited by the speaker as a child from the gravel bed is revealed through a biblical allusion: "Beautiful in or out of the river, /The kingdom of gravel was inside you too" (21 − 22). For him, the spiritual experience is being one with the „eternal" ecosystem of the gravel bed. The river and

the gravel bed as a sacred agent of purification is repeated in the biblical allusion: "As you went stooping with your barrow full/ into an absolution of the body, / The shriven life, tired bones and marrow feel" (26 − 28). The river as sacred inherent in the Gaelic culture is reflected in the biblical allusions in the poem. Thus the sacredness of the water surpasses the religious borders in Heaney"s poems through the amalgamation of Gaelic spirituality, Latin mythology and Christian spirituality.

The select poems state the language of water as inherited from the interaction with the ecological uniqueness of Northern Ireland as well as from the Gaelic rootedness of cultural ecology adopted by the poet as a native of Ireland. The perception of water as sacred is acquired from Gaelic spirituality which keeps the cultural ecology closer to the natural world. Thus the select poems deconstruct the anthropocentric notion of culture as detached from nature.

Works Cited

Connolly, S.J, editor. The Oxford Companion to Irish History. Oxford UP, 2002.

Finke, Peter. "Identity and Manifloldness: New Perspectives in Science, Language and

Politics." The Ecolinguistics Reader: Language, Ecology and Environment, edited by

Alwin Fill, Peter Muhlhausler, Continuum, 2001.

Grimm, Jacob. Teutonic Mythology. Vol. 4. Translated by James Steven Stallybrass.

Routledge, 1999.

Heaney, Seamus. Death of a Naturalist. Faber, 1966.

---, Station Island . Faber, 1984.

---, Seeing Things. Faber, 1991.

---, The Spirit Level. Faber, 2009.

---, Human Chain. Faber, 2010.

Holdridge, Jefferson. "Great Hunger, Unspeakable Home: Landscape, Nature and Original

Sin in Lady Morgan"s The Wild Irish Girl and William Carleton"s The Black

Prophet." Ireland's Great Hunger: Relief,

Representation, and Remembrance, edited by David A. Valone, UP of America, 2009,

p.39. ProQuest Ebook Central, ebookcentral.proquest.com/lib/britishcouncilonline ebooks/detail.action?docID=480092. Accessed 3 Aug. 2018.

Russell, Richard Rankin. "Seamus Heaney's Regionalism."

Twentieth Century Literature, vol. 54, no. 1, 2008, pp. 47– 74. JSTOR,

www.jstor.org/stable/20479837. Accessed 9 May 2020.

Wachtel, Eleanor. "An Interview with Seamus Heaney: An excerpt." BRICK: A LITERARY
JOURNAL, no.86, Laurie D. Graham, 30 Sep.2013,
brickmag.com/an-interview-with-seamus-heaney/.Accessed 16 July 2016.
Xerri, Daniel. Seamus Heaney's Early Work: Poetic Responsibility and the Troubles. Paul
Alto: Maunsel and Company, 2010.
http://library.lol/main/
F33502782B0FF4B3FC16BE7ACEAB22E6. Accessed 8 Mar. 2016.

CHAPTER XXII

NEUROCULTURE AND TRANSDISCIPLINARY APPROACHES

Sona Mathew

ABSTRACT

The last three decades witnessed the rise of neurosciences, a neuroevolution that resulted in emergent disciplines like cognitive literary studies, neuro-novels, neuroaesthetics, neurotheology, neuroeconomics, neuromarketing, neuroeducation, neuroethics, cultural neuroscience and so on. The world is being reshaped with the knowledge of the brain. Neuroevolution resulted in a new generation of scholarship. The acceleration of neuron culture is caused by the advancements in technology such as neuroimaging, fMRI, brain wave measurements, PET etc. The most astonishing factor that scientists have unearthed during their research is that the environment can change brain wiring and synaptic circuits. Neuronovels engage in the exploration of subjectivity and identity in neurological worlds, where the protagonist experiences the world in terms of the symptoms that define the syndrome or disorder. The studies which orient toward the conditioning of subjectivity by brain and environment mutually gave rise to neuroeconomics, neuromarketing and neuro-capitalism. Neuroethics is a field that monitors how the knowledge of the brain is appropriated and applied across different disciplines. Neuroculture and Transdisciplinary Approaches In 1990, an American Obstetrician-Gynecologist, Frank Lynn Meshberger reinterpreted the glorious fresco on the ceiling of the Sistine Chapel.

• • •

Neuroculture and Transdisciplinary Approaches

The Creation of Adam by Michelangelo Buonarroti in terms of neuroanatomy. He identified an anatomically accurate image of the brain behind the God in the painting. Though gazed upon by millions, the fact went unnoticed until Meshberger brought it up in the article "The Interpretation of Michelangelo's Creation of Adam Based on Neuroanatomy" in the Journal of American Medical Association. He points out that God is residing in the central and subcortical regions of the brain. Frank Lynn Meshberger and Tony B Rich illustrate: On close examination, borders in the painting correlate with sulci in the inner and outer surface of the brain, the brain stem, the basilar artery, the pituitary gland and the optic chiasm. God's hand does not touch Adam, yet Adam is already alive as if the spark of life is being transmitted across a synaptic cleft. Below the right arm of God is a sad angel in an area of the brain that is sometimes activated on PET scans when someone experiences a sad thought. God is superimposed over the limbic system, the emotional centre of the brain and possibly the anatomical counterpart of the human region of the brain. ("Explaining The Hidden Meaning")

The last decade of the twentieth century was declared as the 'Decade of The Brain' by the then president of America, to draw attention from the public towards the discipline of neuroscience. The declaration also stimulated brain research globally. Two decades later, neuroscience pervaded academic disciplines beyond biology and anatomy, into science and humanities alike. As Melissa M Littlefield and Jenell M Johnson rightly observed in the introduction of the book The Neuroscientific Turn: Transdisciplinarity in the Age of the Brain, "The application of neuroscience to fields beyond medicine has been characterized as revolutionary, akin to the industrial and information revolutions and evidence of the birth of a 'neuro-society' in which all domains of life and knowledge production are under (or soon will be) the sign of 'neuro'" (1). Academicians acknowledged and welcomed the new methods of knowledge production which consequently led to the development of cognitive culture. Stephen Katz explains,

"It is a culture because the cognitive field, while dominated by the neurosciences, also, extends to business, industry, insurance, economics, the military, the arts, the pharmacology, and education and has created newly hybridized "neuro" disciplines, products and social values" ("Embodied Memory").

The brain studies in the 1990s witnessed considerable improvement and have resulted in several emergent discourses and neologisms including but not limited to neuroaesthetics, neurotheology, neurobiology, neuroanatomy, neuromarketing, neuroeconomics, neuroethics, neuron-season, neuroligin, necropolitics, neuroeducation, neuropsychiatry, computational neuroscience, cultural neuroscience, neurophilosophy, neurogenesis, neuro-society, neuron culture, neuro-subjects, neuro-novels, neuroevolution, neuro turn, neuroplasticity. The academicians of all fields are baffled by the interdisciplinary approach or rather, this transdisciplinary evasion. Scientists owe to the exploratory nature of neuroscience for neuro turn which created a vast amount of knowledge, thanks to the expedition of brain sciences worldwide. The emergent fields of brain science, developmental neurobiology, cognitive neuroscience, neuroinformatics together with neurotechnology work for cracking the most elusive riddle of the human body, the brain.

The knowledge of the brain has seeped from academia into the culture. The world is now running on a neuron culture, driven by the knowledge of the importance and working of the brain. When was the last time you heard about the prefrontal cortex, dopamine or serotonin? The last TED talk you listened to must have mentioned the behavioural patterns and the parts of the brain which drive these characteristics. The tendency to define everything from witnessing a random act of kindness to daily exercise, in terms of effects on the brain is the new norm. Neuroscience pervaded popular culture and we now understand everything in relation to the knowledge of the brain. We might not have viewed our daily activities in a brain augmenting way. With the innovative technology of functional magnetic resonance imaging, scientists identify the part of the brain and the neural circuits responsible for memory, perception, judgement, emotions, reasoning, decision making, reading, writing, speaking etc. The acceleration of neuron culture is caused by the advancements in technology such as neuroimaging, fMRI, brain wave measurements, PET etc.

The world is expanding upon a eurocentric perspective that very often one chance upon videos, web articles and popular magazine articles which describe effects on the brain and how to enhance brain activity contrary to the popular belief that intelligence is fixed. Researchers proved that intelligence can be improved with the right method of learning thus destabilizing the notion behind intelligence tests. The common belief that the brain cannot be changed after it is developed in childhood and adolescence was proved wrong by neuroscientists. The most astonishing factor that scientists have unearthed during their research is that the environment can change brain wiring and synaptic circuits. The capacity of the brain to remodel itself and create new synaptic connections among neurons is referred to as brain plasticity. The brain is capable of making new synaptic connections and structures which is why it is called the plastic brain. Neural plasticity is an idea that drives the neuroscientific world crazy. The book by Norman Doidge The Brain That Changes Itself, which discussed neuroplasticity in detail, was a bestseller among other neuroscience rhetoric and thus the public became aware of the game-changing discovery. Norman Doidge states, "The idea that the brain can change its own function and structure through thought and activity is, I think, the most important alteration in our view of the brain since we first sketched out its basic anatomy and the workings of its basic component, the neuron" (Preface).

All disciplines concerned with mankind and individuals are persuaded and obliged to accommodate the neuro turn and the knowledge created by neuroscientific studies. There is evidently a shift in the cultural paradigm. The popular neuroscience rhetoric led to the emergence of a genre called neuron over, as Marco Roth identifies. Neuronovels explore the contours of neurology. It provides interaction between brain science and literature. "This category names a subgenre of fiction that, while sharing certain formal features with modernist novels of consciousness, engages conceptually with recent interdisciplinary developments in cognitive science, neuroscience, psychopharmacology" (Gaedtke 274). Neuro fiction portrays different neurological disorders and syndromes such as Huntington's, Parkinson's, Tourette's, Capgras, Schizophrenia, Encephalitis Lethargica, Asperger's etc. These disorders occur either due to structural abnormalities in the brain or brain injury. Neuronovels engage in the exploration of subjectivity and identity in neurological worlds, where the protagonist experiences the world in terms of the symptoms that define the syndrome or disorder. Neurofiction includes but is not limited to Ian McEwan's Saturday, Richard Powers' The Echo Maker, Mark Haddon's The Curious Incident of the Dog in the Night-Time, Scott Simon's Sunnyside Plaza.

Cognitive literary studies encompass several different paradigms and approaches from cognitive historicism to cognitive queer studies, including cognitive narratology, cognitive postcolonial studies, and research on emotions and empathy while reading literature. Aristotle's definition of tragedy is an area of interest to researchers in the interdisciplinary field of cognitive literary studies. Tragedy should arise pity and fear among the audience, as Aristotle perceives it. The part of the brain which is associated with fear is Amygdala. Antonio Damasio in his works, Looking for Spinoza and Descartes'Error, explain the emotional aspects of the brain and the associated research tools. The self, which was thought to be an aspect of mind and psychological studies, is no more so. Neurologization of self is in progress.

The mind-brain theories have created a brainfood for neural subjects. The psychological strain in the field of narration has transformed into the more critical field of cognitive narratology. Some researchers check for the several layers of thoughts and emotions in the narration. The Oxford Handbook of Cognitive

Literary Studies edited by Lisa Zunshine presents glimpses of various approaches and practices of the field. Semir Zeki coined the term 'neuroaesthetics' in 1999. He believes in the necessity of discipline because art is perceived and created by the brain. The neural activity of artists and audiences are mapped to identify the specific brain areas associated with the production and consumption of art as well as to make sense of the concepts of perception, creativity, imagination and imaging. Art is approached from a neurobiological viewpoint.

Educators are researching for making learning more effective to which neuroscience has contributed significantly. Before neuroscience came into play, intelligence and the brain were topics of disinterest which the common public cared the least unless they were concerned about the academic levels of students, especially at parent teaching meetings. That would be one important scenario when teachers and parents discuss the intelligence of students, which was believed to be an unchangeable one. As the paradigm shifted, researchers are developing interesting and engaging pedagogy that helps to retain attention and memory simultaneously augmenting the creative capacity of the child focusing on the plastic nature of the brain. The behavioural and psychological aspects of learning have given way to the cognitive and neural aspects. Children are treated not as cultural subjects but rather as neural subjects. The developmental stages of these children are of prime focus because this is the age of developing the amygdala and prefrontal cortex.

Bygone is the era when Bruner and Piaget defined the development of a person in terms of social and psychological parameters. The neuromodulators in the field combining education and brain studies define the development of a child in terms of the development of the areas of the brain like the cerebellum, which is an important part of the brain in charge of cognitive processes, which includes attention, language and emotions, skills, memory and motor control and neocortex, which is a neural tissue which contains most of the neurons and is also critical in decision making, perception and retention. The development of the prefrontal cortex, amygdala, temporal lobe, parietal lobe, frontal lobe, occipital lobe, hippocampus, limbic system and the interconnectedness of various parts are the areas of focus. Neuro pharmaceutical companies are offering medicines for inattentiveness and other learning problems. Classroom control has been a never-ending problem for teachers worldwide for which neuroscience may find a solution. Often neuroplasticity is paralleled and compared with philosophical assumptions. These juxtapositions range from ideas of Rousseau to Deleuze and Guattari. Rousseau in Emile proposed the idea of the perfectibility of human nature, which in other ways can be called conditioning. The postmodern theorists Deleuze and Guattari proposed the notion of becoming, the instability of subjectivity. Another philosopher, Brian Rotman, perceives plasticity as an opportunity for multiple subjectivities. The studies which orient toward the conditioning of subjectivity by brain and environment mutually gave rise to neuroeconomics, neuromarketing and neuro-capitalism.

It examines capitalist societies in which cultural, economic conditions are favourable for fashioning or otherwise, manipulating. The business sector is collaborating with neurosciences to improve marketing techniques and accelerate the rate of consumption. In the field of advertising and business, predicting and influencing the behaviour of the customers are the most important factors. The behavioural and psychological segments of marketing have started to rely on neurosciences to predict and influence the target market. Neurosciences help to reduce the uncertainty in predicting market behaviour as it understands the choices and interests as neural activity and circuits. "The field of neuromarketing - sometimes known as consumer neuroscience - studies the brain to predict and potentially even manipulate consumer behaviour and decision making" (Harrell "Neuromarketing"). Tech giants Facebook, Google and Microsoft have set up neuromarketing units. Neuroeconomics combines the fields of neuroscience, psychology and economics. Functional Magnetic Resonance Imaging, Electroencephalograph and Positron Emission Tomography are used to observe blood flow, neural activity and biochemical stimulants before, during and after making decisions and choosing from alternatives. "Neuroeconomics has the possibility of improving the accuracy of economic theories by factoring in social, cognitive, and emotional factors into economic decision making" (Chen"Neuroeconomics").

Neuroethics is a field that monitors how the knowledge of the brain is appropriated and applied across different disciplines. "Neuroethics focuses on ethical issues raised by our continually improving understanding of the brain, and by consequent improvements in our ability to monitor and influence brain function" (Roskies "Neuroethics"). The scope of this discipline is also extended to the knowledge of the role of the brain in ethical thought and actions. The International Neuroethics Society is constituted to discuss the implications of neuroscience beyond research labs, in classrooms, offices and homes all around the world. Several sub-disciplines have emerged, each with a different approach to ethics which Illes Judy duly noted in the American Journal of Bioethics - Neuroscience as reflective neuroethics, clinical neuroethics, research neuroethics, women's neuroethics, empirical neuroethics, pluralistic neuroethics and other fields of study. The ethics of neuroenhancement is a major field of contention. Neuro enhancement is based on the concept of neuroplasticity and the use of knowledge of the brain to enhance/ condition human beings. The treatment of diseases, malfunctions or disorders with cognitive intervention diminishes human agency and leads to the rise of disparities between the different economic classes. Neuroethics also takes into consideration the threat posed by cognitive enhancement to cognitive liberty. It also aims to equip humans to function with higher cognitive capacity. The thin line between normality and disease is open to question and is a concern of discussions.

Cultural neuroscience is an interdisciplinary field that studies the relations between culture, brain and mind. It studies how culture as an amalgam of values affect individual brain and gene expression. Cultural neuroscientists argue that the inner working of the brain is affected by the environment and the environment is complete only with the individual brain's perception of the outside. The socio-cultural experience is an important factor that is involved in genetic expression and brain working. This field puts forward an innovative approach to bridge social sciences and biological science. Robert Sapolsky's Behave: The Biology of Humans at Our Best and Worst is a bestseller in popular science that throws light upon individual and group behaviour in terms of neural circuits. Cultural neuroscientists are interested in politics also. In the US, cultural scientists conducted fMRI of Republicans and Democrats and identified different cognitive styles and neural structures. The ideological differences correlate to differences in neural activity. The emergent field of spiritual neuroscience focuses on the relationship between the brain and religion. "Neurotheology is multidisciplinary in nature and includes the field of theology, religious studies, religious experience and practice, philosophy, cognitive science, neuroscience, psychology and anthropology" (Sayadmansour, 52). The study aims to uncover the responses of the brain towards the positive and negative aspects of religion. Transcendental spiritual experiences like stigmata and afterlife vision are also areas of interest for the researchers.

The objectification of the brain should be perceived with caution. The neuropharmacological innovations mostly result in the well being of society, the question of ethics is something that needs attention. The interventions in the brain have the potential to control and minimize the autonomy of individuals. Individuals are assessed on the basis of intelligence, emotional and spiritual quotients. Exposure to the knowledge created by the neuroscience of religion may lead to the loss of the spiritual self. The tendency to reduce everything in terms of the brain should be discouraged. " While no one doubts that popularizing neuroscience is a positive good, neuroethics has been legitimately worried about the possibilities of misinformation. These include worries about the 'seductive allure' of neuroscience and of misleading and oversimplified media coverage of complex scientific questions" (Roskies "Neuroethics").

Works Cited

Chen, James. "Neuroeconomics." Investopedia, 6 Sept 2021,
www.investopedia.com/terms/n/neuroeconomics.asp

Doidge, Norman. Preface, The Brain That Changes Itself: Stories of Personal
Triumph from the Frontiers of Brain Science. Kindle ed., Viking Press,
2007.

Gaedtke, Andrew. "Neuromodernism." Modern Fiction Studies, vol. 61, no. 2,
Summer 2015, pp. 271-294. JSTOR,
www.jstor.org/stable/10.2307/26421793.

Harrell, Eben. "Neuromarketing: What You Need to Know." Harvard Business
Review, 23 Jan 2019,
hbr.org/2019/01/neuromarketing-what-you-need-to-know

Katz, Stephen."Embodied Memory: Aging, Neuroculture and the Genealogy
of Mind." Occasion: Interdisciplinary Studies in Humanities, Stanford
University Division of Literatures Cultures and Languages, vol 4, 2012
arcade.stanford.edu/sites/default/files/article_pdfs/OCCASION_v04_Ka
tz_053112_0.pdf

Littlefield, Melissa M., and Jenell Johnson. "Theorizing the Neuroscientific
Turn - Critical Perspectives on a Translational Discipline." Introduction.

The Neuroscientific Turn: Transdisciplinarity in the Age of the Brain,
University of Michigan Press, 2012, pp 1- 25.
Meshberger, Frank Lynn, and Tony. B Rich. "Explaining the Hidden Meaning
of Michelangelo's Creation of Adam." Microneurosurgical International
Group,
www.microneurosurgery-roma.com/explaining-the-hidden-meaning-of[1]michelangelos-creation-of-adam/
Sayadmansour, Alireza. "Neurotheology: The relationship between brain and
religion." Iranian Journal of Neurology vol. 13,1 (2014): 52-55.
Roskies, Adina. "Neuroethics." The Stanford Encyclopedia of Philosophy, 3
March 2021, plato.stanford.edu/entries/neuroethics/

• • •

AN ANALYSIS OF ENGLISH LANGUAGE CURRICULUM AND EXAMINATION AS A TOOL OF EVALUATION BASED ON THE PRINCIPLES OF EDUCATION

Soya Francis Puvathingal

Assistant Professor, Department of English

Yeldo Mar Baselios College, Kothamangalam,

Affiliated to MG University & IELTS Trainer

Milwaukee Academy, Kothamangalam

ABSTRACT

This paper critically analyses the present curriculum, its mode of delivery, syllabus and the examination as a tool of evaluation followed in the English language teaching-learning process in the undergraduate levels based on the five principles of education that govern the efficiency of activities in the English language pedagogy. The Five Principles of education taken into account are as follows: (1) Principle of Learning by Doing (2) Principle of Child-centredness (3) Principle of Multisensory Appeal (4) Principle of Utility (5) Principle of School environment. Suggestions for improving the design and mode of delivery of the Curriculum, Syllabus and Examination system in the English language teaching-learning process to enhance the learners' proficiency in all four language skills, Speaking, Listening, Reading and Writing, are discussed.

Keywords: Curriculum, Syllabus, Examination, Evaluation, Pedagogy, English language teaching-learning, Learning by doing, Child-centredness, Multisensory appeal, Utility, School environment, Speaking, Listening, Reading, Writing.

● ● ●

An Analysis of English Language Curriculum and Examination as a Tool of Evaluation Based on The Principles of Education

1. Introduction

According to Arthur Cunningham, "Curriculum is a tool in the hands of the artist(teacher) to mould his material (pupils) according to his ideals (aims and objectives) in his studio (school)." (Dr K.Sivarajan, 2007, 406). The term 'Curriculum' is derived from the Latin word 'current which means 'path'.In this sense curriculum is the path through which the student has to go forward to reach the goal envisaged by education. (Dr.K.Sivarajan, 2007, 405). However, the curriculum is understood in a narrow sense as a group of subjects prescribed for study in a particular course. The curriculum is not synonymous with the syllabus. The curriculum is a broad term as it encompasses the resources of an educational institution including its infrastructure, library, teachers and instructional materials, classroom activities, co-curricular activities and evaluation system, that is the totality of experiences an educand is exposed to within and outside the campus. The syllabus is specific as it includes the details of the study, the hierarchical order of presenting the content and forms the basis for writing textbooks, preparing teacher's guide and planning lessons. The syllabus is an integral part of the curriculum. `Evaluation´ is the process by which we judge the quality of something. It is the process of determining the extent to which an objective is achieved or the thing evaluated possesses the qualities envisaged."(Dr.K.Sivarajan, 2007, 03). Evaluation is the continuous assessment of the overall development of the personality of the educand. Examination, one of the tools of evaluation, measures only academic achievement. (J.C.Aggarwal, 2001, 355).

2. A Critical Analysis of the Curriculum, Syllabus and Examination followed in the English

Languages classes in the Undergraduate Level :

This paper evaluates the Curriculum, Syllabus and Examination based on the five principles of education. The Principle of Learning by Doing emphasizes the importance of an Activity-centred curriculum. Learning a language, being an artist requires a lot of practice to master it. (Dr.K.Sivarajan, 2012, 512). According to Comenius, "Whatever has to be learnt must be learnt by doing." (Dr K.Sivarajan, 2007, 410). But, unfortunately, teachers, in a rush to finish the syllabus tend to forget the importance of acting as a medium of imparting knowledge, attitude as well as skills and adopt verbal teaching. As Pestalozzi declared "Verbal system of teaching neither suits the faculties of the child nor the circumstances of life." (Dr K.Sivarajan, 2007, 411). The Syllabus is also designed in such a way that verbal teaching is given emphasis.

According to the principle of Child-centredness, the classroom activities should be child-centred, not teacher-centred or subject-centred. (Dr.K.Sivarajan, 2012, 513). In the English classrooms, the educand hardly gets an opportunity for discourse and he or she is usually fated to remain a passive learner. The Principle of Multisensory Appeal is very significant in language learning. Proficiency in language means proficiency in the four skills; Listening, Speaking, Reading and Writing. (Dr.K.Sivarajan, 2012, 512). Speaking and Listening are interrelated while there is a close relationship between Reading and Writing. Speaking and Listening skills are to be developed simultaneously Similarly, the Reading and Writing skills are to be acquired simultaneously. But, the present mode of curriculum delivery is inadequate in providing a multisensory appeal in English Language classes.

According to the Principle of School environment, the school environment should promote the speaking, listening, reading and writing abilities of students. (Dr.K.Sivarajan, 2012, 515). Most of the educational institutions lack the resources and infrastructure to promote the four language skills. The lectures are usually delivered in the mother tongue even in English classes in most of the institutions. Since the medium of communication and instruction is mostly in the mother tongue, students are denied an opportunity to develop the four language skills. Besides, during the examination, there is a provision for the students to write the answers to the questions in the subjects in their mother tongue. The Principle of Utility states that the students will show genuine interest in learning English if they are convinced of its utility in future life. (Dr K.Sivarajan, 2012, 515). Unfortunately, no initiatives are taken to make the students understand the importance of the English language as the window to the world, especially to the west and hence students are least interested in developing the four language skills (Speaking, Listening, Reading and Writing) in the undergraduate level.

3. Suggestions for restructuring the Curriculum, Syllabus and Examination to enable the students to master the four skills of Language.

A shift from the teacher-centred curriculum to the child-centred curriculum is the need of the hour for grooming the students to use the English language in real-life situations. So, apart from including prose, poetry and drama in the syllabus of the English Common Course, the syllabus should also include activity-oriented materials that enhance speaking, listening, reading and writing skills like Note making, Notice writing, Letter writing, Essay writing, Story writing, Writing scripts for mini mellow dramas, Writing reviews of books and films, Writing Reports, Listening and Reading comprehension, Tips for Effective Public Speaking and so on. English movies can be included in the syllabus as it is an attractive strategy to teach all four language skills and thereby providing a multisensory appeal. Students should be given ample opportunities for discourse in English in the classroom. This would enable the learners to enrich their vocabulary and learn the rules and principles of language by themselves. In the acquisition of English as a second language, a language laboratory equipped with electronic devices provides the learner with an opportunity to listen to the right accent, pronunciation, tone and rhythm of the English language. So, a Language Laboratory is mandatory in educational institutions. ICT enabled classrooms are important to deliver the curriculum effectively.

Teachers should convince the students of the growing importance of acquiring proficiency in the English language as it is a language for higher education, employment, trade, library, Science and technology. Since most of the students wish to do their higher studies in the European countries, it is mandatory for them to clear IELTS (International English Language Testing System) in which all the four language skills are assessed. Hence, the existing Curriculum and Examination pattern that give undue emphasis on memory, promoting rote learning should be restructured in such a way as to evaluate all four language skills. Oral tests should be given to students and if possible with a native speaker as the examiner. This would definitely boost the confidence of the students. Moreover, the medium of instruction and communication should be in English to provide the educand, an environment conducive for English Language learning.

Conclusion

Since Curriculum is the heart and crux of an educational institution, the resources and infrastructure of an educational institution should support the effective implementation of the curriculum. To make an objective evaluation of the effectiveness of a curriculum in terms of the achievement of its immediate as well as long term objectives, a curriculum evaluation is essential. It should not be done for evaluating students solely for the purpose of certification. The modern teaching-learning process calls for a child-centred approach. So, it is the need of the hour to remove the deadwood and update an existing curriculum so that the learners can slot in anywhere around the globe.

Works Cited

Dr.K.Sivarajan. Trends And Developments In Modern Educational Practices. University of
Calicut, 2007.

J.C.Aggarwal. Principles, Methods and Techniques of Teaching. Vikas Publishing House Pvt
Ltd, New Delhi, 2001.

Dr.K.Sivarajan. English Language Education. University of Calicut, 2012.

Hopkins, Dave. Smooth Moves. TEFL International.

Curriculum and Instruction. Indira Gandhi National Open University.

• • •

THE UNHEARD VOICE OF DALIT MOTHERS: A COMPARATIVE STUDY OF THE SELECT POEMS OF WAMAN NIMBALKAR AND JYOTI LANJEWAR

Ms. Jeremy Jain Babu

Assistant Professor, Department of English

Kristu Jyoti College of Management and Technology, Changanacherry.

ABSTRACT

Dalit literature is about the seemingly endless struggle of humanity for justice and survival. Dalit women when compared to Dalit men are marginalised both as the lower caste and the other sex. Being Dalit writers, Waman Nimbalkar and Jyoti Lanjewar explicitly presents the suppressed, the oppressed and the degraded position of their mothers in the poems which are titled alike as "Mother". Both the poets portray their mothers as strong women who despite hardships and discrimination provide food and education to their children. The hope within the mothers for a better world devoid of discrimination is the highlight of the poems. The aesthetic quality of this Dalit poetry is its humanist ideology and the mode of expression of the familiar but unfamiliar content. This article is a comparative study on the doubly marginalised state of women as depicted in the two poems "Mother" by Waman Nimbalkar and "Mother"by Jyoti Lanjewar. It emphasises the need for the upliftment of Dalit women through the elimination of caste and gender prejudice and the role of post-colonial feminism in creating a world where all people have equal rights and opportunities.

Keywords: Dalit poetry, Double Marginalisation, Dalit feminism.

• • •

The Unheard Voice of Dalit Mothers: A Comparative Study of the Select Poems of Waman Nimbalkar and Jyoti Lanjewar

Introduction

The gruesome system of discrimination formed by the intersection of caste and gender discrimination makes a Dalit woman victim of severe violence. They are denied choices and freedom in all spheres of life. Denial of justice, education, health and other services are presented in the personal narrative poems of Waman Nimbalkar and Jyoti Lanjewar. It focuses on creating awareness about the obstacles faced by Dalit women. Both the poems "Mother" by Waman Nimbalkar and "Mother" by Jyoti Lanjewar are English translations of Marathi Dalit poetry. Dalit literature as stated by Darshani Dadawala in *Dalit Literature-Concept, Origin, Features* "...is characterised by its fundamental criticism of the caste system and all kind of discrimination and by its call for destroying social hierarchies. It is the literature of social and political commitment that challenges the status quo." (13) This research article projects Dalit women who are the untouchables as different from the upper caste woman who enjoys Brahminical privileges. Those unheard voices and soft whispers speak a lot about the neglect faced by women who are oppressed on different levels of the hierarchical society. Their caste, creed, race, religion suppresses them in addition to the gender role that the patriarchy entails upon them.

Dalit Women as Daily Wage Earners

Waman Nimbalkar reflects a pessimistic note and hopelessness in waiting with an empty stomach when the neighbouring houses have the kitchen fires burning. The poet persona goes back to his childhood, recollecting nuances from his daily routine of waiting for his mother to return from her work. The aroma of food gives a pleasant feast to the children's nostrils when the stomach burns in darkness.

Kitchen – fires too. Bhakris beat out.

Vegetables, gruel cooked.

In our nostrils, the smell of food. In our stomachs, darkness (4-6)

The mother collects firewood from the forest which is then sold so that the children never remained hungry. The mother in Jyoti Lanjewar's poem is portrayed as a strong lady who takes up different kinds of daily wage works to look after her family. She works with the road construction crew, with the building construction crew and as household help. She ignores her growling and grumbling stomach and the thirsty throat while burning her energy to feed her children. The poet has never seen her wearing a gold necklace and bangles, fancy sandals and gold-bordered saris. Gold as a materialistic prospect is unattainable for a Dalit woman. The minimum wage that they receive for working the whole day under the scorching sun is inadequate and insufficient for buying enough groceries. She keeps herself half- fed so that there is something remaining for the breakfast.

To make coarse bread and a little something

To feed everybody, but half-fed yourself

So there'd be a bit in the morning... (39-41)

Amanat Khullar in his article in *The Wire*, "Average Dalit Woman Dies 14.6 Years Younger than Woman from Higher Caste" highlights the United Nations recent report on the 2030 Agenda for Sustainable Development regarding Indian Dalit women: According to the report, in India, a woman aged 20-24 from a poor, rural household is over five times as likely as one from a rich urban household to marry before the age of 18. There is also an over 30 times likelihood of the former as compared to the latter to have never attended school, 1.3 times not having access to money of her own and 2.3 times not having a say in spending.

Poverty and Deteriorating Health Condition of Dalit Mother

Waman Nimbalkar visualises his mother as a shadow that is heavy with the burden on her head which makes her leg stagger. The burden could be the weight of the bundle of the firewood that she carries on her head or the weight of the responsibility of the family that she has to manage almost single-handed. She is thin and dark due to a lack of nutritious food and tiresome work. Dalit women are undernourished and thus the chances for them to meet with death during childbirth are high. Poverty is at its peak that the Dalit mothers sacrifices their pleasures for their children to see them happy and in good health. Jyoti Lanjewar's mother hangs her little ones in a cradle on the acacia tree near her workplace so that she could give "a sweaty kiss to the naked child"(14) amidst her work. A Dalit family commonly has children due to a lack of family planning and proper education. These women are subjected to several numbers of pregnancies and delivery of the babies in an unhealthy atmosphere that deteriorates their health. They are automatons that perform multiple works like taking care of children, doing household chores and earning money through odd daily wage jobs.

Dalit Women as Victims of Sexual Assault

A turn of events takes place in Waman Nimbalkar's poem when the mother is bitten by a snake. The two women who brought the mother back to the house with her leg bandaged explained, "He raised his hood. He struck her. He slithered away."(17) This refers o the dangerous work atmosphere in which a Dalit woman has to work. This line could also be a connotation for rape where the 'He' mentioned is the snake who is the rapist. A similar situation is also faced by the mother of Jyoti Lanjewar where she covers herself with the sari which is torn and stitched several times asking the one who looked at her with lustful eyes, "Don't you have a mother or a sister?"(49) She boldly chased away everyone who nudged at her with her slippers. Sexual advances are made by the employer which the Dalit woman could possibly not avoid in certain situations due to fear of losing her job which could ultimately lead her family to starvation and death. Dalit women are thus crushed under the wheels of the caste system, the internal patriarchy inside their own community and the external patriarchy of the mainstream society. When the mother of Waman Nimbalkar failed to protect herself the mother of Jyoti Lanjewar sets an example for other Dalit women to be bold and courageous in protecting themselves.

Dalit Women as Self Sacrificing Mothers

There is grief in the tone of Waman Nimbalkar when he explains the failed attempt in trying charms, spells and medicine to cure his mother and sadness in the words of Jyoti Lanjewar when she says that she could never see her mother in a gold-bordered sari. There is guilt in this daughter in her inability to buy her mother a gold-bordered sari when she attained financial stability years after the death of her mother. As a dutiful daughter, she fulfils her mother's last wish to fight for Baba until her last breath through her creative poetry. On the other hand, Waman Nimbalkar overcomes his grief by buying firewood, whenever he spots a thin woman with firewood on her head in remembrance of his mother and her struggles to feed him and his siblings. The mother's only aim was to see her children joyful and successful. Saving a little for her children to buy candy was the only thing that she could gift them. She advised them to get an education and hence to transform the society. They live in shacks that lack basic propriety development. Their huts remain in darkness when the 8neighbouring houses are bright with power supplies. With the money she earned by washing clothes and cleaning utensils at different households she could only afford the essentialities like salt and oil.

> I have seen you
> evenings, untying the end of your sari
> for the coins to buy salt and oil,
> putting five-paise coin
> on a little hand
> saying "go eat candy"(27-32)

Unlike the self-sacrificing deeds of an upper-caste mother, a Dalit woman's struggle as a mother is more sacrificial because of her marginalised state as a lower caste woman. The candy that the little one buys with the five-paise coin given by the mother is more of value than the box of chocolate that a well off child gets as a present. Swayamdipta Das upon concluding her research article "Dalit Feminism and Baburao Bagul's Short Story 'Mother'" projects the mother's state of being. "Her suffering, humiliation and final estrangement from her son also reflect how the forces of caste and gender are linked together and work in inter-related ways. Thus this story is not only an attack against the caste system in India but also the male patriarchal system which together works in many inter-related ways. Caste, class and gender differences work in an inter-related way to keep a few sections of the society suppressed in the hierarchical system. This stratified ranking of the members is a result of the power structure that rules the world only to benefit the people in the higher levels of the system. Thus the relation between the minority and majority is always strangled since the social structure always favours the majority.

Dalit Women and Liberation Movement

The breeding ground for Dalit feminists was the Long March of March 1979, the Marathwada Riots and the Worli Riots in which many Dalits were killed. Women participated in the protest movement opposing the government, in their decision not to rename Marathwada University in honour of Dr. Babasaheb B.R. Ambedkar. The mothers in both the poems are universal and they represent each and every Dalit mother. The pillar of the revival movement of Dalits from their oppression, Dr. Babasaheb B.R. Ambedkar was commonly and affectionately nicknamed Baba and Bhim. The mother in Jyoti Lanjewar's "Mother"fought for her rights, went to jail with upright head and shoulders and remarked boldly to the police on the martyrdom of her only son, "If I had two or three sons, I would be fortunate / They would fight on" (73-74). In spite of illiteracy and tedious labour, she dedicated her life to her children and their future by being a strong factor in the Dalit liberation movement started by Ambedkar. She was generous enough to give the money she earned toDhikshabhumi, the site of conversion to Buddhism as it propounded unity and equality unlike the caste system of their religion. Her final words in the death bed were:

"Live in unity...fight for Baba...don't forget him..."
And with your very last breath

"Jai Bhim"(80-82)

Being a staunch follower of Ambedkar, she encouraged her children to fight for equality and justice. She reminded them that the only means to attain freedom is to be well educated because education has the power to change the world into a better place. The plight of Dalit women and their children and the struggle to overcome it, expressed in the first-person narrative is the essence of the poems "Mother"by Waman Nimbalakar and "Mother" by Jyoti Lanjewar.

Conclusion

Voicing the problems faced by Dalit women, Waman Nimbalkar and Jyothi Lanjewar creates a pathway for the future dalit feminists to follow their foremothers in gaining equality in terms of caste and gender. The two Dalit women are portrayed from the perspective of a man, the son as in Waman Nimbalkar's poem and from the perspective of another woman the daughter as in Jyoti Lanjewar's poem makes the reader analyse the suppression from different viewpoints. Robert J.C.Young in *Postcolonialism: A Very Short Introduction*,throws light on the issues that are still being faced by these women "it will highlight the degree to which women are still working against a colonial legacy that was itself powerfully patriarchal- institutional, economic, political and ideological". Equity and equality cannot be achieved without universal sisterhood and universal sisterhood can only be possible if women of all race colour and creeds come together and fight as one. Postcolonial Feminism ensures ways by which people stand by each other to uphold their rights and needs. Art and literature as a mainstream field of study paves way for the success of this true cause with a higher social, political and economic impact. When these structures of discrimination are demolished completely; the world will become a better place not just for some people but for all.

Works Cited

Adarkar, Priya, translator." Mother", *Poisoned Bread: Translations From Modern Marathi Dalit Literature,* Arjun Dangle, editor. By

Waman Nimbalkar, New Delhi, Orient Blackswan Private Limited, 2009.pp 43,44

Dadawala, Darshini. "Dalit Literature- Concept, Origin and Features." *IJELLH*, Vol. IV, Issue II, February 2016. pp 11-13

Das, Swayamdipta. "Dalit Feminism and Baburao Bagul's Short Story 'Mother'". *Indian Ruminations*, 5 Jan.2015, http://www.indianruminations.com/research-article-contents/dalit-feminism-and-baburao-baguls-short-story-mother-swayamdipta-das-kolkata/

Khullar Amant."Average Dalit Woman Dies 14.6 Years Younger than Women from Higher Castes". *The Wire,* 15 Feb.2018, www.thewire.in/224546/averge-dalit-woman-dies-14-6-years-younger-than-women-from-higher-castes-finds-un-report/

Martinez, Sylvie, et.al., translators. "Mother", *An Anthology of Dalit Literature.* Mulk Raj Anand and Eleanor Zelliot, editors. By Jyoti Lanjewar, New Delhi, Gyan Publication

House, 1992. pp 99-103

Young, Robert JC. *Postcolonialism: A Very Short Introduction.* New York. Oxford

University Press. 2003

Bio-Note

Ms. Jeremy Jain Babu is an Assistant Professor in the Department of English at Kristu Jyoti College of Management and Technology, Changanacherry. She pursues her research degree as a part-time scholar at Newman College, Thodupuzgha (affiliated to Mahatma Gandhi University, Kottayam), under the guidance of Dr. Jinu George (Associate Professor, St. Peter's College, Kolencherry). Her interest and area of research reside in Food Literature, Transnational Culture Studies and Gender Studies. She has qualified GATE (Graduate Aptitude Test in Engineering) for Humanities and Social Sciences awarded by IIT, Bombay in 2021. She graduated with remarkable scholastic records in M. A. English Literature from Loyola College (Autonomous) Chennai in 2018. She has one research publication and several research papers to her credit. Her expertise extends also to the field of blogging and journalistic writing. She served as a journalist intern at The Times of India Bureau, Thiruvananthapuram in 2017. As a passionate writer, she blogs at www.theathoolikaonline.wordpress.com

• • •

CHAPTER XXV

DISCOURSE OF MUSLIM WOMEN: READING LATIFA'S MY FORBIDDEN FACE

Anet Susan John

Assistant Professor, Department of English

Ilahia College of Arts &Science, Pezhakkappilly

• • •

Women have been a ground where different ideologies and various socio-culture and political movements have been communicated, defined and redefined and manifested themselves they have been using this ground and turning it towards their own gain she had different names and identities under various contexts. Symbols of women have been the products of narrations and histories, representation of various contexts manifestation of ideological desires and constructs of discourses and intentions it is generally " understood' that US invasion of Afghanistan is justified and legitimized by propagating the notion of emancipating Muslim women the particular policies of emancipation is not a contemporary phenomenon as it has similarities to the 19Th-century colonialism in India and Algeria were domination was naturalized in the name of saving women from the native, as Gayatri Chakraborthy Spivak commented, " Why men saving brown women from brown men" (Spivak 1988-280). *My Forbidden Face: Growing Up Under Taliban: A Young Women's Story* written by Latifa is a particular text that visualizes the contemporary role of western feminism in supporting US invasion in Afghanistan under the rhetoric of saving women it also attempts to introduce the idea of Islamic feminism and dimension in thoughts and discourse.

Postcolonial feminist discourses came into existence by location colonialism as a cultural phenomenon in which women become subjectivities and one of the chief instruments that serve to maintain power. Generally, feminist postcolonial theory is more concerned with the problematic relationship between western women and broadly indigenous women (Levis and Mills 172). These theorists mainly look at the language and way of enforcing the stereotypes of colonized women which work parallel to imperialism. Critics like Ania Loompa and Gayatri Chakraborthy Spivak accuse feminist discourses of having supported the 'liberating mission' of colonial Britain through which the legitimacy of colonialism is maintained.

Feminist postcolonialism has been often concerned with the modes and extends to which representation and languages are crucial to identity formation and construction of subjectivity. Feminist critics like Spivak looked into the literature of the 19th century within the context of colonialism and its impacts on making colonial subjectivity. In her essay, " Three Women's Text and a Critique of Imperialism" (1985) Spivak recovers the marginalized character of Bertha Mason a Jamaican born female who produces the white subjectivity of the white Jane the recapturing of sidelined characters and the political mission that these characters accomplish are the main concerns of feminist postcolonial critics.

My Forbidden Face, the memoir written by Latifa, tells the story of a young girl from Kabul and her life under the domination of the Taliban. It documents the eventful Taliban rule in Afghanistan in 1996 till the invasion of Afghanistan by the US. Written autobiographically the novel archives the personal story of Latifa along with the Taliban rule and its after mark, especially on women the novel was written after Latifa's escape to France with her family through a secret mission operated by a French-based Afghan resistance group and magazine Elle.

While recording her own story under the Taliban rule Latifa explores the entire modern history of Afghanistan and sagas of wars and foreign invasions she vividly explains the Russian invasion in Afghanistan and the native resistance against it. Her own brother, Wahid, has been actively participating in these national political processes. According to Latifa, her family has been a microcosm of the changing socio-political context of Afghanistan in her family Wahid who was settled in Russia was once a pro-Russian supporter and became a reputed officer in the army. Her elder sister, Chakila was a journalist and a great source of information and motivation for Latifa, her mother is a doctor who is in her late years working for poor patients. Besides them, she has a sister and brother and her father was a businessman who was supportive to all of his children.

She also narrates the resistance against Taliban operated by conducting secret schools and gatherings inside the households. She herselfcomes forwarded to teach small children secretly in her own home as it was banned by the Taliban and punishments for violation included death sentences too. Actually, this mission gives a new hope in her life which she thought to be closed under the Taliban. In the meantime, she gets an invitation from a French association that requests her to visit France and give an honest account about the Taliban rule her family forces her to accept the request and with her father and mother she flees to France where she meets many persons and continues her ambassadorial mission. This infuriates the Taliban and they control her house and announce public order against her and her family. Her memoir ends when the US invasion was about to take place in Afghanistan and she desires to go back to her homeland with dreams of freedom and democracy for her country, Afghanistan.

In classical European colonialism, a particular kind of knowledge about a specific race of people produced by a particular group of writers has been a significant phenomenon that has specific purposes and intentions to the broad discourse of colonialism. The discourse of Orientalism, a specific form of knowledge about the oriental produced and articulated by Orientalists underwent serious critical analysis by Edwards Said in his pioneering work *Orientalism*. This particular kind of knowledge that compromises the European fantasy of the 'other' was important in legitimizing the domination and colonial rule. These groups of writers were the products of colonial ideological machinery that constructed languages and discourses to justify its existence and power. Hamid Dabashi conceptualizes the idea of 'native informer' in relation to western, American invasions of the Middle East. According to him, native informers' are a group of intellectuals/ writers who have "digested and internalized" language of rationalized orientalists of early European colonialism and they, native informers speak it with the authority of natives. Debashish conceptualizes 'native Informer' as a group of diasporic writers having Muslim origin actively writing on conditions of Muslim women in the Middle East and demanding the political intervention in the homeland (Dabashi 12).

The diasporic writers who serves the US imperial project of Middle East invasion by providing authentic knowledge through their narratives went under the critical reading of feminist scholars like Leila Ahammed, Seba Mahamood and Lila Abu Lughod. Dabashi takes another angle by terming these writers as 'native informers' due to their crucial position in producing knowledge about the Muslim countries in facilitating the 21st century's imperial project in this context the 'native informers' role is to provide an authorial voice on the behaves of these rights and shape public opinion and building consensus and facilitating war. Native informers are there to convince the public that invading and bombing, occupying the homelands of others is a good and very moral thing in terms of human rights, and, especially woman's rights. After the official announcement of the war on terror and the invasion of Afghanistan as its immediate offshoot, the global readership has received a series of books narrating the lives and experiences in Muslim countries. What is interesting is that most of them are about Muslim women and are written by women writers. These writers, as Dabashi's analysis shows, provides serious raw materials that vouchsafe for human rights violations and woman's rights based on which the invasion has been justified. Thus, the writings of Muslim women and their texts must be analyzed critically and located in this context.

Latifa's memoir about her life under Taliban rule becomes problematic in this critical context of the role of native informers and their role in providing support for the invasion, especially in Muslim countries with its rhetoric of women's rights. Latifa and her work have serious resonance with some other texts which are also published in this period, especially in the selection of their genre and themes they tried to narrate. *My Forbidden Face* has to be critically in the broad context of imperialism and its new conceptual machinery of the native informer. In spite of these external / wider complexities *My Forbidden Face* fails itself in the text and confronts serious biases in her perspectives from her description about her family, it is clear to the reader that she was born in a well established middle-class family where everybody was well educated and well settled. She describes herself as a liberal and so is her family, and, she has been exercising considerable freedom in the family. But the way, Latifa tries to establish her identity as a liberal, modern city dweller, middle class and independent is to be looked at critically. She draws her images of modern and liberal by making a sharp contrast with typical Afghan Women. She makes a dichotomy between herself and 'other women. While she describes her family she makes one thing clear: " I have had the good fortune to be born into a loving and united family, at once religious and liberal" (Latifa 6).

Here Latifa seems to be very proud in a family which is liberal as well as religious. She tries to establish herself as not a traditional nor a conservative person especially in terms of her dress, she always make a comparison between her "jogging trousers, a polo neck or pulls over and trainers" and the burqa wore rural women as "voluminously robbed figures in the street" and giving nicknames like "bottles" or "upside-down cauliflowers" and "storage sacks". (21 78 134) it is quite surprising that Latifa who observes everything about her country, its political history, assassinations and the foreign invasion seems to be ignorant of the relation of Afghan society to the ideology of Islam and their cultural and social traits and specificities. Latifa as an ambassador of afghan women flees to France with help of a magazine and she is forced to stay there as their home is captured by the Taliban. Staying there in France she dreams of democracy and liberation of Afghanistan that is achieved with the international intervention in her homeland she predicts the future of her country in this way: " ...as soon as the last Tali hung up his black turban and I can be free women in a free country " (Latifa 179). As she finishes her Taliban saga thus: " I finish my modest tale at the hour when guns begin to speak in my place. They always have" (Latifa 175).

Though the tale started pessimistically, she comes to an end where she is optimistic about the new changes in the country. Both the starting and ending of her memoir have a single feature in which both are in relation to two great events in Afghan history. She starts her story the very day the Taliban had established their rule and she ends it in the context of the US invasion of Afghanistan. What makes it interesting about the author is that she, after 13 years (2001-2014) , remains in anonymity even after the overthrow of the Taliban which is accused as a major hindrance in identifying the real name of Latifa. Latifa cannot answer any questions as she was hidden in her "forbidden face" and too covered to see the new white Talibs without black turbans in her homelands.

To some extend it's significant that few critics of feminism have attempted to redefine the accepted perspectives that have been used in defining Muslim women and in addressing their issues. had it been the veil that prevented women in Afghanistan from exercising their rights and the main imposition of the Taliban then why wouldn't the women throw away their veil even after the removal of the Taliban? It is important to be in conformity with what we are supporting and what the issues are that have gone into it. Saba Mahmood wants the entire feminist scholarship for being in support of imperial strategies and be participatory in the war market by [proving necessary support in the ideological rhetoric of women's rights and saving them. She reminds us how the discourse of feminism has been hijacked to serve an imperial project and goes on to want that " Unless feminisms rethink their complicity in this project... feminism runs the risk of becoming more of the handmaiden of empire in our age than a trenchant critic of the

Euro-American will to power" (Mahamood 808)

Works Cited

Abu-Lughod, Lila."Do Muslim Women Really Need Saving? Anthropological Reflections on Cultural Relativism and Its Others." *American Anthropologist* 104.3(2002):783-790. Web.10 May 2009.

---*Remaking Women: Feminism and Modernity in the Middle East.* Princeton, NJ: Princeton UP,1998

Ashcroft, Bill, Gareth Griffiths, Helen Tiffin.Post-*Colonial Studies: The Key Concepts.* Abingdon, Oxon: Routledge,2013.14-240.

Dabashi, Hamid. *Brown Skin, White Masks.* London: Pluto, 2011

Latifa, and Chekeba Hachemi.*My Forbidden Face: Growing Up Under the Taliban: A Young Women's Story.* New York: Hyperion, 2011.

Lewis, Reina, and Sarah Mills. *Feminist Post Colonial Theory: A Reader.* Edinburgh:Edinburgh UP,2003.

Mahmood, Saba. *Politics of Piety: The Islamic Revival and The Feminist Subject.* Princeton, NJ: Princeton UP,2005.

Said, Edward W. Orientalism.London: Penguin,2003 (1978).

Spivak, Gayathri Chakraborthy. "Three Women's Texts and A Critique of Imperialism." *Critical Inquiry* 12.1,1985.243-26. Web 15 May 2019

---A Critic of Postcolonial Reason: Toward A History of the Vanishing Present. London: Harvard University Press. 1999.

CHAPTER XXVI

GENDER SUBVERSION

Jitha Mohan MA, M.Ed, NET- JRF

Wikipedia defines Subversion as " a process by which the values and principles of a system in place are contradicted or reversed, in an attempt to transform the established social order and its structures of power, authority, hierarchy, and social norms" (Web, Anonymous) It can be as simple as clothing or as great as a public act of defiance. But those are not the only ones. Art, sculptures, speeches, songs or lifestyle choices can also become acts of subversion.

Gender has played a very important role in how people live and how people look at life. The most common form of distinction that human beings are subjected to is that of gender. People are expected to act and react in the way suitable to their gender and that has shaped society today. "The Filipino woman of the pre-Hispanic era was a chanter, a priestess, and a warrior. Her predominant role was unquestioned. As priestess and healer, she performed ritual dances and songs during weddings and funerals"(Web, Tarrayo). With the arrival of the Spanish, this changed. Women were seen as secondary citizens, her place was at home, looking after the children and her man. In many cases, the board room for the man and the kitchen for the women became a golden rule.

Gender Subversion is one of the most common forms of subversion owing to the fact that the society has become patriarchal or in some cases masculine gender oriented. Laurie A. Rudman and Peter Glick, professors of Psychology in their book The Social Psychology of Gender state that the "Differences between men and women trace back to culture more than nature. These differences nevertheless become real because social forces compel men and women to enact or perform gender". (8) Questioning the stereotypes of gender or standing against it doesn't often happen in loud and bold ways. Sometimes it happens in very simple or subtle ways that are often overlooked.

The subversion of gender that happens in different stages of a Filipino woman's life is discussed in this paper. A woman goes through different phases in life as a maiden, wife, mother, widow etc. In each of these junctures, she is expected to behave in a certain way and there are some women who subvert from the role that is devised for them.

The short story Desire was written by Pas Latorena talks of stereotyping a woman's body. There is a deeply existing cultural message embedded in almost all cultures and countries of the world that a woman is expected to have a particular body type to attract men. There are references to age-old practices in which a woman is insisted to learn particular things in order to groom herself in a particular way. Ovid's Art of Love, written in the 2nd century BC goes into great detail on how a woman is to conduct herself, what type of makeup she has to use in order to look presentable, how to sit, walk and talk in order to position themselves in the poses that are most attractive to their physical appearance. "Women the world over are pushed toward impossibly high standards of beauty and receive strong cultural messages that their bodies are unacceptable as they are, thus promoting a variety of body-altering procedures." (Jackman, 1999 SPG) The binding of feet in the Chinese culture, the usage of corsets etc are some examples of how women have risked themselves to alter their bodies to better suit society's expectations. There were recorded cases of feet so bent that the women were unable to walk without assistance and cases of asphyxiation due to excessive pulling of the corsets. This modification of body in order to be socially acceptable or desirable has continued to modern days in the form of high heels and push up bras in the lowest forms to cosmetic surgeries and breast implants in the extremities.

Desire talks of a woman with an enthralling body but a homely face that is more masculine with a broad forehead and slanted eyes. She feels dirty as men look at her with lust rather than love which she deeply desires. To prevent herself from being the object of fascination for men, she wears loose and shapeless clothes. This turns away the men who admired her as they thought she became fat and shapeless. She turns to write to vent out her feelings. Her airy sketches catch the eyes of a white man. He is attracted to her humour and writes a letter of appreciation to encourage her. Her nonsensical answers endear him and they start a correspondence that quickly escalates into friendship. The first time they meet, she is convinced that he will see her ugly face and shapeless body and their correspondence will stop. Much to her surprise he sees her as a very different woman, a brilliant mind with a comely body and thinks nothing of it. As their relationship grows and she is finally sure that he sees her for her inner beauty and not just outward appearance, she decides to dress properly as she wants him to know all aspects of who she is. But that desire to be loved comes crumbling down when he sees her in a dress that flatters her body. His eyes, which normally looks into her eyes raked her body. He confessed that he loved her body the moment he saw her in the dress that properly highlighted her curves.

The protagonist is a woman whose body is naturally so beautiful that she is always approached by men out of lust. Her face had what was called masculine traits but from neck down, she was a beauty that sculptors would dream of making. From her neck to her small feet, she was perfect. Her bust was full, and her breast rose up like twin roses in full bloom. Her waist was slim as a young girl's hips seemed to have stolen the curve of the crescent moon. Her arms were shapely ending in small hands with fine tapering fingers that were the envy of her friends. Her legs with their trim ankles reminded one of those lifeless things seen in shop windows displaying the latest silk stockings. (Lorena, 1) She was what society deemed to be the epitome of feminine beauty, except for her face. The men flocked around her for her body and not for the woman she was inside. She longed for simple things that other women had, a lover who loved her for what she was and not for how she looked.

In a world where women go to great lengths to accentuate their beauty and physical appearance, she wanted to hide her physical attributes. She wanted to be liked and admired for her soul and for who she is. As a rebellion against society and the men who looked at her only for her outward appearance, she decides to cover up that which makes her desirable in the eyes of men. "She started wearing long, wide dresses that completely disfigured her. She gave up wearing the Filipino costume which outlined her body with startling accuracy" (Latorena, 3). As time passed, society had come to look at her as a figureless woman and thought that she has grown fat and shapeless.

She showed her subversion in refusing to dress up as society dictated. Though her looks were approved by society, she stood up for what she deemed to be important for her, not to be an object of desire but that of pure and unadulterated love. She is subversive, as she refuses to accept the belief of the society which states a woman is expecting women to catch the eye of men and hold it using any means possible. She looks for a man who looks at her soul that is permanent not the body that is temporary. She goes out of the way to ensure that.

Summer Solstice by Nick Joaquin is a story of how women use rituals as an act of subversion. The patriarchal society used religion with its dominant doctrines to push women to the margins. On the other hand, women use some of the religious rituals to take it back. They use it as an act of subversion as most pagan rituals are constructed in a way to maintain the balance between the masculine and feminine. "The Goddess movement is claimed to offer self-empowerment through an articulation of the female experience as divine, and to protest what are perceived to be patriarchal values that promote gender inequalities." (...)

The Moreta's family prepare to celebrate the Feast of St.John and Dona Lupeng finds that her cook is missing. She goes in search of her only to find her in a compromising position. The cook Amanda, who is normally timid with her husband is vocal and Entry, her husband who usually beats her at the slightest provocation is obliging to her wishes. Dona Lupe recounts the incident to her husband, You know how the brute treats her: she cannot say a word but he thrashes her. But this morning he stood as meek as a lamb while she screamed and screamed. He seemed actually in awe of her, do you know—actually afraid of her! (Joaquin, 2)

When she enquired Entoy said that Amanda was the representation of Tadtrin the night before and hence she should be treated with the reverence she deserves. The Tadtrin is a three-day pagan fertility ritual that takes place around the summer solstice which was later adapted to coincide with the festivities of St.John's day, dedicating the festivities to the Christian saint. Amanda who is always seen as subservient to her husband gains the upper hand in the relationship on the days of Tadtrin as the people believed that on the days of the summer solstice, when the women gather around the Beltane tree, women become one with the spirits and nature, therefore men have no claim over her as her husband and lord. She represents forces of nature and fertility in a concrete manner. Entoy further says, "The spirit is in her. She is the Tadtarin. She must do as she pleases. Otherwise, the grain would not grow, the trees would bear no fruit, the rivers would give no fish, and the animals would die."(Joaquin, 2)

Dona Lupeng is appalled at the idea that man has no control over women on the days of a ritual. As the family make their way to Paeng's grandfather's house, the procession of St. John crosses them. The procession is made of men and boys, screaming and dancing holding up a statue of St.John. She looks at the display of male arrogance and thinks of how men are courageous because the women give them the space to be so and how women are pushed to the background. Men occupy the place of prominence, not because they deserve it but because they are given the place by the women. It is then that she is reminded of the incident she witnessed in the morning. "She recalled, vindictively, this morning's scene at the stables: Amada naked and screaming in bed while from the doorway her lord and master looked on in meek silence." (Joaquin, 2)

In the evening as the children ran around the house playing, Guido, Paeng's cousin finds Dona Lupeng and strikes up a conversation about the festivities. He admits that he had been to the Tadtrin rituals the day before and the woman who was the representation of Tadtrin was beautiful. She laughs at that idea, stating that she was her cook and that she was fat and ugly. Gudio defends himself saying that she was beautiful as an old tree. There is the beauty of embracing nature. He goes on to describe the ritual, "I do not know. I can only feel it. And it frightens me. Those rituals come to us from the earliest dawn of the world. And the dominant figure is not the male but the female." (Joaquin, 2) He feels that the ritual is heavily centred on women. She denies it claiming that the festivals are a part of St.John's day to which he replies that the lord worshipped by those women are ancient gods who belonged to a time women were more powerful than men.

Guido acts as a subversive as he claims that it is the women who were powerful than men, contradicting the popular belief that men hold the power in the world while women are meant to be man's subordinates. He says, "The queen came before the king, and the priestess before the priest, and the moon before the sun." (Joaquin, 2). It was in later days that this popular belief was replaced with the thought process that men hold power over women. As the height of subversive behaviour, he kisses her shoes as she gets up to look for her children. "The young man, propping up his elbows, dragged himself forward on the ground and solemnly kissed the tips of her shoes. She stared down in sudden horror, transfixed—and he felt her violent shudder."(Joaquin, 2)

She is disturbed by the act as it stood against everything she was taught and told but at the same time, she was intrigued by the concept he put forth. She is silent and contemplative the entire ride home and her husband notices her silence and pensive look. He enquires if she was disturbed or offended by the presence of Guido. She replies in the affirmative and reveals that he had kissed her shoes. The couple gets into an argument on how a man should treat his woman. "A gentleman loves and respects woman. The cads and lunatics—they 'adore' the women."(Joaquin, 2) She asks what is wrong with a man adoring his woman. She was lost in thought about the conversation and asked to witness the last day of the ritual. When Paeng refuses to take her, she threatens to go with Amanda and her husband. Paeng agrees and takes her to the plaza to view the procession. The women came dancing, singing, and holding an image of St.John aloft. The Tadtrin, an old crone walked calmly before the crowd holding a wand in one hand and seedling in the other.

The ritual proceeded with the Tadtrin lying down in an imitation of death. Her body was covered in a shroud and the women around her covered their heads and wailed. After a beat and a silence, the woman woke up and held the seedling and the wand. The women surged around, singing, laughing and dancing. Soon the spectators joined them, Dona too shook her husband off and joined the primal urge, moving her limbs in a dance as old as the primitive Gods. He tries to hold on to her but she shakes him off and runs further deep into the crowd. He runs after her but when he is in the middle of the crowd, searching for her, he is beaten black and blue by the women as he came into the procession meant for women. He is rescued by his carriage driver who then sends people to retrieve Lupeng.

They reach their home, she with a smile on her face and he with his wounds aching and bleeding. He threatens to have her whipped for her behaviour stating, "Because you have behaved tonight like a lewd woman."(Joaquin, 2). She replies that he is not going to whip her for her behaviour but for the fact that he was injured by women because he went after her. She challenges him to whip her or accept that he adores her. He refuses to whip her stating that he loved and respected her. He threatened to do so in the spur of a moment. But she insists that neither of them can live in peace until they clear the matter between them. He finally gives in, sinks to his knees. "And he, in his dead voice: 'That I adore you. That I adore you. That I worship you. That the air you breathe and the ground you tread is so holy to me. That I am your dog, your slave"(Joaquin, 2). She asks him to crawl to her and moves slowly away from as him as he crawls to her without a moment's hesitation. She stands and offers her leg to him and he repeats what he called was the behaviours of rakes and cad, he kisses her feet. "He lifted his dripping face and touched his bruised lips to her toes; lifted his hands and grasped the white foot and kissed it savagely – kissed the step, the sole, the frail ankle"(Joaquin, 2)

In a time period where men had control over his wife to the extent of him being called her lord, master and husband, women had only a few instances in which she could state through her actions or words that she is not to be owned or subdued. Men had enough power that they could openly threaten to whip his wife when they went against his wish. Amanda and Lupeng, to an extent all the women who were a part of the Tadtrin rituals took it as an opening to reclaim their space as in the past. Entoy shows his reverence to Amanda and Paeng accepting that he adored and worshipped Lupeng stand as the result of the strong women who subverted from the behaviour that is considered acceptable by society.

The Maternity Leave by Ligaya Victorio Reyes is a story that portrays the dilemma of a woman who struggles to choose between financially supporting her family and having a child. Lucia is seen talking with her colleagues from the school she works as a teacher. She reveals that she is pregnant again and each woman gives her cent on maternity. The women also talk about how maternity leave and the subsequent lack of salary could affect the family. Numerous examples of former teachers who lost their job because of their maternity or women who suffered because of lack of pay are also discussed. On the walk home, Lucia thinks about the financial condition of her family. She thinks how the lack of her salary could affect them for the four months that she has to stay at home. The fact that she could potentially lose her job, thereby creating a financial deficit keeps her disturbed. Just as she was about to open the door, she decides to abort the baby and turns away from her husband who is seen bending over the crib to coo at their six-month-old child. "A complete woman is a woman who is a mother and manages all other roles." (Anonymous, web). From times immemorial, the primary role of a woman is to become a mother and nurture the family. Motherhood is seen as the most important thing in the life of a woman. A woman is expected not only to have children but also to be ecstatic about the prospect of being a mother. There are a lot of cultures that condemn women without children as inauspicious or incomplete. A child is required for a woman to be made to feel complete by society. Moreover, it is seen as a blessing. The Maternity Leave looks at pregnancy not through the lens of motherhood but through the lens of reality.

Lucia and her husband are school teachers who depend on their monthly income for running their family. The laws on maternity leave are not favourable towards the pregnant woman who depend on the income they receive for the daily expense of their families. Lucia announces the news of her pregnancy to a group of colleagues who meet up. The initial reaction is that she should be thrilled to be a mother as motherhood after marriage is the most natural thing. "What's wrong with having babies if one is lawfully wedded? Babies are so cute" (Reyes, 2). The reaction is a typical reaction of the society that looks at women as a way of furthering and continuing the existence of the species. The condition of the woman in question is not taken into consideration. It is assumed that she will go through the pregnancy because what kind of woman doesn't want to have children. The expected behaviour of a married woman would have been similar to the one the protagonist recalls about a fellow teacher Rosing, There was Rosing, a cousin of Ester's who married in her late thirties and was anxious to have a child. She practically lived at the doctor's clinic, asking questions and treasuring answers which would ensure her safe motherhood. (Reyes, 1).

Lucia on the other hand is real and thinks about the situation she is under. The government is not sympathetic towards pregnant women. The time period being that of Japanese colonization of the Philippines, the expecting mothers are allowed to take maternity leave but they are not paid for the duration of their absence. If they don't return to work in four months there is a huge possibility that they will be fired from their job. The urge of society to beget children clashes with the urge to provide for the family that she already has. Liz gives words to Lucia's internal struggle "If you are a teacher, and married to another teacher, you should think thrice before you have babies in a hurry," she said in her bitter voice. "Two times sixty is better than sixty, and baby can be an awful expense." (Reyes, 2).

Lucia thinks through her condition on her way home and decides to abort her baby to care for the current family she has. "All other considerations vanished from her mind. It was so easy, once one had arrived at a decision. She was going to be free from a whole year of worry. This was going to be simple."(Reyes, 4). She subverts from the general attitude and expectation of the society that woman has to embrace motherhood. She gives up a future child to afford the children she has.

The short story Woman with Horns written by Cecilia Menguera Brainard is about a widow and a widower, exploring how they cope up with the loss of their spouse. Gerald Macalister was the American public health director of the fictional city of Ubec. He lost his wife three years ago and still hasn't got over it. He immersed himself completely in work in order to distract himself from the pain of losing her. It is in the hospital that he meets Agustina, who lost her husband a year back. She is rumoured to have been a child of the river spirits, born with horns which her mother paid a carpenter to have sawed off. Agustina lives with her daughter and loves to live her life. They cross paths at a few societal gatherings and he is taken aback by the way she is. The people around her criticise her for not being demure as befitting a widow. He is left to rethink his life as he goes through his wedding album. He accepts that it is good to move on and the two are seen making a splash in the river on a full moon night.

The concept of widowhood differs with gender. The life of a widow is very different from the life of a widower. The fact that women live longer lives when compared to men and that men tend to marry women who are younger than them. are some of the reasons. Even in the case of a widower, the possibility of him remaining in the same state is very narrow as men tend to remarry rather quickly. Most cultures deem it important that the men remarry after the death of his wife as he needs the comfort of a companion. The wife on the other hand is most of the time blamed for the death of the husband. She is forced into widowhood rather curtly and socially shunned as someone whose bad luck killed her husband. "It is significant that it the widow who was tainted with the scent of death, not the widower. This symbolic construction of the image of the widow, the emphasis the woman, reappears throughout the history of mourning ritual, it is an effect of the symbolic violence of gender domination" (Web, Barbnay)

In a few societies, widows were forced to go through rituals that crushed their spirit and sense of independence in addition to the grief of losing their husbands. They are brought into a mentality that they should undergo certain behavioural modifications in order to better fit into society in their new role as a woman without her husband.

Agustina, who lost her husband was treated with open hostility as she presented herself as an independent, outgoing and happy woman. "The people don't approve of her,' Gerald commented when he noticed women gossiping behind their fans, their eyes riveted on Agustina." (Brainard) Her husband had been sick and she had nursed him throughout it. But the people complained and spread around stories that she had affairs with other men during the time her husband was sick, as she quickly went back to a normal schedule. The story of how she was the daughter of the river spirit, born with horns on her head which were sawed off on her mother's orders did nothing to help the matters. "She patiently nursed her husband. They said she had lovers but for five years, she took care of him."(Brainard) As a woman, she was expected to confine herself to the memories of her husband, curb her feelings, curtail her emotions, contain her curiosity about the world and have a bleak look at the things around her.

On the other hand, Gerald who was a widower under similar circumstances was expected and advised to get on with his life. "You don't smoke; you don't have women; you are a shell. Bringing you here was a chore. You look like a god from Olympus – tall, blonde with grey eyes. You're not forty, yet you act like an old man." (Brainard) His own admission of adultery with the nurse who came to take care of his sick wife does nothing to change the views of society on his behaviour. The irony is that the very same society accused a woman who lovingly nursed her husband in his sickbed, of adultery just because she got on with her life after her husband's death.

The widows had a very controlled foray into society. "They were forced to withdraw completely from the social life of the community and were made to follow a severe discipline which made their existence a virtual social death." (Anji, Web) Most of the cultures considered a widow as inauspicious and controlled their activity in social and cultural gatherings to the maximum. They had to be dependent on the men in their families to support them.

Augustina, on the other hand, went about the day doing what she wants to get done. She typically stood against everything dictated by society. She pushes against the boundaries that have been laid to keep them in line. Dr Gerald sees her in the playground playing with her daughter on the swing, the mother and daughter taking turns to push each other on the swing. "The child pushed her hard and Agustina's infectious laughter rose above other sounds."(Brainard) She doesn't let the assumptions of the people about her and how she should behave get in the way of her happiness. She doesn't confine herself to the stereotype that society created to maintain a hierarchy in which men occupy the place of honour and women have no say in what happens to them. She breaks them and creates the space not just to be independent but also happy. "I can see why the people would despise a widow who carries on the way she does," (Brainard)

Augustina stands as a subversive, who takes her stand in what she wants, not sticking to the substandard views of the society that shushes the widows into metaphorical closets while their male counterparts are urged to find happiness, remarry and live their life. She doesn't just socialise or come out into the places where widows are frowned upon but finds ways to be happy there.

Widowed for only a little over a year, would laugh, be happy, even flirt outrageously with him. Why was she not consumed with grief? Why did she not sit at home crocheting white dollies? Why did she not light candles in the crumbling musty churches, the way proper Ubecan widows did? He was outraged at her behaviour. He condemned her for the life that oozed out of her (Brainard). Society has set roles for her play, as out forth by Brainard through Dr Gerald's words but she doesn't fit into a mould rather breaks all stereotypes. The feminine gender has been subjected to typecasting and they find ways to subvert themselves from the dictated roles that they are expected to play.

Works Cited

Anji, A and Dr. K. Velumani."Contemporary social position of widowhood among Rural and urban area". International Journal of Advancements Research & Technology 2.10 (2013): n.pag. Web. 27 Nov 2020.

Anonymous, "Women Quotes". Brainy Quotes. Web. 27 Nov 2020.

Ayashiro, Hatsuho "Deconstructing Dominant Discourse Using Self-
deprecating Humour: ADiscourse Analysis of a Consulting with
Japanese Female about Hikikomori and NEET". Wisdom in Education
5.2. web. 21 Dec 2020.
https://scholarworks.lib.csusb.edu/wie/vol5/iss2/2
Balen, F. Van and H. M. W. Bos. "The social and cultural consequences of being childless in poor-resource areas". Facts Views Vis Obgynv. Web.
30 Nov 2020.
www.ncbi.nlm.nih.gov › PMC › articles › PMC4251270

Barnaby, Mary The social location of widows. Diss. U Plymouth, 1997.

privately published, Web. 24 Nov 2020.

Clymer, Kenton J. Protestant Missionaries in the Philippines, 1898-1916: An

Inquiry into the American Colonial Mentality. Urbana, IL: University of

Illinois. 1986. Print

Daly, Martin and Weghorst, Suzanne J. "Male sexual jealousy". Science

Direct: Aetiology and Sociobiology3.1 (1982): 11-27. Web. 14 Dec

2020.

Foucault, Michel."Michel Foucault: Discourse". ed. Rachel Adams. Critical

Legal Thinking(2017). Web. 3 March 2021.

https://criticallegalthinking.com › 2017/11/17 › Michel-...

Hall, Stuart. The west and the rest. Discourse and power North Carolina: Duke

UP, 1992. Print.

Hare-Mustin, R. T. "Discourses in the mirrored room: A postmodern analysis

of therapy". Family Process. Web. 3 March 2021.

https://doi.org/10.1111/j.1545-5300.1994.00019.x

Hilton, James, and William Von Hippel. "Stereotypes." Annual Review of

Psychology (1996). Web. 6 March 2021.

Holy Bible. New King James Version, Nashville: Thomas Nelson, 1982. Print.

Joanne Pearson, "Witches and Wicca, in Belief Beyond Boundaries" Wicca,

Celtic Spirituality and the New Age. Web. 18 Nov 2020.

Jocano,F. Landa. Filipino Catholicism: A Case Study in Religious Change

Diss. U Philippines Dilima. privately published, Web. 24 Nov 2020.

Litonjua, M.D. "1898 and America's Empire in the Philippines: Race,

Religion, Imperialism, and Colonialism". Academia. Web. 23 Nov 2020.

Porter, Catherin. "When Did Philippine History Begin?" American Historical

Association.Web.23 Nov 2020.

www.historians.org   ›   em-24-what-lies-ahead-for-the-Philippines-(1945)

Reyes, Michelle. "A Personal Note from a Therapist's Perspective".

Motherhood. 15 Oct 2018. Web. 27 Nov 2020.

https://mothergoodco.com › home › 2018/10/15 › a-pe…

Rudman, Laurie A. and Peter Glick, The Social Psychology of Gender: How

power and intimacy shape gender relations. New York: Guliford, 2010.

Print.

"Self-preservation" Cambridge Dictionary .Cambridge UP, 2021. Online.

Web. 17 Dec 2020.

Sitoy, Valentino. A History of Christianity in the Philippines. Quezon City:

New Day Publishers, 1985. Print.

"Subversion". Cambridge Dictionary .Cambridge UP, 2021. Online. Web. 15

Nov 2020.

Tarrayo, Veronico Nogales. "The Woman in the Mirror: Imaging the Filipino

Woman in Short Stories in English by Filipino Woman Authors"
Research Gate. Web. 17 Nov 2020.

Wallace,Diane. "Whispers of the Crone: Meeting our personal crone".

Grannysage at The Crossroads. Web. 24 Nov 2020.
https://grannysage.weebly.com › whispers-of-the-crone

• • •

245

www.ingramcontent.com/pod-product-compliance
Lightning Source LLC
Chambersburg PA
CBHW061241120726

48001CB00001B/91